MW01505537

You Are That Temple!

Other books by Kevin Vost
from Sophia Institute Press:

Memorize the Faith!

Fit for Eternal Life!

The One-Minute Aquinas

Unearthing Your Ten Talents

Aquinas on the Four Last Things

12 Life Lessons from St. Thomas Aquinas

The Seven Gifts of the Holy Spirit

The Catholic Guide to Loneliness

How to Think Like Aquinas

The Seven Deadly Sins

Hounds of the Lord

Kevin Vost, Psy.D.

YOU ARE THAT TEMPLE!

A Catholic Guide to Health and Holiness

SOPHIA INSTITUTE PRESS
Manchester, New Hampshire

Copyright © 2022 by Kevin Vost

Printed in the United States of America. All rights reserved.

Cover design by Updatefordesign Studio.

On the cover: Vitruvian man illustration (5602491) © microone / Freepik.

Unless otherwise noted, Scripture quotations in this work are taken from the Revised Standard Version (RSV) of the Bible: Catholic Edition, copyright © 1965, 1966 the Division of Christian Education of the National Council of the Churches of Christ in the United States of America, and are used by permission of the copyright owner. All rights reserved.

No part of this book may be reproduced, stored in a retrieval system, or transmitted in any form, or by any means, electronic, mechanical, photocopying, or otherwise, without the prior written permission of the publisher, except by a reviewer, who may quote brief passages in a review.

Sophia Institute Press

Box 5284, Manchester, NH 03108

1-800-888-9344

www.SophiaInstitute.com

Sophia Institute Press is a registered trademark of Sophia Institute.

paperback ISBN 978-1-64413-596-9

ebook ISBN 978-1-64413-597-6

Library of Congress Control Number: 2022942255

First printing

To Rick and Karen Branham,
temple-tending friends for more than forty years now

Contents

Part III

Temple-Building Instructions
(Proper Exercise to Build and Maintain Sturdy Temples)

Part IV

From Steeple to People
(Special Concerns for Special Groups)

Appendices

Caveat Flexor et Qui Comederit
(Warning!)

You've probably heard the phrase *caveat emptor* — "Let the buyer beware!" I'd like to make clear from the start a few warnings for the person who exercises (*flexor*) as well as for the person who eats (*qui comederit*). The information in this book is for healthy men and women and for those who would like to improve their health. But even people without known health problems should consult their physician before starting any new exercise or dietary program. There are many unsettled issues in nutritional and exercise science in general. Further, individuals may vary greatly in their responses to particular kinds of food or exercise regimens.

The material in this book is not a substitute for the advice of one's own health-care professionals, such as physicians, dieticians, pharmacists, psychologists, and so forth. People taking prescribed medications, in particular, should be sure to discuss with their physicians any major dietary changes, as such changes could significantly impact the appropriate dosage. Any application of the advice in this book is at the reader's sole discretion and risk. As is customary for books involving discussion of health- and fitness-related issues, the author, publisher, and all contributors involved disclaim any liability — personal, professional, or otherwise — resulting from the application or misapplication of the information in this book.

God's Call to Keep Our Temples Holy (and Healthy)

Do you not know that you are God's temple and that God's Spirit dwells in you? If any one destroys God's temple, God will destroy him. For God's temple is holy, and that temple you are.

— 1 Corinthians 3:16–17

God Commissions Holy (and Healthy) Bodily Temples

In the passage above from his First Letter to the Corinthians, St. Paul could hardly have said it more clearly, that *you* are the temple of the Holy Spirit. And yet he reemphasizes and elaborates on the point three chapters later: "Do you not know that your body is a temple of the Holy Spirit within you, which you have from God? You are not your own; you were bought with a price. So glorify God in your body" (1 Cor. 6:19–20). Note well that in this passage, he elaborates four essential points:

1. Your *body* is the temple. (Holiness resides not only in the human soul.)
2. Your body and soul are gifts *from God* and are *not your own*. (Who among us gave ourselves our own body or soul?)

3. A *price* was paid for you, in body and soul. (It is thanks to Christ's Passion, death, and Resurrection that you may one day enjoy eternal life in both body and soul.)
4. Therefore, we should *glorify God* through our bodies. (We should show our gratitude and magnify God's glory through how we honor and use the bodies that house and manifest God's Holy Spirit.)

The first three points refer to tenets of the Faith that we need to *know*, and the last point refers to what we need to *do* about them. That last is primarily what this book is about: a how-to book of sorts on how to glorify God in our bodies. St. Paul gets us started with advice on how *not* to degrade or destroy our bodily temples through sexual sins that denigrate the dignity of our bodily temples. "Shun immorality. Every other sin which a man commits is outside the body; but the immoral man sins against his own body" (1 Cor. 6:18).

The Church has long warned of the seven deadly, or "capital," sins that can lead to death of the soul: "pride, avarice, envy, wrath, lust, gluttony, and sloth or acedia" (*Catechism of the Catholic Church* [CCC], no. 1866). Church Doctors have long classified five of them as *spiritual* sins (pride, avarice, envy, wrath, and sloth) and the last two (lust and gluttony) as *corporal* or physical, bodily sins. If we are to glorify God in our bodies, we must avoid the corporal sins that directly dishonor the body, and we must also avoid using our bodies as vehicles to carry out actions prompted by spiritual sins.

The sins most directly relevant to our theme in this book will be gluttony and sloth. Indeed, some consider them the fundamental causes of so many widespread physical health problems around the world today, but we will very carefully consider in just what sense they may (or may not) be the two true deadly culprits.

Of course, while we must fight against various vices and sins so our bodily temples will not be dishonored, there are a great many things that we can do to actively honor our bodily temples and glorify God in the process. This is the realm of virtue, holiness, and healthy behaviors that we will examine in great depth.

We should note from the start that the Catholic Church is quite clear on the nature of human beings and on the value of the human body. We can all attest from personal experience that we are beings of both matter and spirit, ensouled bodies. The *Catechism* elaborates that "the unity of soul and body is so profound that one has to consider the soul to be the 'form' or the body.[1] ... Spirit and nature, in man, are not two natures united, but rather their union forms a single nature" (365).

Recall, too, that Jesus commanded His followers to "be perfect" (Matt. 5:48). The English word *perfect* derives from the Latin *per* (thoroughly) and *facere* (to make) and means "complete." Given our body-soul natures, it follows that we must strive to be *perfect* according to our entire nature: soul *and* body. This does not mean that we must spend inordinate amounts of time trying to attain "the perfect body" any more than we should become paralyzed with scrupulosity, obsessively striving to perfect our souls, by cleansing them of even the slightest possible (or imaginary) sins. Rather, we are to try to perfect the form and the function, the health and the fitness of our physical bodies as best we can, within the context of a well-rounded spiritual life.

Christ told us above all else to "love the Lord your God with all your heart, and with all your soul, and with all your strength, and with all your mind; and your neighbor as yourself" (Luke 10:27). In the chapters ahead, we will zoom in on all those components of what we have to offer to God, issues literally related to hearts, souls, strength, and minds. Further, we will not neglect that second phrase, containing the second great commandment: to love your neighbor *as yourself*.

---

[1] Cf. Council of Vienne (1312): DS 902.

The great St. Thomas Aquinas, who seems to have written on every important issue under the sun, has shined the light of his intellect upon each implication of that command, revealing that through it, *Jesus has commanded that we love our own bodies.* In examining the great theological virtue of charity (*caritas*, or love), Thomas tells us that we should love our own bodies out of charity. What God has made is good, and we are to use our bodies "as instruments of justice unto God" per Romans 6:13.[2] Although our bodies cannot know and love God, it is by the works of our bodies that we are able to come to know God. "Hence from the enjoyment in the soul there overflows a certain happiness into the body,"[3] and since the body has a share of this happiness, it can be loved with charity.

We must remember, too, that God Himself, in the person of the Word, His Son, took on a body for our sake. Bodies can clearly be good, godly, and, in one case, intimately conjoined with the divine nature! The Church teaches that Mary, the Blessed Mother of God, was assumed into Heaven body *and* soul, and indeed, after Christ's Second Coming, the souls of *all* people who have died will be reunited with their bodies for eternity. (Indeed, we will touch on the fascinating nature of the glorified bodies in Heaven in our last chapter before the conclusion.)

So, even from the very beginning (as we read in Genesis, again and again), God declared that created, physical, bodily things are "good" — indeed "very good" (Gen. 1:10, 12, 18, 21, 25, 31). He deemed that human beings have dominion over all of the creatures of the earth and are to serve as His grateful stewards, caring for all of creation (including ourselves, in body and soul). He has clearly called us to be holy — and healthy. Now let's take a quick look at how we'll attempt to answer that call and live it out in our daily lives.

[2] See also the *Summa Theologica* [*ST*], II-II, Q. 25, art. 5.
[3] Ibid.

Understanding How to Plan, Build, and Maintain Our Holy Temples

As the architect (well, author) of this book, I'll lay out for you our blueprints for constructing and maintaining holy, health temples, glorifying the Spirit within them all the while.

In part 1, we'll prepare the temple grounds, digging into such issues as the widespread threats that our physical, mental, and spiritual temples face from a variety of growing public health issues: COVID, obesity, diabetes, heart disease, dementia, and more. We will examine to what extent sins such as gluttony and sloth may contribute to our crumbling temples, and we will take a first glance at some possible means of renovation. Jesus told us of the importance of building upon sturdy foundations (Matt. 7:24–27). We will begin to lay down a sturdy foundation by examining the "virtues of fitness" that will help us to know what's true, do what's good, and fortify our bodily temples for the glory of God.

Having prepared the ground and established the foundation, when we work our way to part 2, we will start to collect the materials we need to build and perfect our bodily temples. We'll be looking for the bodily equivalent of the finest and sturdiest marble, precious metals, and gems, while learning how to avoid the "fool's gold" of what some have called "fake foods" so prevalent today. We will inspect, weigh, and measure the heavy materials we may need, such as the macronutrients of carbohydrates, fat, and protein, as well as the micronutrients, such as vitamins and minerals, that provide our finishing touches. We will find what can happen if we choose materials of poor quality, if we choose too little or too much of any of them, or if we use them too often or not often enough. We will also get practical with suggestions for eating plans based on the best materials (as God made them), and we'll throw in some simple sample recipes.

When we arrive at part 3, we will shift our focus from materials to labor and will find out just what kind of work it takes to build and maintain a holy, healthy temple. Recalling that Christ calls us to love God with all of our *strength*, we will examine three modern methods of physical strength training — building the muscles, bones, and connective tissues that will make our temples as sturdy as Gothic cathedrals strengthened by flying buttresses. In order to love God with all our *hearts*, we will look at what many call "cardio" training, methods to perfect our hearts, lungs, and limbs and to provide the power to light our temples and to render us veritable "dynamos of charity." Knowing there are many ways to skin a cat (as the old, perhaps infelicitous saying goes), we will also take a quick look at many other ways to build and energize our bodily temples, from kettlebells to sports to organized group fitness classes. Realizing, too, that "real work works," we will look at the temple-tending benefits of normal daily physical activities, such as tending your temple's yard or garden.

We will also focus on "minding" our temples, first by looking at the myriad of benefits modern research has shown to accrue to our brain tissues and to our mental functioning courtesy of proper exercise and nutrition.

In part 4, we will move from "steeple to people" (for those who remember that little childhood rhyme recited while rearranging and wiggling one's fingers). We will zoom in on special concerns for special groups of people extending even beyond the "womb to tomb" focus psychologists refer to when describing the field of "life-span" developmental psychology. We will delve into issues from "zygote to eternal life," as we examine health issues of expectant mothers, the preborn, infants and young children, adolescent and young adults, and middle-aged adults and the elderly. We will consider similarities and differences in temple tending between the two sexes, and we will not forget the needs of so many people with significant physical and mental disabilities.

Finally, when we conclude, we'll put that Holy Spirit within our temples, front and center, reminding ourselves that all that we do to build and maintain the great gifts of our temple is to honor that great Gift and Giver, the Holy Spirit Himself — in unity with the Father and Son.

KISS — Keep It Simple, Samson (or Sarah)!

If you happen to have read *Fit for Eternal Life* (not at all necessary for understanding this book), you might recall that I used the acronym KISS and modified it a bit from the less than fully charitable original meaning of "Keep it simple, stupid!" to "Keep it simple, Samson!" with our emphasis in mind. Here I will expand it to "Keep it Simple, Samson (or Sarah)!" to emphasize that these lessons apply to people with either male or female bodily temples and to honor Samson, God's physically mighty and Spirit-filled strongman described in the book of Judges, as well as Sarah, Abraham's loving wife, the long-lived, faithful, fruitful matriarch we meet in the book of Genesis.

Now, I used the phrase in my previous book to emphasize that exercise in general, and strength training in particular, are often presented as overly complicated and thereby may appear daunting to some would-be exercisers, whereas strength training is really far closer to "rock science" than rocket science. (Indeed, one can become strong by merely lifting rocks!)

Here, I will also present a new, rather more complicated and sophisticated method of training I did not know about then. My goal, though, will still be to keep it as simple as possible without going too far and oversimplifying things. (You can let me know later how I did.)

My real challenge in this book will be to apply the KISS principle not to the field of exercise but to the field of *nutrition*. Indeed, the day I opened up this Word document to get down to business on this text, I came across this simple line in a brand-new research study: "The field of nutritional science is notoriously complex."[4] Does anyone disagree?

---

[4]   Peter J. Foley, "Effects of Low Carbohydrate Diets on Insulin Resistance and the Metabolic Syndrome," *Current Opinion in Endocrinology,*

You Are That Temple!

I wonder if any of you have seen that humorous little skit in which a couple are eating breakfast in their 1960s-era kitchen when a man arrives on the scene and tells them he is from the future.[5] The husband is ready to dig into a breakfast of steak, eggs, toast, orange juice, and coffee when the man from the future warns him not to eat the *eggs*. The wife asks why; the man says because of *cholesterol* (which the couple had not heard of).

Next, as the wife prepares to toss out the eggs, the man from the future returns in more modern attire. "Wait!" he instructs her and explains that "we were wrong about the eggs." Now he tells her they've found out about "good" and "bad" cholesterol, and she must throw out only the *yolks*.

Lo and behold, he's back in an instant to tell her "We were wrong about the eggs." "Again?" says the wife. He explains that science has found that the cholesterol in one's bloodstream is not significantly affected by the cholesterol one consumes (and the body produces lots of its own cholesterol). Still, "Wait!" he exclaims once more. The man must not eat the *steak*, since red meat increases the risk of heart attacks!

Off he goes, and the husband wisely makes his wife pause before tossing out the steak, because the time-traveling dietician is back and exclaims, "We were wrong about the steak.... It's the *toast!*" He says we should eat only what our paleolithic ancestors ate (and they really liked meat!). The husband eats the toast anyway, and here comes our dietician again.

Now he says we should probably be eating *more bread*. Then he says they should ignore everything he said and just *exercise*.

Diabetes, and Obesity 28, no. 5 (October 2021): 463–468. https://journals.lww.com/co-endocrinology/Fulltext/2021/10000/Effect_of_low_carbohydrate_diets_on_insulin.7.aspx?fbclid=IwAR3qDQw_mWW8qLy56So9nwFs8qNai-YmTc3lAegY47ebZSC1KlDEgqZV2qs.

5   Funny Or Die, "This Is Why Eating Healthy Is Hard" (Time Travel Dietician), YouTube video, 4:26, https://www.youtube.com/watch?v=5Ua-WVg1SsA.

On his final appearance, he proclaims that it turned out to be all a matter of *genetics*. He concludes by apologizing for spoiling their meal! I find that video very funny, but the sad part is that it is based on historical fact regarding the confusing and conflicting advice we've been given by experts over the last several decades. Too often, we've been given advice on the basis of partial and very imperfect evidence.

We will examine some of this history. I'll note, too, that my own ideas have changed over time, including some of the nutritional advice I've given in the past. In these pages, I'll do my very best to make the key issues as simple as they can be. All of my opinions are based on a great deal of research. While I'll try not to bog us down with too many footnotes, I will provide them for essential research findings. Appendix 2 will reveal where you can go if you really want to dig deep into the mountains of research behind the conclusions.

Oh, and if I were to make this nutrition advice as simple as possible, I'd boil it down to three words: "Eat real food!" Chapters 4 through 11 will flesh out just what that means and how to do it.

Who Am *I* to Say?

One of my favorite lines from St. Bonaventure comes from one of his "collations" (lectures) on the gifts of the Holy Spirit. When considering the gift of wisdom, he cites this scriptural reference: "Wisdom has built her house, she has set up her seven pillars" (Prov. 9:1). Before he supplies his exegesis, the good saint asks an amusing rhetorical question: "But what are the seven pillars of this house? Should I make them up out of my own head?"[6] No, he says, because the pillars of wisdom are also right there in Scripture: "But the wisdom from above is first pure,

---

[6] St. Bonaventure, *Collations on the Seven Gifts of the Holy Spirit*, trans. Zachary Hayes, O.F.M. (St. Bonaventure, NY: Franciscan Institute Publications, 2008), 188.

then peaceable, gentle, open to reason, full of mercy, and good fruits, without uncertainty or insincerity" (Jas. 3:17). He then expounds on each pillar with additional insights of his own.

Now, since even the great Seraphic Doctor would not presume to make up things out of his own head to explain the pillars of the house of wisdom, I will do my best not to make up out of my own head the pillars of our holy temples! My role will be to attempt to describe the evidence produced and compiled by the real experts, but I will indeed present some of my own opinions based on my evaluations. For that reason, I'd better take a page or two to explain to you just who I am to say things about such things.

Let's make clear from the start that I am not a medical doctor, a nutritionist, a dietician, a pharmacist, a dentist, a nurse, a physical therapist, or an exercise physiologist. Further, *my opinions are not intended as any kind of one-on-one personalized health-care advice.* For that you must turn to your health-care providers, though you could certainly share with them some of the ideas you encounter in this book or other recommended books, if you care to. As for what I am, or at least what experience I have, three areas are most relevant.

First, my formal educational training was as a clinical psychologist with a specialization in neuropsychology. My doctoral dissertation was on the early detection of Alzheimer dementia, and we will touch upon Alzheimer's in later chapters. Further, I was trained in the construction, performance, and statistical analysis of social science research, which is helpful in assessing the various kinds of epidemiological and experimental studies performed in the fields of nutrition and exercise. As for my years of college teaching, the courses I taught most often were Life-Span Developmental Psychology, Psychology of Adolescence, and Psychology of Aging. This knowledge should prove helpful in the chapters of parts 3 and 4 that look at health in body, mind, and soul as we progress through the stages of life on earth.

Second, I've been involved in strength and fitness training in one way or another since I saw a weightlifter on TV when I was in second grade in 1968. I immediately insisted that my dad buy me a barbell set. (Thankfully, he was happy to comply.) After playing with the weights off and on for a few years, I've been training with them seriously since the seventh grade in 1973, going on fifty years now. I also competed in Olympic weightlifting, bodybuilding, powerlifting, Highland Games heavy athletics, distance running, and even on ten-man tug-of-war teams over the years.

I taught my first weightlifting course at a YMCA as a teen in the late 1970s, and I worked as a part-time lifting and fitness instructor at two gyms while I was in college. In 1999, I was fortunate to win a writing contest sponsored by the International Association of Resistance Trainers (an organization that certifies person fitness trainers). I went on to write some health psychology articles for their magazine *Exercise Protocol* and was on their certification board. Since then, I've written three books that relate to strength training and fitness (*Full Range of Motive, Fit for Eternal Life,* and *Tending the Temple* — a devotional I co-authored with my friends Shane Kapler and Peggy Bowes).

Over the years, I've written fitness articles for various magazines and websites. I'm delighted to show friends hard copies of magazines in which my fitness articles have appeared and which feature my favorite and perhaps most unlikely pair of "cover models," so to speak. One is an issue of *Exercise Protocol* on whose cover appears the massive body of multitime Mr. Olympia winner Dorian Yates. Another is a cover article for *Liguorian* magazine, which displays a photo of a beaming Pope John Paul II in his prime — albeit blessing, not flexing.

I'm sixty as I write this, and I still train three or four days per week. I have also tried to keep abreast of breaking research on nutrition over the years, and, in the last 321 days, as I write today, I have read several dozen new books and have viewed videos every single day to dig into what was a relatively new nutritional topic to me that I'll lay out in the pages ahead. I'm excited to write about it, having lost thirty pounds in 160 days, kept it off since then, dropped my waistline by six inches, dropped my blood pressure by more than twenty points, and normalized my blood lipid values.

There is one last area of relevant background that I have not brought up before when writing on faith and fitness, but which is more relevant than ever for this particular book on proper care of our temples. In our very first chapter, we will consider what I've called the biggest pandemics of all. These refer to health problems that have skyrocketed over the last several decades — primarily obesity and diabetes, but also a host of related disorders, including non-alcoholic liver disease.

Well, I spent the years 1984 to 2016 employed full-time in the adjudication of physical and mental disability claims for the Social Security Administration. During my first two decades as a disability adjudicator (or examiner, as some states call it) I decided five hundred to seven hundred cases every year, reviewing comprehensive medical records of children and adults, while working with medical doctors, psychologists, nurses, and speech pathologists to determine whether the applicants' conditions had rendered them unable to work or, for children, to function in an age-appropriate manner. During my last decade as a supervisor of adjudicators and a brief stint as the supervisor of the people who train the adjudicators, I usually supervised eight to ten people and reviewed the medical records of several thousand children and adults every year. I've seen these epidemics up close as they developed, and I've seen exactly how they impact living and breathing individuals. I will share these experiences when relevant.

Well, that's enough about me! (For now, anyway.) Let's take a quick look at some more interesting folks.

Who Are *They* to Say?

I am delighted to reveal that this book will be greatly enhanced by an appendix featuring twenty-three personal vignettes, "Temple-Tender Tales," that tell the stories of real-live Catholics in our day and the ways they have found to keep their bodily temples healthier and holier. They are a wonderfully diverse group of men and women, from thirty-somethings to septuagenarians, with a fascinating array of backgrounds and expertise.

In *Fit for Eternal Life*, I wrote that one need not be a Mr. Universe or a runway model to care for one's temple properly. Well, this book will feature a vignette from a real-life Mr. Universe winner! There are also two vignette providers who are Catholic priests, and one is in diaconate formation.

Many of the people who share their vignettes have been seriously involved in physical fitness as personal fitness trainers, exercise-class leaders, kettlebell instructors, or competitive athletes in sports as diverse as bodybuilding, Olympic weightlifting, powerlifting, Highland Games, Greco-Roman wrestling, long-distance running, martial arts, skateboarding, tennis, and even Sumo wrestling! Others are ordinary men and women who have lost considerable body weight and restored or maintained their health through what they have learned about exercise and or diet. Some will emphasize how proper training and eating have helped them in body, and some will emphasis the effects on the mind or spirit. Some of these people I've had the pleasure to know through the wonders of modern social media; others I've met face-to-face and have known for many years.

I must note as a caveat, too, that they will provide a variety of insights and approaches to health, fitness, and holiness that have worked for them. *The presence of their vignettes does not imply that they agree with all of the nutritional or exercise recommendations that I provide.* Bearing that in mind (and exculpating them from any errors of my ways), I think you will enjoy and profit greatly from their temple-tending tales.

So, without further ado, let's get busy. We've got a lot of learning (and eating, working, and praying) to do if we are to build healthy, holy temples!

Part I

⸺⸱⸱⸱⸺

Preparing the Ground for Our Temples
(Digging into Disease, Sin, and Virtue)

Health and soundness are better than all gold,
and a robust body than countless riches.

— Sirach 30:15

1

The Biggest Pandemics of Them All

Obesity is a common, serious, and costly chronic disease. Having obesity puts people at risk for many other serious chronic diseases and increases the risk of severe illness from COVID-19.

— Centers for Disease Control[7]

As I write today — All Souls' Day 2021 — we are still in the midst of the great COVID-19 pandemic, an epidemic occurring in *pan* (Latin for "all") places around the world, though in some places more so than others. It appears that virtually anyone can contract the virus, even the vaccinated. Further, while some of the people it savages are young and healthy, most readers are probably aware that those most likely to suffer serious illness or die from it are the elderly and those with comorbidities. I'll provide some details from the Centers for Disease Control and Prevention (CDC) in our next section. This chapter will examine some of those comorbidities, or "pre-existing conditions" in insurance language, that may well be the biggest, most enduring, and

[7] Centers for Disease Control and Prevention (CDC), "Obesity, Race/Ethnicity, and COVID-19," CDC, last reviewed May 20, 2022, https://www.cdc.gov/obesity/data/obesity-and-covid-19.html.

most destructive to our temples and the most quickly proliferating pandemics of all.

Overweight and Obesity:
Temples or Oversupply Warehouses?

Take a look around you (or perhaps even down to your own belly), and you will see that many of us seem to be building not temples of the Holy Spirit but oversupply warehouses for the foodstuffs we have overstuffed ourselves with, so to speak. But please note well, I intend no slight or disparagement toward those who are obese or overweight (as more than two-thirds of Americans are right now, and I was overweight within the last year). Anyone over fifty will recall that even in your lifetime, obesity was not nearly so prevalent in the recent past. A modern comedian showed photos of groups of typical young people from the 1960s and contrasted them with photos of groups of young people today. He said they do not seem to be the same species! The average American adult today weighs about twenty-five pounds more than the average American adult did forty years ago.

Indeed, one huge modern pandemic is skyrocketing *obesity*, which, in turn, leads to other destructive comorbidities. As for the relationship between obesity and ill effects from COVID, here are some highlights from the CDC, under the heading "Obesity Worsens Outcomes for COVID-19":

- Obesity increases the risk of severe illness (and even being overweight may as well).
- Obesity may triple the risk of hospitalization.
- Obesity is linked to impaired immune function.
- Obesity reduces lung function and can make ventilation more difficult.
- Studies suggest that the more obese one is, the more risk rises for hospitalization, intensive care unit (ICU) treatment,

mechanical ventilation, and death, with the effects most profound for those *under* age 65.

- Thirty-two percent of all hospitalizations in the U.S. for CO-
VID have been for obese patients.
- Children eighteen and under who are obese had 3.07 times
greater chance of hospitalization and 1.42 times greater risk
of severe illness.[8]

Obesity is clearly serious business during the COVID pandemic,
but it is also potentially serious business all the time. Let's take a quick
look at how obesity has expanded over the last several decades.

Although there is a wealth of data on obesity rates in the United
States and around the world, looking at it from a variety of angles and
demographics, such as country by country, state by state, by sexes, age
groups, ethnicities, income brackets, and so forth, I'll zoom in on the
overall picture in the United States. But first we must define "obesity"
and "overweight."

The cutoff point for obesity is a body mass index (BMI) of 30.0 or
greater. It is based on the formula of weight in kilograms divided by
the square of height in meters, but you can easily dispense with the
mathematics and the metric system by using one of the many free BMI
calculators online. All you will need is your height and weight. To give
you a simple example, at my height of 5 feet 9.5 inches, my BMI would
reach 30.0 at a weight of 206 pounds. Generally, "morbid" or "severe"
obesity is defined as a BMI greater than 40.0 (for which I would have
to weigh 275 pounds).

Further, the category of "overweight" begins at a BMI of 25.0
(for me, 172 pounds). Now, we should bear in mind that the BMI
does not differentiate between fat and lean tissue. Some athletes
may have BMIs well into the obesity range because of the size of

---

[8]   Ibid.

their muscles, while they may carry far less fat than a person of even normal BMI. (I'm leaner than I've been in years, and my BMI today at 5 feet 9.5 inches and 190 pounds is 27.7.) Still, for the typical person, BMI can serve as a fairly valid predictor of whether one is carrying too much fat.

Now, on to the stats![9]

Years	Rates of Obesity in Men	Rates of Obesity in Women
1960–1972	10.2 percent	15.7 percent
1971–1974	12.2 percent	16.9 percent
1976–1980	12.3 percent	17.1 percent
1988–1994	20.6 percent	26.0 percent
1999–2002	28.1 percent	34.0 percent
2007–2010	34.4 percent	36.1 percent

Although a quick perusal of the CDC's website did not provide a quick comparison of separate obesity percentages for males and females, the overall percentage of obese Americans is reported as 42.4 percent for 2017–2018 (the most recent reported dates). Indeed, the combined percentage is greater than it was for females alone up to 2010, and recent findings show that 40 percent of young adults ages twenty to thirty-nine are now obese. Truly, obesity continues to grow

---

9   This table was previously available through the CDC but is no longer available. I report the numbers as cited in Tim Noakes, Jonno Proudfoot, and Sally-Ann Creed, *The Real Meal Revolution: The Radical, Sustainable Approach to Healthy Eating* (London: Little, Brown Book Group, 2015), 256.

by leaps and bounds. Moreover, if we add in the nonobese who are nevertheless in the "overweight" range, a full 73.4 percent of American adults, according to the CDC, are carrying too much weight.

According to these numbers. obesity has *tripled* in the United States even since I was born (1961), to the point that now only *one person in four* is at a healthy body weight. And sadly, children have not been spared. Whereas in the early 1960s, fewer than 5 percent (one out of twenty) of U.S. children and adolescents were obese,[10] by 2017, 19.3 percent (one out of five) children were classified as obese.[11]

Obesity carries serious consequences for most people, even when COVID is nowhere to be found. Let's move on to our second chronic pandemic: *diabetes* (and prediabetes).

Diabetes and Prediabetes:
Sour Truths about Too Much Sugar

Some researchers have observed that as rates of obesity rise in a population, rates of diabetes mellitus tend to rise five or ten years later, since it takes some time for the self-destructive mechanisms that obesity unleashes to take their tolls on our temples. First, let's define diabetes mellitus.

Type 1 diabetes is a relatively rare form of diabetes that occurs most commonly in children and younger people. In this type, the pancreas does not secrete enough of the hormone insulin to regulate amounts of glucose (sugar as it appears in human blood). This

---

[10]   CDC, "CDC Grand Rounds: Childhood Obesity in the United States," figure 1, "Prevalence of Obesity among Children and Adolescents, by Age Group — United States, 1963–2008," *Morbidity and Mortality Weekly Report* 60, no. 2, January 21, 2011, https://www.cdc.gov /mmwr/preview/mmwrhtml/mm6002a2.htm#fig1.

[11]   CDC, "Childhood Obesity Facts," CDC, https://www.cdc.gov/ obesity/data/childhood.html.

prohibits the cells' ability to use sugar for energy or storage in the body tissues. Untreated type I diabetics will therefore excrete sugar in their urine. In fact, the word "diabetes" comes from the Greek *diabainein*, meaning to "go through" or "siphon," and the Latin *mellitus*, for "sweet." Untreated type 1 diabetes can produce many symptoms, including fatigue and weight loss, and can seriously affect the skin, eyesight, and neurological system.

Type 2 diabetes is growing increasingly common in adults and now, sadly, even among children (it *used to* be called "adult-onset" diabetes). Here, the pancreas may still be producing insulin (at least for a while, even for many years), but the body tissues have become insensitive and unresponsive to insulin's normal action of lowering blood sugar. Untreated or uncontrolled type 2 diabetes can produce a wide variety of serious physical complications. I recall from my disability-evaluation days that some of the most severe complications included blindness from diabetic retinopathy, caused by damage to the tiny blood vessels that feed the eye, and the need for amputations of the toes, feet, or lower legs due to damaged small blood vessels.

How common has type 2 diabetes become? Am I exaggerating by calling it a pandemic? Let's see.

Though I don't see the data to compile a chart like the one for obesity, information I found from the CDC cuts to the chase with some disconcerting findings.[12] In 1958, less than 1 percent (0.93 percent) of Americans were diagnosed with diabetes, whereas by 2015, the number had risen to 7.4 percent — almost an eightfold increase. Let's bear in mind that these are percentages, so the growth in population did not make an impact. In terms of raw numbers, where population matters, the CDC reports that in 1958, 1.6 million

---

[12] CDC, "Long-Term Trends for Diabetes, 2017." CDC https://www.cdc.gov/diabetes/statistics/slides/long_term_trends.pdf.

Americans were diabetic, and in 2015, 23.4 million were — almost a fifteenfold increase! And speaking of *pan*demics, the World Health Organization (WHO) reports that from 1980 to 2014, the number of people in the world with diabetes rose from 108 million to 422 million[13] (a nearly fourfold increase worldwide, while total population increased from about 4.5 billion to 7.3 billion, well less than a twofold increase).

And sadly, as for children, the CDC reports "the rate of new cases (or incidence) of diabetes in youths younger than 20 years increased in the United States between 2002 and 2015, with a 4.8 percent increase per year for type 2 diabetes and a 1.9 percent increase per year for type 1 diabetes."[14]

Prediabetes is another rapidly expanding pandemic. "Prediabetes" refers to higher-than-normal blood sugar that does not yet fall into the range classified as diabetic.[15] It is often a precursor, a warning sign that full-blown diabetes may be brewing to rear its sugary head later on. The CDC reports that 34.5 percent of Americans had prediabetes in 2018.[16] What is going on here?

---

[13] "Diabetes," World Health Organization, November 10, 2021, https://www.who.int/news-room/fact-sheets/detail/diabetes#:~:text=The%20number%20of%20people%20with,stroke%20and%20lower%20limb%20amputation.

[14] CDC, "Rates of New Diagnosed Type I and Type II Diabetes Continue to Rise among Children and Teens," CDC, last reviewed February 11, 2020, https://www.cdc.gov/diabetes/research/reports/children-diabetes-rates-rise.html.

[15] I will not report such exact numbers here, since such numbers obtained in the laboratory for any individual are best discussed between the patient and his or her health-care provider.

[16] CDC, "Prevalence of Prediabetes among Adults," CDC, last reviewed December 29, 2021, https://www.cdc.gov/diabetes/data/statistics-report/prevalence-of-prediabetes.html#:~:text=An%20estimated%2088%20million%20adults,A1C%20level%20(Table%203).

Teetotallers Beware:
The Rise in Nonalcoholic Fatty Liver Disease

Nonalcoholic liver disease triggers a personal memory for me. I recall opening a new disability case in the late 1990s and seeing that one of the person's allegations was liver disease. I instantly (and erroneously) assumed that the person suffered from alcoholism, since that had been the case for virtually every liver disease case I had worked in the past. It was my first exposure to nonalcoholic fatty liver disease (or NAFLD). I mentioned this case to my co-workers, and they were surprised too.

The disease is diagnosed when more than 5 percent of the liver's weight is composed of fat. Historically, this was almost always found in alcoholics because only the liver can metabolize alcohol; therefore, too much alcohol consumed over time overloads the liver and causes it to store excess fat. If NAFLD worsens, a person may go on to develop nonalcoholic steatohepatitis (NASH) as the liver becomes inflamed and scarred. If the damage continues to the point at which the scarring significantly damages liver tissue and function, this is called cirrhosis of the liver. Finally, in some cases, patients will even develop liver cancer. (Cirrhosis and cancer were what my co-workers and I often saw in disability claims.)

Now, here lies the scary rub for *nonalcoholic* liver disease. While the condition was almost unheard of in the 1980s, when I began my career of disability evaluation, it was estimated to affect 15 percent of the worldwide population by 2005 and 25 percent by 2010.[17] Indeed, it is by far more common now than *alcoholic* liver disease, which was estimated to affect 4.7 percent of the U.S. population in 2015 and

---

[17] Souveek Mitra, Arka Dee, and Abhijit Chowdhury, "Epidemiology of Non-Alcoholic and Alcoholic Fatty Liver Diseases," *Translational Gastroenterology and Hepatology* 5, no. 16 (April 5, 2020), https://www.ncbi.nlm.nih.gov/pmc/articles/PMC7063528/.

2016. NASH is also the leading cause of the need for liver transplantation in the United States, the United Kingdom, and other developed countries. It bears noting, too, that *obesity* is highly associated with NAFLD. Indeed, it is reported that more than 95 percent of patients who undergo bariatric surgery for weight reduction — the severely or morbidly obese — have NAFLD.

God crafted our temples with livers capable of metabolizing the nutrients we eat, of excreting a variety of chemicals and hormones, of producing bile to carry away waste and digest fats, and of synthesizing the proteins we need to keep our temples strong. And yet a growing pandemic is destroying this vital structure deep within our temples. Indeed, researchers say that "liver diseases are fast emerging as global health priorities."[18] Why? We'll dig deeper into that mystery in the chapters ahead, but first we'll take a quick look at one prime suspect.

Unmasking the Mysterious Syndrome X

Is there a common denominator underlying conditions as diverse as obesity, diabetes, nonalcoholic liver disease, and perhaps a host of other health disorders, such as heart disease, cancer, and even Alzheimer's disease? Some believe there may well be. Many researchers have found that soon after native populations around the world have been exposed to the lifestyles of modern developed countries, once relatively unknown conditions, such as those mentioned above, started to rear their sickly heads. Hence, these diseases have been called "diseases of civilization" by some. But what about "civilization" would produce such disease in those native peoples and rise to pandemic proportions within the developed nations themselves?

Well, the WHO recognizes a syndrome that may well explain it. There are estimates that nearly nine out of ten American adults have

---

[18] Ibid.

at least one feature of this syndrome.[19] Early on, it was known as "Syndrome X," when introduced by researcher Gerald Reavan, M.D., in 1988, and now it is called "Metabolic Syndrome." Here are its five key features, building upon the WHO's criteria established in 1998:

A person must have at least two of the following:

- High blood pressure (greater than 140/90 — though some health organizations show greater than 130/85)
- Dyslipidemia (abnormal blood lipids such as triglycerides and cholesterol)
- Central obesity (fat stored around the middle, sometimes shown as greater than forty inches for males and greater than thirty-five inches for females)[20]
- Microalbuminuria (a urine abnormality suggesting kidney dysfunction)

In addition, a person must have insulin resistance, which plays a central role. Indeed, at one time the syndrome itself was also called "insulin resistance syndrome." You may have observed that obesity has cropped up once more, though in this case, in the form of "central" obesity. (More on that later.) Recall, too, our brief discussion of the rising pandemic of diabetes mellitus. The key factor in type 2 diabetes is indeed the body's resistance to insulin.

One of insulin's many functions, and the primary function of interest here, is to regulate levels of glucose, the sugar in our bloodstream,

---

[19] Joana Araújo, Jianwen Cai, and June Stevens, "Prevalence of Optimal Metabolic Health in American Adults: National Health and Nutrition Examination Survey 2009–2016," *Metabolic Syndrome and Related Disorders* 17, no. 1 (February 2019):46–52, National Library of Medicine, https://pubmed.ncbi.nlm.nih.gov/30484738/.

[20] The cutoffs are 35 inches for Asian men and 33.5 inches for Asian women per William Y. Shang, M.D., *The FIRST Program: Fighting Insulin Resistance with Strength Training* (n.p.: Shang Publishing, 2021), 8.

and a most delicate process it is. A 155-pound person has all of about four grams (one teaspoon) of sugar circulating in his or her blood at any time. To put things into perspective, a typical twelve-ounce can of soda contains thirty-eight to forty-six grams of sugar! Drink one of those, and your pancreas had better start cranking out the insulin to move that sugar out of your bloodstream.[21] Now, where does that excess sugar go? As we'll see in more detail later, small amounts can be stored in our muscles and liver, but the major storehouses are our poor overloaded fat cells.

The body can become resistant to insulin if the pancreas is stimulated to overproduce insulin over the years in response to too much sugar in the blood. Then the cells of various tissues in the body, such as the adipocytes (fat cells) and the cells in the muscles and the liver, become unresponsive to the insulin, unable to absorb the blood sugar, and hence, greater concentrations of blood sugar remain circulating in the blood. When these concentrations reach a certain level, we call it diabetes. I should note, too, that the most common test for diabetes is a fasting blood-glucose level. Unfortunately, in many individuals, insulin may rise for decades to keep the blood glucose level low. By the time it can no longer maintain a normal blood-sugar level due to insulin resistance, what appears to be a new problem may have been mounting for quite a long time. There are other tests for blood sugar that can tell us more, like the hemoglobin A1C level, but insulin levels themselves are rarely tested.

Now, as we saw, if untreated, diabetes can damage the blood vessels and virtually every body tissue they serve (including the heart,

---

[21] I'll note in passing that both table sugar (sucrose) and high-fructose corn syrup, the most common sweetener in sodas today, are both nearly equal combinations of glucose and fructose. Fructose has a story of its own that we will delve into later (especially as it relates to nonalcoholic liver disease).

the eyes, the lower limbs, and the brain). Ironically perhaps, a common treatment for severe diabetes is injectable insulin. The body has grown unresponsive to the insulin levels the pancreas can produce, so more is pumped in from outside. This can indeed lower blood sugar in diabetics and possibly stave off severe complications, but what might the long-term effects from more insulin be? Perhaps further insulin resistance, and in the majority of patients, almost certainly increased body fat.

A Cause for Alarm, but Not for Despair

I've started us off with a look at some of the biggest pandemics that threaten our bodily temples today, and real threats they are. As prevalent and alarming as these growing health pandemics may be, in the rest of this book you will see there is always hope and never a need to despair.

Indeed, though I've been involved in fitness and endurance training for nearly fifty years and have retained a fair measure of muscle mass, strength, and cardiovascular endurance for an old guy, within a year of writing these pages, I suffered at least two of the symptoms of metabolic syndrome myself. Indeed, in February 2021, my blood pressure was 159/91 and my waist was 40.5 inches. Within six months of following the nutritional practices of this book's part 2, my blood pressure was 124/68 and my waist was 34.5, and all this at age sixty.

There are laws of biology and physiology that apply to every one of us, and yet there are also significant individual differences between us. God made us this way in His image and likeness, as members of the human race, but as unique individuals too. I hope that in the pages ahead you will find plenty of information and inspiration to shore up and spruce up the temple God gave you to better glorify *Him* in *your* body.

Now let's get down to business to see how we can shrink these pandemics (and if need be, ourselves) down to size.

TEMPLE-TENDING TENET #1

The biggest pandemics of all in our time involve the rapidly rising rates of obesity and associated metabolic disorders, including diabetes and nonalcoholic fatty liver disease. While temple-threatening on their own, they also function as dangerous comorbidities that make us more vulnerable to damage from acute pandemics. The good news is that changes in the way that we eat and live can help reverse these chronic conditions and rebuild sturdy bodily temples.

2

Gluttony and Sloth: Guilty as Sins?

The vice of gluttony does not regard the substance of food, but in the desire therof not being regulated by reason. Wherefore if a man exceeds in quantity of food, not from desire of food, but through deeming it necessary to him, this pertains, not to gluttony, but to some kind of inexperience. It is a case of gluttony only when a man knowingly exceeds the measure in eating, from a desire for the pleasures of the palate.

— St. Thomas Aquinas, *Summa Theologica*, II-II, Q. 148, art. 1

Gluttony, Sloth, and Our Health Pandemics

We saw in our first chapter that obesity is a rapidly rising pandemic tied into related pandemics, including diabetes. Indeed, I did not even mention that research has suggested that men under age fifty-five with BMIs greater than forty have ninety times the chance of developing diabetes than men of normal weight, and women with BMIs greater than thirty-five have ninety-three times the chance of developing diabetes than women with BMIs less than twenty-two.[22] The fact that

---

[22] Studies cited in Zoë Harcombe, *The Obesity Epidemic: What Caused It? How Can We Stop It?* (Zanesville, OH: Columbus Publishing, 2010), 34.

obesity, diabetes, and related disorders are rapidly rising health threats is not open to debate, but the question of why they are rising sure is!

Modern writers on obesity, such as award-wining science journalist Gary Taubes and nutritionist Zoë Harcombe, Ph.D., are among the many people who have chronicled the history of various medical and scientific theories as to the underlying cause or causes of obesity. Most prominent among them today is the simple "energy balance" or "calories in–calories out" theory, which holds we become fat because we regularly take in more calories than our bodies require for maintenance and energy needs. The most basic advice to the obese, or to those who would hope to avoid obesity, is thus to eat less and move more.

This kind of thinking may carry with it both psychological and spiritual implications. Do the overweight and obese have some kind of obsession with food, some kind of psychological "eating disorder"? Do they have some kind of character flaw or lack of self-discipline that leads them to eat whatever they want, or, on the other side of the energy equation, to be too lazy to get up and burn off the food they eat? Do they suffer from the spiritual vices or sins of gluttony or sloth? Can we weigh the gluttony or sloth in people's souls by placing their bodies on sets of scales? Well, I'm going to provide reasons to take issue with the simple "energy balance" theory of obesity and to answer no, for the vast majority of cases, for both our psychological and our spiritual questions posed above.

Since our primary goal in reading this book is to glorify God through honoring our bodily temples, I'll begin by addressing the spiritual issues, specifically the vices and sins[23] of gluttony and sloth.

---

[23] Thomas Aquinas tells us that *vices* are tendencies, dispositions, or habits we build within ourselves to perform *sinful actions*, in just the same way that *virtues* are tendencies, dispositions, or habits we build within ourselves to perform *virtuous acts*. (More on the virtues of health and holiness will come in our next chapter.)

First, as we noted earlier, they are indeed real vices and sins — serious, "capital," and "deadly" ones — but they must carefully be defined. As for gluttony, St. Thomas Aquinas tells us that it is an inordinate, unreasonable desire for food that can entail more than simply desiring to eat too much. There are different "species" or varieties of the vice of gluttony that include the tendency to eat *too much* but also include the habit eating *too greedily* by wolfing down our food, eating *too hastily* by eating *too often* (a species we'll look at more closely in chapter 9, on fasting and feasting), as well as eating *too sumptuously* or *too daintily*, demanding gourmet foods while showing ingratitude for plain and simple fare.

Gluttony's potential toward deadly sin comes from the fact that it removes our attention from God by focusing so much on what goes into our bellies. Also, many philosophers and theologians saw it is a "gateway sin" of sorts toward sins of lust by weakening our control over our bodily appetites. Gluttony is potentially serious business but not, as I'll soon endeavor to show, the underlying cause of our obesity pandemic.

How about sloth or laziness? Are people becoming obese because they are too darn lazy? And does this implicate the vice or sin of sloth? Once again, I don't think so, and to understand why, we must see what the deadly sin of *sloth* really is. It is commonly confused with garden-variety laziness. Indeed, in a secular television series on the deadly sins years ago, its episode on sloth ended with the words: "If Christian tradition is to be believed, the simple act of laziness can send you to Hell!" I don't know about you, but if that truly is the case, I'm in big trouble!

Sins of sloth are infinitely more serious than simple laziness, though laziness about certain matters can certainly flow from it. The key to understanding sloth starts with the word the *Catechism* gives us as its synonym — namely, "acedia," which comes from Greek words meaning "without care." The deadly sin of sloth specifically means *spiritual sloth* — in essence, saying through our thoughts and actions: "God, I don't care!" It is a spiritual boredom and apathy for the things of God, rather than merely laziness of indolence that avoids physical exertion. Indeed, a superlean exercise fanatic may be spiritually slothful if he or she zooms around the gym or the open roads for hours at a time while failing to give God His due. True sloth can be serious business indeed. In fact, Thomas Aquinas tells us it directly opposes the first great commandment: to love God with all that we are. Still, it's not sloth — or even physical laziness — that causes us to grow fat and sick.

The same, I believe, applies to the psychological or character-flaw theory of obesity. While some people may well experience little discipline over what they eat, and may be very little inclined to get up and exercise, I will argue that, in a very real sense, their problem is more than just mind deep, and there is some research out there to back this up.[24] Let's dig into some alternative explanations, again using the wise St. Thomas as our guide.

In the thirteenth century, Thomas wrote the following: "Experience shows that some understand more profoundly than do others; as one who carries a conclusion to its first principles and ultimate causes understands it better than one who reduces it to its proximate causes."[25] Nearly eight hundred years later, nephrologist and obesity expert Jason Fung, M.D., wrote: "Excess calories may certainly be the *proximate* cause of weight gain, but not its *ultimate* cause. What's the difference between proximate and ultimate? The proximate cause is

---

[24] M. V. Roehling, P. V. Roehling, and L. M. Odland, "Investigating the Validity of Stereotypes about Overweight Employees: The Relationship between Body Weight and Normal Personality Traits," *Group & Organization Management* 33, no. 4 (May 28, 2008): 392–424, https://doi.org/10.1177/1059601108321518.

[25] *ST*, I, Q. 85, art. 7.

immediately responsible, whereas the ultimate cause is what started the chain of events."[26]

Consider this insight from obesity writer Gary Taubes:

> Thermodynamics tells us that if we get fatter and heavier, more energy enters our body than leaves it. Overeating means we're consuming more energy than we're expending. It says the same thing in a different way. Neither happens to answer the question why. Why do we take in more energy than we expend? Why do we overeat? Why do we get fatter?[27]

When we strive to answer *why*, we strive to arrive at more profound levels of understanding by ferreting out ultimate causes. Applying this thinking to obesity, yes, we can say that people become fat when they consume more energy than they expend, which, at first glance, suggests that the reason they've accumulated too much fat is that they have simply eaten too much and exercised too little. Taubes and Fung have both pointed out, however, that this doesn't really tell us much. To say that a person is obese because he eats too much is like saying a person is an alcoholic because he drinks too much. True enough, but what does that tell us about why those people eat or drink too much — and how to get them to stop? We would not expect much success if we merely advised an alcoholic not to drink so much, though often the obese are merely advised not to eat so much and to get up off the couch more often — i.e., "Eat less, move more."

But have we explained very much? Are we operating upon the most "proximate" and superficial of causes? Could there be a more

---

[26] Jason Fung, M.D., *The Obesity Code: Unlocking the Secrets of Weight Loss* (Vancouver, Canada: Greystone Books, 2016), 10.

[27] Gary Taubes, *Why We Get Fat and What to Do about It* (New York: Alfred Knopf, 2011), 75.

fundamental underlying reason *why* an overweight person's energy balance seems so out of whack, perhaps despite repeated arduous efforts to do something about it through diet, exercise, or both? Surveys in recent years show that more than half of overweight Americans have tried time and again to reduce their weight. Taubes poses the perhaps mind-twisting question of whether people become fat because they eat so much and move so little, or whether people eat so much and move so little because they have become fat. (Chicken or egg, anyone?)

I, like a growing number of modern physicians, nutritionists, health care providers, clinicians, and researchers of many stripes, believe we can dig deeper to find underlying causes in our own bodily temples, physical disturbances that give rise to what may appear to be psychological and spiritual problems. Let's take a look.

It's the Hormones, Samson (or Sarah)!

The theory that views obesity as simply a matter of too many calories coming in from food versus too few going out through energy expenditure is based upon a misapplication of the laws of thermodynamics, such as the first law of the conservation of energy: the idea that energy within a closed system can be transformed but cannot be created or destroyed. This gives rise to the oversimplified notion that "a calorie is a calorie," calories being units of the heat energy stored within foods, regardless of whether it comes from protein, carbohydrate, or fat (each of which will be examined more closely in part 2).

Based on this idea, for several decades the dietary advice for those who would hope to lose weight was to go on a low-calorie, lowfat (partly because fat has more calories per gram) diet and to exercise more, which certainly seems sensible enough on the face of it. Unfortunately, decades of research have shown that the vast majority of obese individuals who lose substantial weight on such regimens end up regaining most or all of it.

Although a calorie is a calorie when foodstuffs are burned in laboratory equipment, the human body is far more carefully crafted and
complex than any machine, operating not only according to laws of
physics but according to laws of physiology too. We need to ask questions like these:

- What if certain kinds of foods are stored or burned at different
  rates in the human body?
- What if certain kinds of foods signal the body to store fat
  rather than to use it for energy?
- What if certain foods stimulate our hunger, prompting us to
  eat more — serving as fuel for gluttony, so to speak?
- What if a chronic diet of such foods makes us tired and prompts
  us to conserve more energy, to move and exercise less (e.g.,
  cranking out our recliners' footrests so sloth can stretch out
  and rest)?

Well, it seems that certain foods do indeed do such things. We'll
look at those foods in the chapters ahead, but right now we will zoom
in on just how they can do these temple-tainting things.

As we move from physics to human biology, our first — and, in
some sense, most important — stop is at our endocrine system, the
group of organs (such as the hypothalamus in the brain, the pituitary
gland, the adrenal glands, the pancreas, and the gonads) that produce
and regulate our body's hormones. Hormones are the body's internal
messengers that act upon various organs to regulate processes including growth and body development, reproduction, sexual development,
energy use and balance, and the volume of fluid salts and sugars in the
blood. That hormones can play a primary causal role in the accumulation of calorie intake, output, bodily growth, and deposition of body
fat can be seen in a great number of ways. Below are several examples
from Gary Taubes's book *Why We Get Fat* that illustrate how body-fat
accumulation is more complicated than simply a matter of calories

in and out, depending on a variety of genetic and other biological processes, foremost among them being the role of hormones and the enzymes (digestive chemicals) they stimulate.

Identical twins, who share the same genes, even if they have been raised apart, have a high correlation in bodyweight.[28] Researchers conclude that genetic influences far outweigh (so to speak) environmental influences on bodyweight. Some of us, through no fault of our own, simply fatten far more easily than others.

Within our own bodies, certain tissues are lipophilic (fat-loving or fat-storing) and others are not. Whereas we accumulate fat around our middles or hips or chins, we do not store it to any significant degree on the tops of our hands, our feet, or our foreheads.

Men and women, with differing levels of the hormones testosterone and estrogen, tend to store fat differently; most men store it primarily in the abdominal region and most women in the hips, buttocks, and thighs. After menopause, when estrogen is reduced, women have a greater tendency to start accumulating fat in their abdomens as well.

During later childhood and early adolescence, appetites grow and more calories come in, as any grocery-buying parent can attest. But, at least until recent decades, the children and teens grew bigger and taller, but not obese. Boys, with their surges in testosterone, tend to grow more muscular, and girls, with the surges in female sex hormones, such as estrogen, tend to accumulate more body fat, but in the specific areas that God intended for them, as in the breasts and the lower body. Children and teens do not grow simply because they are getting hungry and eating more. They are getting hungry and eating more because

---

[28] See A. J. Stunkard, J. R. Harris, N. L. Pedersen, and G. E. McClearn, "The Body-Mass Index of Twins Who Have Been Reared Apart," *New England Journal of Medicine* 322, no. 21 (May 24, 1990): 1483-1487, https://pubmed.ncbi.nlm.nih.gov/2336075/.

genetically programmed surges of hormones are stimulating body growth, and such growth requires plenty of building material!

Pregnancy provides yet another clear example that applies to half of the human race. Pregnant women do indeed tend to take in more calories and exercise less, but that is not why their tummies are growing!

As a final, dramatic example, consider the thankfully rare disorder of progressive lipodystrophy, a disease found in both sexes, but about four times more likely in women. During childhood, those with this disease suffer a progressive *loss* of fat, in the face, neck, trunk, and upper extremities. Some of these patients will gain so much weight over time, though *only below the waist*, that their BMIs reach the level of obesity. As Taubes has stated (and provided photographic evidence), it can be as if they have the upper body of a marathon runner and the lower body of a Sumo wrestler. How does the calories in–calories out model explain these people? Are their lower bodies gluttons while their upper bodies are anorexics?

Clearly then, genetic factors and hormones play a huge role in why some of us — actually the majority of us today — are carrying too much fat and why where the fat is placed in our bodies puts us at risk for a host of related chronic health impairments. We've touched on the roles of sex hormones such as testosterone and estrogen. Human growth hormone plays a huge role as well, especially during adolescence. But when it comes to how much fat we will store in our temples, the key hormone in charge of construction appears to be insulin. Insulin is a good thing, with a variety of essential functions, from the anabolic, cell-building functions of healthy tissue growth to (as we saw last chapter) the regulation of blood sugar. We've all heard the old warning that "too much of a good thing is a bad thing," and we'll spell this bad thing out in the chapters ahead, along with quick, effective methods for once again allowing insulin to help us build the lean, healthy temples God intended.

In sum, true gluttony and sloth are guilty as sins but are most often innocent as primary causes of obesity and poor health. Most of us who become overweight and unhealthy do so not because of psychological flaws of food obsession or physical laziness or sinful tendencies toward gluttony and sloth but because we have been taught by experts and persuaded by food manufacturers to eat food that makes us hungry and tired.

After a new look at the virtues of fitness in our next chapter, we will search for the true guilty parties, the "first principles" and "ultimate causes" in Thomas's language, to explain the health pandemics. Standing up side by side in our first suspect lineup will be real foods and ultraprocessed "food-like substances."

Temple-Tending Tenet #2

Neither gluttony, sloth, nor psychological problems are the primary causes of the epidemic of obesity and related disorders; rather, hormonal responses to the foods we eat are the causes.

3

The Virtues of Fitness

Virtue, inasmuch as it is a suitable disposition of the soul, is like health and beauty, which are suitable dispositions of the body.

— St. Thomas Aquinas[29]

But if a man uses exercise, food, and drink in moderation, he will become physically strong and his health will be improved and preserved. It is the same with the virtues of the soul — for instance, fortitude, temperance, and the other virtues.

— St. Thomas Aquinas[30]

Four High-Flying Cardinals of Health and Holiness

Drawing on St. Thomas Aquinas's parallels between virtues in the soul and health, beauty, and strength in the body, we can see how the cardinal virtues "perfect our powers," both spiritual and bodily powers.

---

[29] *ST*, I-II, Q. 55, art. 2.

[30] St. Thomas Aquinas Commentary on Aristotle's *Nicomachean Ethics* (*NE*) (Notre Dame, IN: Dumb Ox Books, 1993), 89, addressing Aristotle's *NE*, bk. 1, chap. 2.

Fortitude, our capacity to overcome or endure difficulties to obtain worthwhile goals, is the guiding virtue we employ in physical strength training (literally overcoming heavy obstacles) and cardiovascular or aerobic training (literally enduring uncomfortable things) to achieve the goal of bodily fitness.

Temperance, our capacity to rein in our desires for bodily pleasures, is the guiding virtue regarding what we eat to maximize our health.

Prudence, or practical wisdom, is the virtue that helps us craft realistic, practical regimens of eating and exercise that make sense for us as individuals, with our unique bodies, preferences, and life-commitment responsibilities.

Justice, the social virtue in which we give others their rightful due, will be employed in chapters attempting to give rightful due to the needs of particular groups of individuals — namely, women and children, the elderly, and people with physical and mental disabilities.

Dynamos of Charity

These natural, cardinal, moral virtues are used as *means* to help us do what we need to do to grow in faith and fitness. But as Christians, we are recipients of an even higher class of virtues, the three supernatural, theological, or infused virtues of *faith, hope,* and *love* that God breathes into our souls at Baptism. As St. Paul put it so well, "So faith, hope, and love abide, these three; but the greatest of this is love" (1 Cor. 13:13). Love (or charity, from the Latin *caritas*), is the greatest of these three virtues. Indeed, as we read in James: "As the body apart from the spirit is dead, so faith apart from works is dead" (2:26). Thomas Aquinas says it is charity that "quickens," or brings to life, faith, that inspires loving works; and indeed, charity is the "mother of the virtues." The "order of charity" or love sets up the *ends* or goals for which all other manner of natural and supernatural virtues serve as the *means.*

Charity is the ultimate "virtue of fitness" as well. We should all strive to become veritable dynamos of charity, so that in growing strong, enduring bodies, we will be better able to actively serve God and the physical and spiritual needs of our neighbor. *Charity* is also the queen and mother of all virtues. Indeed, it flows from the very presence of the Holy Spirit (one of whose names is Love, per St. Thomas)[31] within our bodily temples.

Still, in this book, I'd like to introduce yet another set of virtues that are particularly important when it comes to understanding the complexities of human health, nutrition, and the role of exercise.

Intellectual Virtues for Physical, Mental, and Spiritual Health

Aristotle wrote (and St. Thomas agreed) that moral virtues (like the cardinal virtues and the panoply of virtues that assist them) help us do the good, while there is another class of natural virtues that help us know the true. So, if we are to do our bodies good, so to speak, we must come to know what is truly good for our bodies. Ancient Greek philosophers called these truth-seeking virtues "intellectual" virtues and designated three as science (or knowledge — since *scire* is Latin for "to know"), understanding, and wisdom.

They are right there together in Scripture as well. For example: "By wisdom a house is built, and by understanding it is established; by knowledge the rooms are filled with all precious and pleasant riches" (Prov. 24:3–4). Since we are trying to build fitting temples to house the Holy Spirit within us, it seems we should certainly try to stock up on some science, understanding, and wisdom! Let's look at them separately in brief:

- Science, or knowledge, pertains to the comprehension of cause-and-effect relationships.

---

[31] *ST*, I. Q. 37 "Of the Name of the Holy Spirit, as Love."

- Understanding pertains to the grasp of fundamental, underlying principles.
- Wisdom pertains to the judgments made regarding the highest of causes and the most fundamental of principles.

St. Thomas described their relationship like this: "Science depends on understanding as on a virtue of higher degree: and both of these depend on wisdom, as obtaining the highest place, and containing beneath itself understanding and science, by judging both the conclusions of science, and of the principles on which they are based."[32]

Without a doubt, to cut through all the complexity so we can better understand the fundamental causes of our health pandemics and better judge what we can do to correct them, we're going to need heaping helpings of all three intellectual virtues. Let's start with a quick look at the virtue of *science*, since health and nutrition are ideally grounded in sound scientific research.

How to Be Enlightened, Not Blinded, by Science

As we work through the pages of this book, we will encounter many kinds and classes of scientific evidence that bear on human health and disease. The branch of science that deals with health, disease, and related factors, such as nutrition, as they appear in populations is called epidemiology, from the Greek *epi* (among), *demios* (people), *logia* (theory or study of). Let's take a very quick look at the pros and cons of its most commonly used research methods.

Observational and correlational studies. These are the most commonly used studies with the greatest number of research subjects. Researchers gather data from different groups on things such as diet (often through giving research subjects food questionnaires to fill out about

---

[32]   *ST*, I, Q. 57, art. 2.

their eating habits) as well as evidence on various measures of health or health outcomes — everything from cholesterol levels, to heart attacks, strokes, and overall mortality. These may be cross-sectional studies in which several groups are compared at one point in time. Some of the most influential studies in nutrition have compared the diets and health outcomes from people of different nations around the world, as we will see when we examine the work of Ancel Keys. Some studies are longitudinal, meaning that they follow one or more groups over time, perhaps even decades, often gathering new data at certain intervals. One of the most famous we will examine is the Framingham Heart Study, which has been going on since 1948! Observational studies are relatively easy to perform because the subjects are not required to do anything different. Their normal habits and outcomes are simply observed and measured. The fundamental limitation is that while such data shows correlations — that is, which features of diet are more strongly associated with certain health outcomes — a valid maxim of social science holds that "correlation does not prove causation." Other factors may explain why certain factors are correlated. For a simple example from the nutritional literature, many studies in the twentieth century that associated increased fat intake with health problems did not control for the fact that the same kinds of Western diets that were high in fat included large amounts of processed foods that were also high in sugar. So which was the culprit? (We'll look at that soon.) Further, results of correlational studies should provide starting points for deeper investigation where possible, but many of the massive changes in nutritional recommendations in the United States and around the world at the beginning of our obesity and diabetes epidemics in the 1970s and 1980s were based almost exclusively on observational studies.

Experimental studies. Thousands of experimental studies have been performed in the field of nutrition and exercise and their relation to obesity, to a variety of diseases, and to positive health outcomes. Here, the goal is to get at actual cause-and-effect relationships (as the virtue of science nods its head in approval!). In the field of nutrition, this is accomplished by assigning people in a certain group or groups specific kinds of dietary changes and comparing them with control groups without dietary changes, or perhaps on different kinds of diets. We will consider one nice example, the A to Z study, in chapter 6. It is all for the better when people in each group are assigned there randomly, to ensure that the dietary intervention, and not some inherent difference between the people in each group, is the cause of whatever results are obtained. Best of all, when it is feasible, is the double-blind study, wherein neither the research subjects nor the researchers know which groups the subjects are in while the study goes on. A problem with scientific studies is that it is not always feasible or ethical to assign people certain interventions, which could prove to be harmful. Consider the link between cigarette smoking and cancer, for example. People were never randomly assigned to groups where some were to smoke some certain number of cigarettes per day so the researchers could see what happened! Rather, the correlational or observational data was so consistent and so great in magnitude that cigarette smoking was rightly implicated as a highly likely risk factor for cancer, even though some people may well smoke all their lives and never get cancer. Still, while dietary studies rarely show even a twofold difference in risk for various diseases, cigarettes were routinely found to increase people's risk of lung cancer by fifteen- to thirtyfold.

Systematic reviews. Systematic reviews provide the results of researchers' analyses of multiple past studies performed in a given field. A key principle in science is that valid findings should be capable of replication — that is, they should show up consistently in subsequent studies and thereby be less likely to represent some kind of error or fluke.

Systematic reviews look for this consistency or lack thereof, as well as the strength of the findings.

Meta-analyses are systematic reviews in which statistical procedures are performed that effectively combine the limited power of previous studies with their limited number of subjects into one grand study with as many subjects as all of the previous studies combined. Meta-analyses have been described as the best and depicted as the peak of the pyramid when it comes to nutrition and exercise science studies. Potential problems with meta-analyses and systematic reviews can arise, though, depending on the criteria researchers use to rule in or rule out studies fit for review or meta-analysis. This can stilt the results.

Animal studies. Sometimes experimental studies performed with animals are used to provide evidence potentially applicable to human nutrition, and sometimes it may prove more applicable than others. We will see in chapter 6, for example, how the first studies leading to recommendations that we reduce cholesterol and animal fats in our diets came from deleterious effects of massive amounts of dietary cholesterol in, of all species, rabbits — plant eaters! On the other hand, we will see that studies of the natural eating habits of the lowly locust may have provided highly important information on how even you and I seek out protein in our daily diets.

Cellular level or in vitro studies. Though such evidence has sometimes been overlooked in its application to human obesity and related disorders, evidence that comes from examining the metabolism within particular cells of our bodies, such as fat, muscle, and nerve cells, can tell us a great deal about the effects of various nutrients and hormones on cellular structures such as mitochondria and cell membranes, which may have significant bearing on just what we should or should not eat. (The findings on the impact of insulin and ketones will prove particularly relevant.) "In vitro," by the way, comes from Latin words meaning "in a glass" (such as a petri dish used in a laboratory).

Anecdotal evidence. Usually considered the lowest rung on the scientific ladder is anecdotal evidence, often in the form of "experiments of one," such as a doctor's case study of a particular patient or our own experiments on ourselves. Sometimes these are called "n of 1" studies, "n" referring to the number of subjects. They are limited as a source of scientific evidence for a variety of reasons. To begin with, we all have significant differences in our unique genetics, so something that seems to work for me may not work for you. Further, we often make many changes to our diets or exercise regimens all at once, so how can we be sure we know what really produced the changes (or failed to do so)? And yet, think about this. We all live our lives as an "n of 1." When it comes to our health, that "1" makes all the difference in the world. In a very real sense, the personal vignettes in the appendix of this book are all "n of 1" studies. What worked for Nick or Laraine might or might not work for you but might provide ideas for new things to experiment with (under the guidance of your health-care professional), and I pray that they will inspire you to find ways to better build, maintain, and sanctify your own bodily temple.

And here is one last point. If we are to make important life changes in the way we eat or exercise based on the findings of scientific studies, we should analyze those studies very carefully, or consult with health-care professionals who can help us do so. All too often, secondary sources such as news outlets will craft startling, eye-catching headlines like these: "New Research Shows Pizza Causes Cancer." (Don't worry; I just made that one up.) In such cases, one would want to turn to the original research report. If such an example referred to an observational study, for example, we'd know from the start that actual *causation* was not even measured.

We should also be aware that a good deal of nutritional and pharmaceutical research is funded by food and pharmaceutical companies that may have a vested interest in setting things up so the results tend toward a certain preferred conclusion. Further, sometimes studies that produce results contrary to the consensus views of the time are rejected for publication by peer reviewers and sometimes are not even submitted for publication by the researchers themselves. Indeed, in a few cases, such never-published research has been discovered, reanalyzed, and finally published decades later. And, finally, sometimes what researchers present as their conclusions are not really supported by their own detailed findings! That is why, if we want to dig deep into the findings of an important scientific study, we must read the entire report; we read only the headlines, the conclusion, or even the abstract (summary) at our peril.

Still, rest easy. I'm hoping this little primer on scientific methods will make things a little easier when we examine some of the findings of such studies and the implications they hold for glorifying God in our bodies. Grounded in the cause-and-effect relationships science can bring us, we will search for those fundamental, underlying nutritional and exercise principles that understanding can grasp, to place before wisdom's judgment seat. And speaking of fundamental, underlying principles, at least as far as eating goes, we are just about to meet the first, and perhaps most important, one.

Temple-Tending Tenet #3

To build healthy, holy temples we need to train ourselves in the moral virtues, to be able to do what is good for us; the intellectual virtues, to know what is truly good; and the theological virtues, to know and do what we do for the love and the glory of God.

Part II

Collecting Quality Building Materials
(Proper Nourishment of the Bodies God Gave Us)

If you are willing and obedient,
you shall eat the good food of the land.

— Isaiah 1:19

4

These Thy Gifts: Enjoying the Foods God Made for Us

And you, take wheat and barley, beans, and lentils, millet and spelt, and put them into a single vessel, and make bread of them.

— Ezekiel 4:9

Enriched wheat flour, water, sugar, yeast, salt, soybean and/or canola oil, defatted soy flour, wheat gluten, calcium, propionate, sodium stearoyl-2-lactylate, sorbic acid, vegetable monoglycerides.

— Ingredient list of one of America's top-ten best-selling breads

Real Food Feeds

Enough now of the background and readying of the soil. It's time to get down to business and start building our temples. We'll begin by examining the materials we'll need. I will cut to the chase, proceed to the virtue of understanding, and lay down our first fundamental principle: *Real food feeds.* Moving next to wisdom and the judgments it proclaims, our most fundamental maxim of nutritional advice is therefore: *Eat real food!* There. It is finished. Thank you for your attention. (But if you would care to know more about just what "real food" is, what kind of "foods" are not "real," and why we should stick as much as possible to the real ones, please keep reading along.)

Speaking of the complexities of nutrition, perhaps you have heard of (or tried) dietary approaches such as the Atkins diet, the Blue Zone diet, the Bulletproof diet, the carnivore diet, high carb–lowfat diets, high fat–low carb diets, high-protein diets, the Mediterranean diet, the Ornish diet, the Paleo diet, the primal diet, the South Beach diet, veganism, vegetarianism, the Zone diet, or any other number of diets scattered throughout the alphabet. Some of these approaches could hardly disagree more about the proper materials to build human bodily temples. Some argue for high or low intakes of fat, carbohydrate, protein, animal foods, or plant foods. Some condemn red meat, while others are built upon it. Some, such as vegetarianism, eschew fish. Others, such as the Blue Zone, advise it in moderation.

Most approaches focus on providing optimal human health, but some, such as vegetarianism and veganism, may also be founded upon ethical, ecological, and religious beliefs. Vegetarianism and heavy ingestion of grain is endorsed, for example, by the Seventh Day Adventists. They operate the Loma Linda University and conduct a great deal of nutritional research. And ever hear of John Harvey Kellogg? He was a famous Adventist when he invented his famous crunchy cereals — though, unlike his successors, he didn't load them with sugar.

Many people have claimed vigorous health and vitality through every one of these dietary approaches. Indeed, I know that many of this book's vignette contributors (including myself) have dabbled in at least a few of them over the years. Still, as diverse as these approaches are, there is indeed one very important thing they all tend to hold in common: the recommendation that we eat real, natural, whole foods as much as possible, avoiding as much as possible overly processed manufactured foods, which some have called "fake foods," "foodlike substances," and even "Frankenfoods"! This has been summarized as eating foods that come from "forests, fields, or farms, not factories," or "foods that do not come with a label or barcode." If I might add to the catchphrase list, how about "foods invented by God, not man"?

These are foods as God made them, and they tend to bubble over with all the kinds of life-giving macro- and micronutrients we'll examine in the chapters that follow. We were created to eat them, and they were created to be eaten by us (see Gen. 1:29–31; Acts 10:9–16). And this is exclusively all that we ate, from Adam and Eve on down — until the last century or so, and particularly until the last forty years and the rise of the health pandemics. We'll get to the stats in our next section.

For now, let's consider this chapter's opening quotations. We start with what we could well call the bread recipe from God's own kitchen. Here's what we need: wheat, barley, beans, lentils, millet, and spelt, along with a bowl to mix them in. Now there is real food that feeds. Though my intention is not to praise or to slam particular brands of products in these pages, I can't help but note that there is a modern food company that does indeed make breads pretty much according to the recipes in Ezekiel. They are called, most fittingly, Ezekiel 4:9 breads.

Next, we move to a very popular and wonderful (so to speak) modern bread recipe, prepared for us by manufacturers. Here's what we would need to make it: enriched wheat flour, water, sugar, yeast, salt, soybean and/or canola oil, defatted soy flour, wheat gluten, calcium, propionate, sodium stearoyl-2-lactylate, sorbic acid, and vegetable monoglycerides. If we find our cupboards bare of wheat gluten, calcium propionate, sodium strearoyl-2-lactate, sorbic acid, or vegetable monoglycerides, perhaps we could borrow some from a neighbor.

Of course, man does not live by bread alone, as Jesus told us metaphorically in reference to feeding on God's word (Matt. 4:4) and in the reality of our daily food intake. Significant differences between real foods as God made them and ultraprocessed foods as man has altered them can be found for almost every kind of food. Let's suppose we have a hankering for orangey deliciousness. At the real, whole-food end of the spectrum we find the humble orange. Ingredient: orange. At the man-made end of the spectrum is a tangy space-age drink I enjoyed from time to time during the space age itself (1960s). Ingredients: sugar, fructose, citric acid, maltodextrin, calcium phosphate, sodium acid pyrophosphate, ascorbic acid (Vitamin C), natural flavor, artificial color, guar gum, yellow 5, yellow 6, xanthan gum. Just add water. As I recall, for some reason Mom always brought the powder home from the store and never once whipped up a batch on her own from scratch. Perhaps because she wasn't a chemist.

What on earth have we been thinking — and eating, and drinking? When people think of the potential hazards of eating too much processed food, in my experience their thoughts often go to all of the artificial ingredients, those additives and preservatives with mysterious chemical names that might wreak who knows what havoc in our bodies years down the line. And the potential hazards go beyond what manufacturers have added and even beyond what they *have taken out*, yielding what some call "empty calories," foods devoid of nutrients that should naturally be there. As Robert Lustig, M.D., a pediatric endocrinologist, has argued, food labels should tell us not only *what is in* a processed food product but *what they have done to the food!*[33]

We will examine real foods in real depth in the remaining chapters of part 2, but let's turn our attention next to the artificial foods that are damaging our temples. You might wonder, for example, what percentage of the American diet is composed of real foods versus processed or ultraprocessed foods. Further, if these percentages are so high and

---

[33] Complete references to two of his books appear in the appendix.

these foods are of such questionable value, why are the manufacturers manufacturing them, and why are *we* eating and drinking them? The answers are next up.

Fake Food Fouls — and Fools

Think about it, dear reader: What percentage of the foods you eat in a day are real foods, animals or plants that exist in nature without a nutritional label attached, versus manufactured ultraprocessed foods — ready-to-eat packaged foods, including pizza, prepacked frozen meals, packaged sweet or salty snacks, and desserts? I don't know about you, but I now shudder to think about my own intake of ultraprocessed foods even a year ago, but that itself is probably a big part of the problem. *We hardly think about such foods. We just eat them!* One study showed that from 2012 to 2017, almost 60 percent of the food consumed in the United States — well over half the food we ate — was of the ultraprocessed variety.

To put the icing on the cake, so to speak, in August 2021, the prestigious *Journal of the American Medical Association* published a study indicating that, whereas in 1999, U.S. children and teens ate a whopping 61.4 percent of their daily diet in the form of ultraprocessed foods, by 2018, it had risen yet further to 67 percent on average.[34] More than two-thirds of the calories of the diets of American children and adolescents now comes from foods that did not even exist one hundred years ago, and the rates are steadily rising. The researchers also found, not surprisingly, that their daily caloric intake of unprocessed or minimally processed food (aka real food) had decreased from 28.8 percent to 23.5 percent. True,

---

[34] Lu Wang, Euridice Martínez Steele, Mengxi Du, Jennifer L. Pomeranz, et al., "Trends in Consumption of Ultraprocessed Foods among U.S. Youths Aged 2–19 Years, 1999–2018," *Journal of the American Medical Association (JAMA)* 326, no. 6 (August 10, 2021): 519–530, https://jamanetwork.com/journals/jama/article-abstract/2782866.

correlation does not prove causation, but it sure can point and shake its finger at it. Might there be some connection here with the meteoric rise in obesity and diabetes in our children and teens?

Now let's dig into the wording of our section heading. When I say fake food "fouls," I mean to argue that most food processing impairs or damages the nutritional profiles of the natural foodstuffs they begin with (without even mentioning the artificial ingredients that are so often added) and consequently fouls our bodily temples too. When I say fake food "fools," I mean to argue that most processed foods have been purposefully engineered to "fool" our bodies' own internal mechanisms that tell us we're full and enough is enough.

First, a couple of caveats. For one thing, God gave us minds, and He expects us to use them! There are advantages to some sorts of food processing. Various methods known throughout the centuries have allowed peoples all around the world to store and preserve foods, helping to feed the hungry during harsh winters, for example. These methods include the cooking, drying, and salting of meat and fish and the canning of fruits and vegetables. Also, speaking as a weightlifter from way back, sometimes positive nutritional elements from whole foods can be extracted with benefit. So I certainly do not want to oversimply things and say that *all* processed food is bad, or cannot be eaten at all, though most of them are very shady characters.

Also, ultraprocessed foods rose meteorically in the United States and other developed countries over the last several decades, partly because of their convenience. I wonder, dear reader, if you have ever sat down with your exhausted spouse in the late afternoon and asked if there was anything "easy" to make for supper? Kathy and I are retired, and we still say it now and then, but the lure of a variety of "convenience foods" is even more tempting for the very busy parents of very busy families. As we've just seen, kids can hardly get enough of the stuff anymore! Hopefully, though, with some teamwork and forethought, such as planning menus a day or two ahead, we can work together to make meals based on real foods a little more convenient.

Now, back to the "fouling." Most ultraprocessed foods tend to remove fiber, which can produce a sense of fullness, and natural nutrients and then add ingredients — the most inexpensive ones possible — that enhance flavor and extend shelf life. Notice, for example, that our wonderful modern bread uses "enriched flour" that must be bolstered with artificially added vitamins because the vitamins naturally present have been mostly stripped away. Further, the excessive milling to produce the fine white flour has rendered it almost free of natural fiber, and this lack of fiber helps our blood sugar to rise quickly. (Rather than using milled flour, the manufactured "Ezekiel" bread I mentioned uses sprouted grains, which retain more nutrients and are digested more slowly, producing a less rapid blood-sugar increase.) Moreover, some of the ultimately ultraprocessed foods hardly have any real food in them whatsoever; call to mind the ingredient list of our tangy breakfast drink, for but one example.

Another major way ultraprocessed foods foul our bodily temples is that because they are typically so low in essential nutrients, we may be driven to consume more and more of them to satisfy our nutritional needs, thus making us fatter and sicker.

As for ultraprocessed foods "fooling us," I think we should all be aware that for several decades, food manufactures have hired special consultants of all sorts, from chemists to psychologists to marketing experts, to try to build upon our natural appetites and override our natural restraints on overeating. With interviews and documents from processed-food producers themselves, including virtually all of the major food and drink companies around the globe, journalist Michael Moss, in his book *Salt Sugar Fat*, lays out in the greatest of detail just how manufacturers do this. Many in the food industry argue that they are not fooling us but, rather, are giving us what we, as consumers, want. But to what extent do processed foods themselves serve to alter what we might come to want?

Extensive research with adults and with children determines, for example, the "bliss point" for sugar in a variety of foods and drinks. They give people perhaps dozens of samples of foods, such as prepackaged desserts and sodas, with varying levels of sugar to find the exact, rather limited range of sweetness most people prefer. That sugar produces such "bliss" is why we find it in perhaps the most unlikely places, from spaghetti and barbecue sauces to almost all bread products, and almost everywhere in between. And perhaps some of my readers will relate to the fact that when we become accustomed to savoring very sweet foods, unsweetened foods usually just don't cut it. (Thankfully, as we abandon sugar, the opposite tends to occur, as we now detect sweetness in food we did not consider sweet before. It has happened to me for butter, cream, and grapefruit, for example.)

But there is far more than the carefully crafted "bliss point" to fool our natural ability to regulate our food intake. Another important component of manufactured foods is "mouth feel." We most desire foods with just the right texture, foods that are said to "melt in your mouth." And while sugar generally rules the bliss point, fat takes the crown for that creamy mouth feel. Hence, ultraprocessed foods and meals are notorious for being both fat- and sugar-bombs. Real foods high in both sugar and fat are virtually nonexistent in nature, with the notable exception of milk, which may serve as the sole food source for mammalian young.

But let's not forget our salty little friend, since food processors do not. Open that bag of potato chips, and even before you begin to crunch (and yes, crunchiness, and even the *sound* it makes, is analyzed by researchers for maximum appeal), you will be greeted by an immediate powerful "flavor burst," courtesy of a carefully crafted dose of salt. No wonder no one can eat just one! Even the lower-fat baked version of a popular potato chip features a lot more than potatoes, including sea salt, sugar and dextrose (sugar), and corn oil (fat) — just like Moss's book title. No wonder his second book on the topic is called *Hooked*.

And speaking of clever psychology, behavioral psychologists have known for many decades the principle of "intermittent reinforcement." We are most likely to repeat behaviors when they bring us a reward, but only sometimes and on a schedule that we cannot predict. This is why slot machines, those old one-armed bandits, rake in so much money. You never know when that very next pull could bring home the jackpot! The same principle probably explains why so many of us compulsively check our cell phones and social media accounts dozens of times a day. You never know when something interesting might show up. So how does this relate to processed foods "fooling" us? Well, a particular brand of crunchy corn-based chips was marketed to folks who like spicy treats. The catch was that only a certain percentage of chips in the bag was heavily spiced, and consumers couldn't identify them just by looking at them. They would have to keep eating the chips until they hit the spicy jackpot. Who knows — your next bite could win!

Well, hopefully none of us wants to gamble with our health. We have holy temples to tend to, after all. Armed with the principle that real food feeds, let's dig in a little deeper to find out the important things that it feeds us.

⟡————————⟡

TEMPLE-TENDING TENET #4

The virtue of understanding comprehends that "real food feeds!" The virtue of wisdom, therefore, advises, "Eat real food!"

5

Carbohydrate (Over)Loading?

Every woman knows that carbohydrate is fattening; this is a piece
of common knowledge, which few nutritionists would dispute.

— Dr. Reginald Passmore, 1962

[Americans are advised to] increase the consumption of complex
carbohydrates and "naturally occurring" sugars from about
28 percent of intake to about 48 percent of energy intake.

— U.S. Senate Select Committee on Nutrition and Human Needs, 1977[35]

The U.S. and Canadian Dietary Reference Intake Steering
Committees are currently developing plans to re-examine
energy, protein, fat, and carbohydrate — the timeline for
these macronutrient reviews has not been established.

— U.S. Departments of Agriculture and Health and Human
Services, *Dietary Guidelines for Americans, 2020–2025*[36]

---

[35] "History of Dietary Guidelines," Dietary Guidelines for Americans,
https://www.dietaryguidelines.gov/about-dietary-guidelines/history
-dietary-guidelines.

[36] U.S. Departments of Agriculture and Health and Human Services,
Dietary Guidelines for Americans, 2020–2025, 9th ed. (Washington, DC: U.S. Departments of Agriculture and Health and Human

Will the Real "Fad Diet" Please Stand Up?

While almost all people who take nutrition seriously agree on the importance of emphasizing real foods in our diet, just which kinds of real foods we should eat could hardly be more contentious, with carbohydrates and fats, and animal foods and plant foods, as the top contenders for both the hero and the villain roles. In recent decades, within subsets of researchers, clinicians, and the general population, there has been growing interest in diets that reduce our intake of carbohydrates, both in the form of simple added sugars (which almost all agree on), and also, some say, even the more wholesome "complex carbohydrates" we can obtain in good quantity from naturally starchy foods such as grains and potatoes.

For several decades, however, such low-carbohydrate and ketogenic diets — diets so low in carbohydrate, under fifty or sixty grams or so per day, that the body significantly increases the production of ketones for energy — have often been labelled "fad diets." In my experience, they are most often associated with the Atkins diet, promulgated first in the early 1970s by Richard Atkins, M.D. Indeed, being steeped in mainstream nutritional literature for decades, I long thought these were fad diets myself.

Writing in 2007, in *Fit for Eternal Life* I disparaged low-carbohydrate diets for several reasons, including the fact that after I trimmed down so excessively from a low-carb diet in preparation for a teenage bodybuilding contest, I binged after the show and regained twenty pounds in just one week! I wrote that I had not tried such a diet in twenty-eight years. Lo and behold, fourteen years after I wrote those words, I did indeed try a "low carb" regimen, lost thirty pounds in 160 days, and have not regained a pound more than 160 days later — and not at age eighteen but at age sixty. So, what gives?

Services, 2020), v, https://www.dietaryguidelines.gov/sites/default/files/2021-03/Dietary_Guidelines_for_Americans-2020-2025.pdf.

Well, as I've done far more reading and research, I realized that the regimen I was on was not merely a low-carbohydrate diet, but a low-fat, low-calorie, and perhaps low-protein diet as well. It was common in those days to prepare for contests by eating little more than tuna, lettuce, Tab diet soda, and vitamin pills, a perfect setup for a massive binging rebound later on. In fact, a common practice for bodybuilders in the 1970s was to "bulk up" massively between contests. No wonder! I had employed not a healthy low-carbohydrate diet, balanced by plenty of nutritious protein and fat, but what is known in the research literature as a "semi-starvation diet," which is virtually guaranteed to produce overeating once it is over. Here are a couple of the first things I learned in response to my earlier critiques:

1. I noted that the second half of the word *carbohydrate* — *hydrate*, that is — refers to this nutrient's relation to water and that if you limit your "carbs," you'll lose water, and weigh less on the scales, but you may not be losing fat. I have learned since, through reading and firsthand experience, that while water is certainly shed at first, fat soon follows as well. Further, many of us may walk around a bit too bloated anyway.

2. I noted, too, that the brain feeds almost entirely on sugars that we derive from carbohydrates and that depriving the brain of carbohydrate could lead to eating binges. It is estimated that the brain uses an average of 120 grams of glucose (blood sugar) per day. This is why some nutritional sources indicate we should take in at least 120 grams of carbohydrate per day. Still, current research makes clear that the brain can obtain the glucose it needs *either* from the carbohydrates in our diet *or* by producing its own from proteins and fats in a process called *gluconeogenesis*. In fact, of the three macro categories of nutrients our bodies use for fuel and tissue building and maintenance — carbohydrate, fat, and protein — carbohydrate alone is the one that is *not essential* for life. Not that I recommend eliminating it completely! Still, I have had fewer than fifty to sixty grams of carbohydrates per day for

321 days in a row as I write. I've not been tempted to binge even once, and my brain seems to be doing okay. Right now, I'm writing this book at the pace of ten pages in every morning's three-to-four-hour session.

In any event, to speak of low-carbohydrate diets as fad diets is to overlook the fact that in many decades past, and well before our obesity pandemic, low-carbohydrate diets were completely mainstream approaches for curing or preventing obesity. Dr. Atkins did not pull his low-carbohydrate diet revolution out of his hat in 1972.[37] Several doctors had written similar books before his, and foods high in sugar and starch were widely considered fattening by the public even in the 1800s.

Gary Taubes cites a passage from Tolstoy's *Anna Karenina* from the 1870s in which a character prepares for a horse race by controlling his weight through avoiding "starchy foods and desserts." In the 1869 edition of *The Practice of Medicine*, British physician Thomas Tanner wrote: "Farinaceous [starchy] and vegetable foods are fattening, and saccharine matters [i.e., sweets] are especially so."[38] In 1862, another British physician, William Harvey, prescribed a low-carbohydrate diet to an obese middle-age undertaker named William Banting who had tried a variety of unsuccessful methods to lose weight, including hours of exercise per day. Banting lost fifty pounds, and so great was his gratitude and enthusiasm that he penned a sixteen-page *Letter on Corpulence*. Banting's public letter caused such a stir that indeed, to this day, "banting" means "a method for dieting for obesity by avoiding sweets and carbohydrates" per the Merriam-Webster dictionary.

Ever heard of the Johns Hopkins Hospital, among the most prestigious medical centers in the United States? One of its four founding

---

[37] His first best-selling book was called *Dr. Atkins' Diet Revolution: The High Calorie Way to Stay Thin Forever*.

[38] Cited in Taubes, *Why We Get Fat*, 151.

physicians was Sir William Osler. In his *Principles and Practice of Medicine* (1901), he advised obese women to "avoid taking too much food, and particularly to reduce the starches and sugars."[39]

This is merely a small sample of the evidence out there from physicians and nutritionists over the last two centuries who have touted the possible benefits of carbohydrate restriction for those who wish to control their weight. But the times, they were achangin', especially in the 1970s and '80s. British obesity researcher Zoë Harcombe, Ph.D., begins her book *The Obesity Epidemic* with a quotation from the *Proposals for Nutritional Guidelines for Health and Education in Britain* (1983). Here it is in part: "The previous nutritional advice in the UK to limit the intake of all carbohydrates as a means of weight control now runs counter to current thinking and contrary to the present proposals for a nutrition education policy for the population as a whole." Harcombe then adds a quotation of her own: "And so started the obesity epidemic."

Britain and most Western countries, however, have followed America's lead when it comes to changing official dietary recommendations. I started this chapter with a quotation from the U.S. Senate Subcommittee on Nutrition and Human Needs from 1977 in which Americans were advised to *increase* their carbohydrate consumption. Three years later, in 1980, the USDA released its first set of dietary guidelines. One of its many bits of advice was as follows: "In trying to reduce your weight to 'ideal' levels, carbohydrates have an advantage over fat: carbohydrates have less than half the calories per ounce as fat."[40] The "food pyramid"

[39] Ibid., 154.

[40] U.S. Departments of Agriculture and Health and Human Services, *Nutrition and Your Health: Dietary Guidelines* (Washington, DC: U.S. Departments of Agriculture and Health and Human Services, 1980), 13, https://www.dietaryguidelines.gov/sites/default/files/2019-05/1980%20DGA.pdf.

was also introduced (and many years later discarded).[41] It recommended basing our diets on six to eleven servings per day of carbohydrate-rich breads, cereals, rice, and pasta. At that time, 15 percent of the U.S. population was obese. Now, as we have seen, it is over 42 percent.

New guidelines are issued every five years, and they have included some changes that we'll consider later, but note that, according to this chapter-opening quotation, in our current guidelines —in effect until 2025 — the experts are considering "re-examining" their carbohydrate, fat, and protein recommendations but have not gotten around to establishing even a "timeline."

To conclude this section, lower-carbohydrate diets may well not be for everyone, but they are clearly far more than a "fad," carrying such a pedigreed history and accumulating such mountains of current scientific evidence that the fad label may one day be applied to the very dietary guidelines that ushered our way into the obesity and diabetes pandemics.

This is certainly not to demonize an entire macronutrient group, however (as has, in fact, been done with fat), so let's see what carbohydrates are and what role they might play in a diet that honors our bodily temples.

Have You Been Getting the Skinny on Carbs?

Carbohydrates do indeed provide about four calories per gram, which is about the same as protein, and indeed, a little less than half of the nine calories per gram found in fat. I don't think we need to get into their chemical formulation, but in general, carbohydrates are found primarily in plant foods in the various forms of sugar, starch, and fiber (which is indigestible and has little, if any, caloric value).

---

[41] Some humorous cartoons have depicted Americans whose bodies subsequently grew to be *shaped like pyramids*.

Sugars, sometimes called "simple carbohydrates," in contrast to the more "complex carbohydrates" in starches, are quickly utilized by the body and tend to cause sharp rises in blood sugar (with fructose as a notable exception because it is digested in the liver). You've probably experienced, or at least heard of, the "sugar high," the burst of energy that may follow ingestion of a sugary food or drink, and which may later be followed by an energy "crash." In fairness, I must note that most of the official dietary guidelines in the United States and in other developed nations have cautioned against excess sugar, even from the start. Our 1980 guidelines from the U.S. Departments of Agriculture and Health and Human Services, for example, advised us to "avoid too much sugar." Interestingly though, they explicitly discounted the relationship between sugar and obesity, diabetes, heart attacks, and blood vessel disease but zeroed in only on sugar's promotion of tooth decay.

There are several kinds of naturally occurring sugars, and their names typically end in "-ose," such as the *glucose* in our bloodstream, the *sucrose* in the sugar bowl (about half glucose and half fructose), the *fructose* in fruits and the high-fructose corn syrups in our sodas (typically about 55 percent fructose and 45 percent glucose), the *lactose* in milk, and the *maltose* we find in grain and products such as corn syrup and beer.

The more complex carbohydrates, such as the starches we derive from vegetables and grain, are composed of long, complex chains of sugars. The body breaks them back down into sugars for energy, but this process takes some time and energy, especially since these foods usually also come laden with fiber. They are generally considered healthier than simple sugars, and the foods that contain them are sometimes rich in vitamins and minerals too.

Although it would appear that complex carbohydrates are less likely to trigger a blood-sugar roller coaster, researchers have also measured foods' glycemic index, which, on a scale of zero to one hundred, ranks how quickly foodstuffs raise one's blood-sugar level (with higher numbers indicating quicker blood-sugar impact). Such indexes for all sorts of foods can easily be found online, but I'll highlight just a few that might be surprising, with full-fat French vanilla ice cream (50 grams) at a glycemic index of thirty-eight, the *lowfat* variety at forty-six, and the humble pretzel (30 grams) at eighty-three.

Another measure used is foods' glycemic load, which factors in serving sizes. A simple example is the delightfully sweet watermelon with a scary glycemic index of eighty. When considering how aptly named the watermelon is, containing so much water, the trivial amount of actual carbohydrate people consume in a typical serving yields a very low glycemic load of five.

Still, we should keep in mind that digestible carbohydrates that are either sugars or complex arrangements of sugar (i.e., farinaceous foods or starches) are eventually converted to glucose in our blood, thus causing blood-sugar increases that trigger release of insulin. Two important exceptions are fiber, which is indigestible, and, perhaps surprisingly, fructose, so let's take a closer look.

Fructose is the kind of sugar predominantly found in fruit, though it is also found in honey and in some vegetables and other plants (especially sugarcane and sugar beets). Because of its association with fruit, fructose may have a healthy ring to it. Further, it is sometimes touted because it does not raise blood sugar and trigger an immediate insulin response the way other ingested sugars do. During the 1970s, consuming fructose tablets during one's workout was a trend in the bodybuilding world. (I tried a few bottles myself, and as I recall, they tasted pretty good!) Sodas and many other manufactured food products are now sweetened primarily with high-fructose corn syrup since it is cheaper than sugar, due to the American agriculture's glut of corn. The leading manufacturer of sodas switched to the syrup in 1980, when 15 percent of us were obese.

Still, the potential problem of excess fructose consumption is related to the reason it does not jack up our blood sugar — that reason being that fructose (like alcohol) is metabolized by the liver. Soda, however, spikes our blood sugar too, since nearly half of high-fructose syrup is still good old glucose. Pediatric endocrinologist David Lustig has worked with a great many obese children over the decades. In his book *Fat Chance*, he described fructose as "a toxin." He warns parents to be aware that while sodas have about 1.7 grams of fructose per ounce, orange juice has 1.8 grams per ounce. Here's yet another reason to favor real foods in their least processed forms. A medium orange contains about 6 grams of fructose, compared with the 13.6 grams in a cup of soda and 14.4 grams in a cup of orange juice.

Now, as for the liver, fructose is processed almost entirely within the liver to produce liver glycogen, a limited energy store of about 100 to 120 grams. The liver also converts excess fructose into triglycerides — fatty acids — which are carried by lipoproteins throughout the bloodstream. High triglycerides are associated with greater risk of heart disease.

Modern researchers have opined that fructose may also be a key determinant in the rise of fatty liver disease in recent decades. One review starts with an interesting quotation from Roman historian Pliny the Elder from the first century AD that reads, in part, "We may employ the same artificial methods of increasing the size of the liver of the sow, as of that of the goose; it consists in cramming them with dried figs, and when they are fat enough, they are drenched with wine mixed with honey, and immediately killed."[42] Pâté de foie gras, a paste produced

---

[42]   Thomas Jensen, Manal F. Abdelmalek, Shelby Sullivan, et al., "Fructose and Sugar: A Major Mediator of Nonalcoholic Fatty Liver Disease," *Journal of Hepatology* 68, no. 5 (May 2018): 1063–1075, National Library of Medicine, https://www.ncbi.nlm.nih.gov/pmc/articles /PMC5893377/.

from the specially fattened liver of a duck or a goose, is still produced by similar methods of forced feeding, typically with grain and fat.

Worse yet, are we turning our own temples' livers into pâté de foie gras? Dr. Lustig also provides data comparing 150 calories of beer with 150 calories of soda made with high-fructose corn syrup (12 ounces each). Recall, if you will, that alcohol, like fructose, is processed by the liver, though beer does contain other sources of carbohydrate too. Well, Lusting calculates that the beer is the greater villain to the liver, requiring that it process 92 calories of alcohol, but soda is not at all far behind, requiring the liver to process 90 calories of fructose. This is part of the reason he calls fructose a "toxin." Surely, if we care for our bodily temples, we will not take in fructose to excess and will prefer the fructose in real foods, where it occurs in smaller quantities while accompanied by other nutrients and fiber.

Reexamining Carbs

If being careful not to overload on carbohydrates was long considered essential for maintaining a healthy bodyweight, why did governmental agencies change their advice in the 1970s? Good question — and one we will touch on briefly in our next chapter. To conclude this chapter, let's dig into the answers to two other questions.

But are not carbohydrates the body's primary energy source? Yes, indeed, for most of us today they are, especially since we've been advised for decades now to embrace more carbohydrates in our diets. Further, do not highly fit athletes routinely carbo-load before endurance competitions? Yes, indeed, for the most part they do, but let's look a little more into this story.

I've found a common trend among doctors and nutritionists who have embraced lower-carbohydrate dietary approaches: that those health-care providers first started noticing their own expanding waistline over the decades, despite trying to follow the nutritional guidelines.

Dr. Atkins himself was among this group. As he gained considerable weight in medical school, he did some research on the low-carbohydrate approach, reduced his own bodyfat significantly, and went on to help thousands of his patients do the same over the next several decades. Dr. Gary Fettke of Tasmania became an outspoken proponent of the low-carbohydrate or ketogenic lifestyle after having been morbidly obese himself and diagnosed with cancer. Dr. Ken Berry from Tennessee also overcame his obesity by significantly lowering his carbohydrate intake. A pioneer and current prominent physician of the low-carb school is Eric Westman, M.D., a former president of the American Obesity Association. He was so intrigued decades ago when two of his patients showed him and told him of their weight loss success with Atkins' methods that he arranged to meet Dr. Atkins and later started the first formal medical research using those methods.

Many doctors and nutritionists have since followed their lead. Journalist Gary Taubes reports that when he started his investigation of low-carbohydrate or ketogenic diets twenty years ago, there were perhaps a few dozen physicians worldwide prescribing such diets for their patients. By the time he was writing *The Case for Keto* in 2020, there were thousands and perhaps tens of thousands doing so. Indeed, he noted that a Canadian Facebook group of women physicians who prescribe such diets had more than 3,800 members in September 2019.

There is another set of low-carbohydrate proponents, some of them also doctors, who were strength or endurance athletes who fared well for decades on the high-carbohydrate recommendations, only to find themselves slowing in speed, spreading around the middle, and developing diabetes or prediabetes in middle age, despite maintaining prodigious amounts of exercise. Among the most notable is Dr. Timothy Noakes of South Africa, who literally wrote the book on running, *The Lore of Running*, in 1986. He included chapters recommending carbohydrate loading that he now strongly disavows. His *Real*

Meal Revolution (2015), written with nutritionist Sally-Ann Creed and chef Jonno Proudfoot, is a best seller in South Africa and one of my favorites in the field. Noakes found that he had developed diabetes, like his father, who died from the disease, and his research led him to the perils of carbohydrates for diabetics. Reducing his carbohydrates to a very low twenty grams per day, he greatly reduced his body fat, his blood sugar levels — and his running times![43]

I fall within the low-carb camp of those who first saw dramatic results in their own bodies. I have lifted and done regular cardiovascular training since the 1970s and have always tried to follow the standard dietary guidelines. Over the years, my adulthood bodyweight has ranged from as high as 234 pounds when doing heavy lifting alone in my early forties to as low as 170 pounds when doing a lot of distance running in my mid-forties. This year, knowing the importance of maintaining maximum muscle strength and size as one ages, I set a strength goal and deadlifted 410 pounds for five repetitions to celebrate my sixtieth birthday. That felt very nice! And yet I weighed 220 pounds, my waist was over 40 inches, my blood pressure was over 150/90, my right knee ached, and I sometimes woke up at night with gastrointestinal reflux.

Within two weeks, I'd had my *Aha!* moment and decided to change things. Having dabbled a bit in the low-carbohydrate literature a few years ago, I dove in headfirst, including a wide variety of books and videos on the benefits of whole foods and the practices of processed-food manufacturers, the nature and history of dietary guidelines, the

---

[43] Sadly, I must note that propounding the low-carb message has been a perilous thing for some of these physicians. Both Dr. Fettke of Tasmania and Dr. Noakes of South Africa were prosecuted by licensing boards for dispensing such nutritional advice, though both were eventually exonerated. For a fascinating read see Tim Noakes and Marika Sboros *Real Food on Trial: How the Diet Doctors Tried to Destroy a Top Scientist* (Zanesville, OH: Columbus Publishing, 2019).

pros and cons of animal- versus plant-based foods, reading books and watching videos every single day until I started writing this book nine months later. The tradition continues to this day. The reason is that I have been astounded by the results — not only the loss of 30 pounds and of 6 inches around my waistline but the lower blood pressure and the complete absence of reflux and knee pain. My sleep has also increased from seven to eight hours per night.[44] Better yet, I enjoy every single meal now and never get ravenously hungry. My wife, Kathy, has gladly joined in and has lost just a few pounds (she had little to lose), and she too feels much better.

TEMPLE-TENDING TENET #5

Carbohydrates are not to be placed on a pedestal, nor are they to be trampled underfoot. Nor are they an essential macronutrient. Different people can tolerate different levels of carbohydrate in their diet, and we all would do well to determine how much works best for each of us.

---

[44] Overweight people are notorious for having sleeping problems from restlessness, to snoring, to sleep apnea. One interesting phenomenon I've learned about recently is not only fatty liver, but fatty *tongue!* Maybe I'm sleeping better because my tongue's not so fat! Check this out: https://www.webmd.com/sleep-disorders/sleep-apnea/news/20200110/slimming-down-tongue-fat-might-help-ease-sleep-apnea#1.

6

Giving Fat a Chance

*Peter went up on the housetop to pray, about the sixth hour. And he
became hungry and desired something to eat; but while they were
preparing it, he fell into a trance and saw the heaven opened, and
something descending, like a great sheet, let down by four corners
upon the earth. In it were all kinds of animals and reptiles and birds
of the air. And there came a voice to him, "Rise, Peter; kill and eat."
But Peter said, "No, Lord; for I have never eaten anything that is
common or unclean." And the voice came to him again a second
time, "What God has cleansed, you must not call common." This
happened three times, and the thing was taken up at once to heaven.*

— Acts 10:9–16

Three Keys to the Disparagement of Fat

Many of us in recent decades have come to be very wary of fats in our
diets. Who among us who is old enough did not notice the onslaught
of "lowfat" and "nonfat" processed foods that started filling the gro-
cery store shelves in the 1980s and '90s? I think this is due to at least
three key reasons.

First, the macronutrient category of fat has the same name as the
body tissue we do not want too much of! It seems a simple enough
conclusion that eating fat will make us fatter. After all, "You are what

you eat!" Right? (Ken Berry, M.D., has suggested a different motto, however: "Eat what you are!" since our bodies are composed primarily of fat and protein.[45])

Second, as we saw in our last chapter, dietary fat does contain nine calories per gram, more than twice the four calories per gram in carbohydrate and protein. We saw that the USDA dietary guidelines advised us that to maintain an ideal bodyweight, we should emphasize carbohydrates over fats for this reason. Fats are "calorie dense." A small volume of fat provides a lot of calories.

Still, the third, and likely the most important, of the three keys was the work of physiologist Ancel Keys, who put dietary fat and cholesterol on the map, and, in my opinion, he placed it on the part of the map with the monsters waiting to consume unwary travelers who might wander past the known world's edge! The details of this story are interesting indeed, showing important connections, for example, with how America reacted to President Eisenhower's first heart attack in the mid-1950s and the dietary changes in fat reduction that he followed, though his heart problems continued to worsen. This story could take up many pages indeed, so I will direct interested readers to Nina Teicholz's amazingly well-researched and well-crafted book *The Big Fat Surprise*.

I will zoom in on just a few of the most important facts. In 1952, Keys produced a chart from epidemiological data he had gathered from six countries: Japan, Italy, Britain, Australia, Canada, and the United States. When "deaths per 1,000" was plotted on the X (vertical) axis and "fat calories as percentage of total diet" was plotted on the Y (horizontal axis), one could see that as the fat calories rose for men in age groups of 45 to 49 and 55 to 59, so did the death rates, in almost a perfect line for every one of the six countries. Unfortunately,

---

[45] Dr. Berry's book is referenced in our appendix.

the biggest loser, so to speak, was the United States. The death rates matched the ordering of the countries I presented above. The greatest contrast was between the United States and Japan, where, for 55- to 59-year-olds, there were about seven deaths per thousand in the United States and less than one per thousand in Japan. True, correlation does not prove causation, but pretty striking findings, no?

Recall, however, our warnings in chapter 3 regarding observational epidemiological data. Many problems have been found with this study, but the most interesting one was brought to light by Jacob Yerushalmy a few years later. He questioned Keys' findings because it was well known that there were exceptions in other countries. People spoke, for example, of the "French paradox," in that the French consumed large amounts of fat but had relatively few heart attacks. So Yerushalmy and his associate Dr. Herman Hilleboe found that nutritional and mortality data was available on twenty-two nations at the time. When the rest of the countries' mortality rates and fat-consumption rates were charted, the purported connection all but disappeared, due to many exceptions besides France. Ceylon and Chile, for example, had higher fat intakes than Japan but fewer deaths from heart disease. Mexico had the fewest cardiac deaths of all the nations but had a higher fat intake than Japan, Ceylon, Chile, and Italy. The Netherlands and Norway had among the highest fat intakes and the lowest incidence of cardiac deaths.

Nonetheless, Keys was undaunted and was funded by the U.S. Public Health Service to do another study, this time a study of seven nations: Italy, Greece, Yugoslavia, Finland, the Netherlands, Japan, and the United States. Unfortunately, these countries were handpicked by Keys, and not "randomized," and that calls into question any results. To make a long story short, the data suggested that for the countries he studied, diets low in *saturated* fat appeared to be correlated to fewer deaths from heart disease, and this is what made the headlines — and influenced public opinion and governmental bodies regarding the purported dangers of fat, especially saturated fat.

Oddly enough, though rarely reported, that seven-studies data did not show any decrease in overall mortality for people who ate lowfat diets. People from the lower-fat-eating nations were less likely to die of heart attacks but more likely to die of other causes. Ironically perhaps, the longest-lived group happened to be none other than our dietary fat-loving Americans! Still, the lore of the dangers of fat was born and grew to enormous size. By January 13, 1961, Ancel Keys was the cover man for *Time* magazine.

One of the most important critiques though, not only of Keys' early studies but of modern studies that look for links between saturated fat and heart disease, is that diets that tend to be high in fat also tend to be high in sugar. Keys himself was aware of this but believed that sugar was basically an innocent bystander that was picked up and carried along on fat's deadly joy ride. Many researchers today believe that sugar was really behind the wheel. I should note as well that some highly qualified but underpublicized nutritional researchers in Keys' day, such as British physiologist and nutritionist John Yudkin, M.D., Ph.D., author of *Pure, White, and Deadly: How Sugar Is Killing Us and What We Can Do to Stop It*, also believed sugar, not fat, was the culprit.

Recalling from our brief look at modern manufacturing practices that processed foods are typically high in both sugar and fat, people who eat diets high in fat typically sprinkle their diets with a lot of sugar on top!

Finally, these early studies implicated not only saturated fat but a substance that saturated fat was believed to increase in our bloodstream. Surely you've heard of *cholesterol*. Indeed, as our worries about cholesterol grew, by March, 26, 1984, *Time* magazine's cover would feature not Ancel Keys but two eggs and a piece of bacon arranged into a frowning face, with the cover line "bad news about cholesterol." Do you recall that video I mentioned, in which the nutritionist of the future warned the couple to toss out their egg yolks but later told them that the yolks were okay? Well, by 1999, our eggs had made it back on *Time*'s cover, this time with a slice of cantaloupe *arranged in a smiley face*, with the cover line "good news about cholesterol." Lo, by 2014, *Time*'s cover image was a delicious-looking piece of butter with the cover line "Eat butter: Scientists labeled fat the enemy. Why they were wrong."

What interesting times we have lived in, but no wonder we've been confused. I will note in passing, for those who were not aware, that previous dietary guidelines cautioned us to avoid foods high in cholesterol (including egg yolks and shrimp), though this advice was rescinded from later guidelines, since it had become clear that the body produces far more cholesterol itself, an essential substance within our cells, than is taken in through diet, and further, that eating cholesterol-rich foods does not necessarily raise cholesterol in one's bloodstream or increase heart-attack risk. The current 2020–2025 U.S. guidelines still recommended trying to limit dietary cholesterol and saturated fat but have removed the three-hundred-milligrams-per-day maximum for cholesterol that appeared in the 2015–2020 edition.

Dietary cholesterol and the various kinds of cholesterol in the blood — or, more precisely, the different kinds of lipoproteins that carry cholesterol and triglycerides — are complicated matters that should be addressed with one's health-care provider if problems should arise. For now, let's take a closer look at fat itself, both in its main varieties and in how it fuels our bodily temples. But first, we'll look back once more at our old friend carbohydrate.

Kindling, Kerosene, and Logs

Carbohydrates, as we've seen, are readily accessed suppliers of energy. We usually carry only 4 to 5 grams of sugar in our bloodstream at a time. Our livers can store sugar energy in the form of glycogen to the tune of up to 100 to 200 grams at one time. Our muscles like sugar energy too, and they can store up to 500 grams or so of glycogen in a person of average size. This yields about 600 to 700 grams of stored glycogen at any one time, and glycogen contains about 4.2 calories of energy per gram. Hence, using the high number of 700 stored grams, one's glycogen stores can provide about 2,940 calories. Endurance events such as long-distance running or biking can burn 100 calories or more per mile; this is why many endurance athletes have tried to carbo-load before competitions, cramming their bodies with as much glycogen as possible and also replenishing along the way with high-carbohydrate food products such as gels.

Now, the average American man has somewhere between 18 and 24 percent body fat. (Women's percentages tend to be higher.) At a body fat percentage of 20 and a weight of 200 pounds (to make the math easy), our man would be carrying about 40 pounds, or 18,144 grams, of body fat.[46] Since body fat, too, can yield about 9 calories per gram, this would yield about 163,296 calories of energy — more than fifty times more energy than what is supplied by his body's glycogen stores.

The question then might become, why do we think we constantly need to fuel our bodies with carbohydrates when we are (literally, if you'll excuse me) sitting on vastly greater energy stores that we'd rather not have in such great abundance? Carbohydrates in general are like kindling. They burn quickly, so we need to keep piling them on our bodily fires. Sugars are more like kerosene: they give an even quicker burst, but the energy they provide is soon gone like a puff of smoke (while the excess energy we cannot burn is shuffled away, courtesy of insulin, into our livers, muscle, and last, but certainly not to the

---

[46] I couldn't help myself, so after I wrote this, I did a quick search to find out what is average weight for the American male right now. The CDC says it is 199.8 pounds, so the numbers in my example should not be too far off! (For women, the average is 170.8.) "Body Measurements," CDC, last reviewed September 10, 2021, https://www.cdc.gov/nchs/fastats/body-measurements.htm.

least extent, into our fat cells). Perhaps we should consider using less kindling, setting aside the kerosene, and pulling from that big pile of logs overfilling most of our temples.

If carbohydrates are the kindling or kerosene of our temple's furnace, fats provide our logs. Ingested carbohydrates cause a rapid rise in blood sugar (because carbohydrates are composed of sugars) and a subsequent quick fall in blood sugar (especially in the increasingly dwindling number of healthy individuals who are not insulin resistant) because it triggers insulin, which moves sugar out of the bloodstream and into body cells. And when insulin remains high, it prohibits cells from emptying their fat stores to use body fat as energy. Some have compared insulin to a key that locks fat inside cells.

Ingested fat, on the other hand, does not by itself trigger any significant rise in insulin. If plotted on a chart with insulin response on the vertical axis and time in hours on the horizontal access, carbohydrate's profile looks like that of a scary roller coaster. It quickly soars very high, and then, *whoosh*, almost straight down it goes. Fat's line, however, looks like the children's toy train ride that plods along slowly on level ground. Protein's line, by the way, looks like a children's starter roller coaster. It does not rise as fast or plummet as quickly as carbohydrate's does. It is almost smack-dab in the middle.

Now, because ingested fat does not trigger insulin, it is able to be used as energy itself, and it does not prohibit the release of fat energy already stored in our fat cells if we need more energy than what we've just eaten. This is one advantage of fat over carbohydrates. But it is twice as energy dense! Yes, it is, but when not combined with sugar, a little fat can go a long way. Fat is more satisfying gram for gram and tends to decrease levels of ghrelin, a hormone involved in stimulating hunger.

In general, people who decrease carbohydrate intake while increasing their intake of fat report that they are hungry far less intensely and far less often. (It has certainly worked out that way for me.) Let's look here at one study among many dozens that may give credence to the fact that this works. And this time, we will give women the center stage.

The "A to Z" study was reported in *JAMA* in 2007.[47] It was called "A to Z" because it compared the results of four diets, from "A" (for the Atkins low-carbohydrate diet) to "Z" (for the Zone diet with its 30-40-30 ratio of protein, carbs, and fat), with "T" for the traditional, or LEARN, diet of Lifestyle, Exercise, Attitudes, Relationships, and Nutrition, which was a low-calorie, lowfat, high-carbohydrate (55 to 60 percent) diet — similar to U.S. dietary guidelines — and "O," the Ornish diet, which was very lowfat (less than 10 percent) and in which the subjects meditated and exercised. The subjects were obese, premenopausal women, ages 25 to 50, who were randomly assigned to the different diet groups. After one year, findings were as follows:[48]

Group	Weight (pounds)	LDL	TG	HDL	Blood Pressure
Atkins	-9.9	+.08	-29.3	+4.9	-4.4
Trad.	-5.5	+.06	-14.6	-2.8	-2.2
Ornish	-5.3	-3.8	-14.9	0	-0.7
Zone	-3.3	0	-4.2	+2.2	+2.2

---

[47] Christopher D. Gardner, Alexandre Kiazand, Sofiya Alhassan, et al., "Comparison of the Atkins, Zone, Ornish, and LEARN Diets for Change in Weight and Related Risk Factors among Overweight Premenopausal Women," *JAMA* 297, no. 9 (March 2007): 969–977, https://jamanetwork.com/journals/jama/fullarticle/205916.

[48] Table adapted from summary in Taubes, *Why We Get Fat,* 191. TG = triglycerides.

Interestingly, the Atkins diet, in which subjects were allowed to eat as much as they desired, as long as they kept their carbohydrates low, at twenty grams or less per day for the first two to three months and fifty grams per day after that, showed the best results by a significant margin in all of these findings, with the possible exception of LDL cholesterol, which is generally considered better when it is lower, though recent research has further subdivided LDL into variant types, some of which are healthier than others. The researchers' own conclusions warrant quoting in full:

> In this study of overweight and obese premenopausal women, those assigned to follow the Atkins diet had more weight loss and more favorable outcomes for metabolic effects at 1 year than women assigned to the Zone, Ornish, or LEARN diets. Concerns about adverse metabolic effects of the Atkins diet were not substantiated within the 12-month study period. It could not be determined whether the benefits were attributable specifically to the low carbohydrate intake vs other aspects of the diet (e.g., high protein intake).
>
> While questions remain about long-term effects and mechanisms, these findings have important implications for clinical practice and health care policy. Physicians whose patients initiate a low-carbohydrate diet can be reassured that weight loss is likely to be at least as large as for any other dietary pattern and that the lipid effects are unlikely to be of immediate concern. As with any diet, physicians should caution patients that long-term success requires permanent alterations in energy intake and energy expenditure, regardless of macronutrient content.[49]

---

[49] Gardner, Kiazand, and Alhassan, "Comparison of the Atkins, Zone, Ornish, and LEARN Diets."

The Skinny on Dietary Fat

Before we conclude, I should briefly describe the main categories of fat for those who are not familiar or would like a refresher:

Saturated fat. The level of saturation in a fat refers to the nature and extent of the chemical bonds in it. Saturated fat is the kind we are often warned about. Because of its chemical structure, it is usually solid at room temperature, as we can see in butter and coconut oil. It is often found in animal foods, such as meat, cheese, cream, and full-fat milk, though some fruit sources are actually higher in saturated fat than animal products are. For instance, there are 12 grams of saturated fat, out of a total of 14 grams of fat, in a tablespoon of coconut oil, compared with 7 grams of saturated fat in the same amount of butter. Believe it or not, a tablespoon of bacon fat, or lard, an old-fashioned cooking staple, contains only 4.4 grams of saturated fat! Note, too, there is not always a direct correlation between ingestion of saturated fat and dietary cholesterol. Different studies have produced different findings. Perhaps surprisingly, as Dr. William Castelli, director of the famous Framingham Heart Study, wrote in 1992: "In Framingham [Massachusetts], the more saturated fat one ate, the more cholesterol one ate, the more calories one ate, the lower the person's serum cholesterol."[50]

Monounsaturated fat. Monounsaturated fat has become perhaps the favorite child of the fat family in recent years. It is found in foods, such as olives, that make up a good part of the popular Mediterranean diet. This fat has been associated with lowering blood cholesterol,

---

[50] William P. Castelli, "Concerning the Possibility of a Nut ...," *Archives of Internal Medicine* 152, no. 7 (July 1992): 1371–1372, https://jamanetwork.com/journals/jamainternalmedicine/article-abstract/616375.

and it might reduce the risk of heart disease. Even here, though, you may find some dietary surprises. While olive oil is about 75 percent monounsaturated fat by volume, even good old bacon fat is 45 to 50 percent monounsaturated fat, with only 30 to 40 percent saturated fat and the remaining fat grams falling into our last class, *polyunsaturated fats.*

Polyunsaturated fat. Polyunsaturated fats have been highly touted in the past but increasingly questioned recently, especially such fats of the ultraprocessed variety that are called vegetable oils but are actually industrially produced from the seeds of these vegetables, such as corn, soybeans, and sunflowers. In the most common practice, the seeds are exposed to high heat, petroleum solvents, chemical deodorizers, and chemical coloring agents during different stages of industrial processing. Some modern nutritional experts consider vegetable seed oil consumption hazardous — even more hazardous than overconsumption of sugar. When we were advised to decrease saturated fats in previous decades, we were advised to replace them with such oils. A classic example was the fall of butter and the rise of man-made margarines — though, if you will recall the 2014 *Time* cover I mentioned, butter is making a comeback! Indeed, from 1999 to 2020, butter consumption rose from 1,307 million pounds to 2,070 million pounds. That's per nation, not per person![51] Margarine consumption has shown a matching decline.[52] Part of the reason the

[51] Total consumption of butter in the U.S. from 1999 to 2020 (in million pounds), *Statistica,* https://www.statista.com/statistics/192624/consumption-of-butter-in-the-us-since-1999/.

[52] U.S. population: Usage of margarine / margarine spread from 2011 to 2024, *Statistica* https://www.statista.com/statistics/280759/us-households-usage-of-margarine-margarine-spread-trend/. (The 2024 data is a projection.)

tide has turned was that artificially altered fats called "trans fats," or "hydrogenated" fats that were created to improve shelf life or texture, were later implicated as health risks in the 1980s. While there are small amounts of similar naturally occurring fats in some foods, manufactured trans fats are best to be avoided whenever possible. It should be noted, too, that one reason fats, unlike carbohydrates, are essential to the human diet is because of the essential omega-6 and omega-3 fatty acids found in polyunsaturated fats. Unfortunately, the promotion of seed oils has greatly altered previous ratios of omega-6 to omega-3 heavily in favor of omega-6s, leaving many people perhaps overloaded in omega-6s and deficient in omega-3s. The most commonly recommended source for omega-3s is fatty fish, such as salmon and mackerel; that is why some people take fish-oil supplements. Omega-3 is also found in egg yolks. Some plant sources include walnuts and flaxseeds.

The Skinny on Body Fat

I'll conclude this chapter with an important note on not dietary fat but the fat that we hold in our bodies. Do you recall from chapter 1 that "central obesity" is among the risk factors for metabolic disease? It is most easily found by simply measuring your waistline, but this does not mean that the fat that might be jiggling along your sides or hanging over your belt is the biggest problem. The waistline measurement is a proxy for internal "visceral fat," the kind of fat deep inside that wraps itself around our internal organs. Ever seen a man with a protruding "beer belly" that's as hard as a rock? This is because internal body fat is pushing against his abdominal muscles, making them protrude. The deleterious effect goes far beyond aesthetics, however. This kind of fat is most metabolically active and most likely to produce the metabolic syndrome, complete with insulin resistance, elevated blood pressure, and skewed lipid levels in the bloodstream. This also explains why, though people with diabetes are far more likely to be obese — more than 85 percent per some estimates — around 30 percent of obese people are *not* diabetic. Further, while thinner people are less likely to be diabetic, around 15 percent of diabetics are of normal body weight. A good part of this phenomenon seems to be explained by just where obese and normal weight people tend to store their fat due to genetic and dietary factors. Some diabetics fall into what has been called the TOFI category — "thin on the outside, fat on the inside." Scans of some people of normal weight who have diabetes reveal a lot of fat hiding *inside*. Some obese people carry most of their fat as subcutaneous (under the skin) body fat, and they may be relatively lean on the inside and metabolically healthy!

The take-home lesson is that central or visceral obesity is something we should strive to avoid regardless of what our scales tell us. The good news, too, is that even small reductions in body fat tend to come first from visceral fat stores, so that loss of even a handful of pounds may seriously improve the health of your bodily temple. Keep it up, and you may fly through your doctor's building inspections (so to speak), with flying colors!

Oh, and here is one last note that might inspire you to keep on making small but measurable improvements in reducing your visceral obesity. A good goal for a healthy waist measurement is no more than half your height in inches. In my case, at 5 feet, 9.5 inches, when I started my dietary changes on February 12, 2021, my 40.5-inch waistline yielded a waist-height ratio of 0.58. It took me 210 days to hit 34.75 inches, for a 0.50 ratio. So, regardless of your starting point, any gradual reduction in waist size is likely for the better and is a better gauge than merely body weight alone, since the scales do not differentiate between fat (which we hope to lose) and muscle (which we should hope to keep). When our waistlines get smaller over time, it is far more likely due to loss of unnecessary fat than necessary muscle.

Temple-Tending Tenet #6

Give dietary fat from real foods a fat-fighting chance! Dietary fat is an essential human macronutrient and the steadiest, slowest-burning fuel source that does not take blood glucose and insulin on a roller-coaster ride. This filling fuel can also help us fight hunger.

7

Protein Does a Temple Good

John wore a garment of camel's hair, and a leather girdle
around his waist; and his food was locusts and wild honey.

— Matthew 3:4

Not Quite the John the Baptist Diet

Well, we've seen arguments for eating simple, natural foods as God made them — and what man of God ate a simpler diet than the cousin of our Lord, St. John the Baptist? But there is no need to worry. I am not about to promote the "John the Baptist Diet," though, sure enough, there are very recent nutritional studies about the health benefits of locusts, albeit in rats, in a powder form comprising 3 percent of their diet, but with possible implications for human consumption.[53] The reason I bring locusts into the picture, besides honoring our great desert saint, is to highlight the fact that a recent theory to help explain the growing

---

[53]   Masaru Ochiai, Mako Inada, and Seiya Horiguchi, "Nutritional and Safety Evaluation of Locust (Caelifera) Powder as a Novel Food Material," *Journal of Food Science* 85, no. 2 (February 2020): 279–288, https://pubmed.ncbi.nlm.nih.gov/31976553/. Locusts, by the way, are more than 50 percent protein.

obesity pandemic came not from medical doctors or nutritionists but from *entomologists*, and their research began with the lowly locust.

To make a long story short, when insect researchers Drs. David Raubenheimer and Stephen Simpson systematically varied protein and carbohydrate contents of the diets of locusts in captivity, the lower the protein content of the food, the more the locusts ate. It was as if their little bodies and brains had some sort of meter that turned off their appetites only when they had obtained enough protein.

Similar experiments were then conducted on a number of other insects and arachnids, including beetles, wolf spiders, and web-spinning spiders, by varying the amount of protein and fats in their diets through feeding them flies that had been fed in such a way that they were either high in protein or in fat, and similar results were obtained. Undoubtedly the most interesting finding involved the web-spinning spiders, since they do not get to run about and choose what they eat. They are stuck with whatever gets stuck in their webs. Even they showed this powerful "protein leveraging" effect, however. How so? Well, these spiders inject special enzymes into the bodies of their prey to liquefy their innards before sucking out their insect soup. They are able to tailor those enzymes to extract the nutrients that fit their needs, so spiders that had previously been fed protein-deficient flies selectively sucked out more protein.

Such innate appetites for protein were then replicated in a variety of animal species, all of which showed what the researchers called the "protein leverage" effect, though different species have different thresholds. Cats, for instance, sought out 52 percent of their calories from protein, while various breeds of dogs sought out between 25 and 35 percent. Indeed, the researchers speculate that the reason dogs may have adapted to a lower protein percentage is that they have hung out with *us* for so long and, until recent times, with commercially processed dog foods, were commonly fed table scraps.

Well, what about us? Through various short-term experiments with humans, Raubenheimer and Simpson also found strong evidence of protein leveraging. Give us low-protein foods for even a few days, and we will eat a greater quantity of food and will seek out food sources higher in protein when we are allowed to eat freely. These scientists also report that throughout the world, people consume approximately 15 percent of their daily calories in the form of protein, and this has given rise to the "protein leverage hypothesis" as a possible cause of human obesity.

We chronicled in previous chapters how recommendations for increased consumption of carbohydrate have accompanied the obesity pandemic. For the most part, as carbohydrate intake went up, fat intake went down, but something else did too. According to United Nations statistics, from 1961 to 2000, the average American diet fell from 14 percent protein to 12.5 percent. Raubenheimer and Simpson then calculated that, to meet the need for protein, Americans would have needed to increase their total calories by 13 percent to make up the difference. This energy surplus resulted in significant body weight gains. Consider, too, how we focused on food processing trends and, as Moss has documented so well, the drive to add salt, fat, and sugar to our foods. The missing ingredient is protein, and no wonder. This is the ingredient most likely to satisfy our appetites and prompt us to eat less food. Intriguing, no?

A modern physician who has applied these ideas and ideas of his own to human health is Ted Naiman, M.D. In the book *The P:E Diet: Leverage Your Biology to Achieve Optimal Health,* he and co-author William Shewfelt stress the importance of having a protein-to-energy ratio that is weighted toward protein. When we consume too much energy in the forms of carbohydrate or fat to obtain sufficient protein, we tend to get fat and sick. Naiman and Shewfelt recommend targeting protein and essential minerals to achieve greater satiety and greater health. This is achieved by acquiring and maintaining high levels of lean body mass, especially muscle stimulated by strength training, which also renders us more insulin sensitive and less likely to succumb to the insulin-resistant metabolic syndrome that brings obesity, diabetes, and so many other disorders.

So, just what is protein, how much should we take in, and does it matter how it is spaced in the day? Good questions. Let's get to some answers.

Protein Wins the Gold!

As nutrition scientists started unraveling the mysteries of the various kinds of nutrients God crafted in our foods, what we now call "protein" got its name from Dutch chemist Gerard Johan Mulder in 1838. The name he gave it was Greek, deriving from *protos*, for "first," and *proteios*, for "primary." He declared this nutrient to be of first or primary importance. Hence, I've called it the gold-medal winner. Indeed, bodybuilders and weightlifters have agreed for many decades, and a growing number of modern nutrition researchers are finding ever new reasons to agree.

Protein, like fat, is essential to life, and in a sense, it is primary because so much of our healthy, functional tissues are built out of it. While fats and carbohydrates function primarily as energy sources — though fatty acids are present as constituents of every cell of the body — protein is the main source for building and repairing body tissues, and not just our muscles; bones, for example, are 50 percent protein by volume. And, being quite versatile, protein can also serve as an energy source, if need be. Remember gluconeogenesis? Well, during periods of fasting or low-carbohydrate intake, our bodies can produce glucose from protein.

Proteins, as you are probably aware, are composed of chains of chemicals called "amino acids." There are nine "essential" amino acids that the body cannot produce on its own and must be obtained through the diet, and there are eleven "nonessential" amino acids that the body is able to produce on its own from the essential amino acids, if need be.

It is important to note, however, that not all proteins are created equal. Within the world of proteins, we might say, some win the gold medal, some the silver, and some the bronze; some do not even make the podium.[54] An index called the "protein efficiency ratio" (PER) was developed in 1919 by comparing the growth of rats that were fed varying kinds of protein. Highest PERs were found for eggs, meat, and casein (milk protein), respectively, and lower PERs were found for plant-based proteins, such as soy, pea, and wheat proteins. The PER in no longer considered the gold standard in measuring protein quality, and, as noted, it was developed by testing rats, not humans.

In 1989, the Food and Agriculture Organization and the World Health Organization proposed a more sophisticated measure of protein quality based on amino acid content and human digestibility that produces a "protein digestibility-corrected amino acid score." Here are some of the findings culled from a report on the National Institutes of Health (NIH) website:[55]

Protein Type	Protein Efficiency Ratio	Protein Digestibility-Corrected Amino Acid Score
Beef	2.9	0.92
Black beans	0	0.75

---

[54] One example here is pork rinds. These are a common snack for some people who like to keep their carbohydrates low (they have 0 grams), and they have 7 grams of protein per serving. Still, the protein, derived from the skin, is especially low in essential amino acids, and food labels are required to note they are "not a significant source of protein." I still like them once in a while, though, not for their protein but because they taste good and can keep me from touching a cracker or a chip.

[55] Jay R. Hoffman and Michael J. Falvo, "Protein — Which Is Best?" *Sports Science Medicine* 3, no. 3 (September 2004): 118–130, https://www.ncbi.nlm.nih.gov/pmc/articles/PMC3905294/.

Protein Type	Protein Efficiency Ratio	Protein Digestibility-Corrected Amino Acid Score
Casein (milk protein)	2.5	1.0
Eggs	3.9	1.0
Peanuts	1.8	0.52
Soy	2.2	1.0
Wheat gluten	0.8	0.25
Whey protein	3.2	1.0

As you can see, for the most part, foods with the highest PERs also scored very well as protein sources for humans, and animal-based proteins outperformed plant-based proteins, with the exception of soy protein, which also obtained the highest score, like casein, egg, and whey protein.

One reason animal-based proteins tend to score highest is that they tend to contain significant amounts of all the essential amino acids. Most plant sources, with some exceptions, such as soybeans, quinoa, buckwheat, and spirulina, do not have complete complements of essential amino acids. Still, some plant foods contain certain combinations of amino acids that, when eaten in combination, do provide the essentials, such as rice and beans and bread and peanut butter.

So, it is possible to obtain adequate protein entirely from plant-based foods, but there is an important possible pitfall. Recalling the protein-leverage and protein-energy-ratio theories, one would have to eat greater quantities of plant foods and take in more calories than if one acquired at least some of one's proteins from animal sources. Consider one example: broccoli, a fine food indeed, and even one favored by those on ketogenic diets, is sometimes noted to be high in protein, and one-third of its calories do come from protein. However, to obtain the 8 grams of protein you can get from *one* cup of milk you would have to eat 3.2 cups of broccoli, and its protein would lack some essential amino acids.

Further, as science progresses, we are finding even newer ways to assess protein quality. The digestible indispensable amino acid score (DIASS) is supported by the Food and Agricultural Organization of the United Nations.[56] According to this system, the highest-scoring proteins are pretty similar, for the most part, with the highest scores going to milk, egg, meat, and whey products, reasonably high scores going to soy and pea protein, and the lowest scores to other grain and vegetable proteins.

The Protein We Need to Build Magnificent Temples

An important and much debated question, even within the narrower world of the low-carbohydrate, ketogenic, and protein-leveraging advocates, is how much protein we need to consume. Some people warn against too much protein because, while it does not drive insulin as much as carbohydrate, it still stimulates insulin to some extent and much more so than fat. They argue that our diets should be high in fat and relatively low in both carbohydrate and protein, albeit with more protein than carbs.

Others, most prominently Dr. Naiman and the protein-energy-ratio proponents, advise us to go heavier on protein. Indeed, there are other proponents, including some prominent physicians and researchers on muscle loss and aging. The official recommended daily allowance for

---

[56] Christopher P. F. Marinangeli and James D. House, "Potential Impact of the Digestible Indispensable Amino Acid Scores as a Measure of Protein Quality on Dietary Regulations and Health," *Nutrition Reviews* 75, no. 8 (August 2017): 658–667, National Library of Medicine, https://www.ncbi.nlm.nih.gov/pmc/articles/PMC5914309/.

U.S. citizens, or USRD, is 0.8 grams per kilogram of body weight, which translates to 0.36 grams per pound. At my current bodyweight of 190 pounds, that would translate to 68.4 grams of protein per day. Though I do not precisely count my intake of protein each day, I estimate I take in just about twice that amount each day.

Still, as you will see in part 3, we will be advised, as dedicated temple tenders, to use and challenge our muscles on a regular basis, and physically active people are advised to take in more protein. Indeed, in the same article I referenced for data on protein digestibility-corrected amino acid score, we find this statement listed as their first key point: "Higher protein needs are seen in athletic populations."[57]

As for possible concerns about risks entailed by eating more protein, for many years some have warned that high intake of protein can damage one's kidneys, but research has not borne this out. While it is true that people with certain kidney diseases must carefully monitor their protein intake, scientific evidence does not show that high protein intake causes kidney disease. Also, some have argued that protein's acidity can cause damage to our bones over time, but this has not been borne out by the research either. Remember, too, that bones are 50 percent protein.

Next, we will briefly zoom down in scale from the big macronutrients of carbohydrate, fat, and protein, to the wee but important micronutrient world of vitamins and minerals.

TEMPLE-TENDING TENET #7

Protein, an essential macronutrient, is indeed of primary importance for building and maintaining our bodily temples and for regulating our appetites. The more physically active we are, the more we are likely to need higher amounts.

---

[57]   Hoffman and Falvo, "Protein — Which Is Best?"

8

No Temple Can Stand without Vitamins and Minerals

RNIs (recommended nutrient intakes) for vitamins and minerals were initially established on the understanding that they are meant to meet the basic nutritional needs of over 97 percent of the population. However, a fundamental criterion in industrialized countries has become one of the presumptive role that these nutrients play in "preventing" an increasing range of disease conditions that characterize affected populations. The latter approach implies trying to define the notion of "optimal nutrition", and this has been one of the factors nudging defined requirements to still higher levels.

— World Health Organization, 2004[58]

Vitamins in Food or Added to Food: Which Ones Win?

This is not the place for an in-depth analysis of particular vitamins and minerals, but since we cannot build bodily temples without them, they

---

[58] World Health Organization, *Vitamin and Mineral Requirements in Human Nutrition*, 2nd ed. (Geneva: World Health Organization, 2004), xiv-xv, https://www.who.int/publications/i/item/9241546123.

are certainly worthy of at least an honorable mention. And judging from the quotation above, I believe the WHO would agree.

Vitamins and minerals are called micronutrients in contrast to the macronutrients of carbohydrate, fat, and protein, because, while essential, we need them in far smaller amounts. While the macronutrients are usually measured in grams, vitamins and minerals are usually measured in milligrams (one-thousandth of a gram) or even micrograms (one-millionth of a gram).

Thanks be to God, the same wholesome foods that provide our macronutrients are chock-full of various micronutrients too. No wonder we thank Him before meals! Problems may arise however, if over half of our diets are composed of not real foods but ultraprocessed foods. As we saw earlier, most of our diets, in the U.S. anyway, *are* composed of ultraprocessed foods. Such processing often removes vitamins that naturally occur in foods. As I noted, processed breads, for example, use "enriched flour" because the milling procedures manufacturers use reduce or remove the vitamins, chiefly B vitamins, that are naturally present. Other processed foods will tout on their labels the presence of various vitamins that are not even typically present in those foods or are present in low amounts but have been added to the foods, such as orange juice enhanced with calcium and vitamin D.

Although vitamins are indeed important, and a multivitamin pill may not be a bad idea, there are real advantages to obtaining as much of our vitamins as possible as they naturally occur in real foods, not in isolation, but in combination with other naturally occurring nutrients; for example, the bioflavonoids in oranges that may aid in the digestion of vitamin C.

Water-Soluble and Fat-Soluble Vitamins

Vitamins are classified as either water-soluble or fat-soluble. The water-soluble vitamins are C and the family of B vitamins. Since they dissolve in water, the body will not store too much, so they may need to be ingested on a regular basis. The fat-soluble vitamins are A, D, E, and K. Since they can be stored in our body fat, it may be possible to overdose on these if one takes them in very large doses. This would rarely happen with foods, since large quantities would need to be eaten on a regular basis to stack them up inside. For example, while one carrot supplies 73 percent of our daily supply of vitamin A, few of us are addicted to eating whole bags of carrots every day.

I'll note just a few more things before moving along to minerals. Regarding vitamin D, while few of us today get so little in our diets that we develop the deficiency-based bone disease called rickets, studies have shown declining vitamin D stores in the bodies of modern Americans. Most interestingly, our greatest natural supplier of vitamin D is literally out of this world, that source being the sun, which stimulates production of vitamin D, from — fasten your seatbelts — the cholesterol in our bodies. We have also been advised in recent decades to stay out of the sun.

We might also note that as we attempt to limit our dietary fats, we run the risk of limiting our bodies' abilities to absorb fat-soluble vitamins and that we increase the likelihood of meeting all our vitamin needs if our daily diets contain a variety of real foods.

"Animal, Vegetable, Mineral"

In the game 20 Questions, one player thinks of some item and other players are allowed twenty questions to try to determine the answer. In some variants, the person reveals whether it is an animal, a vegetable, or a mineral, and if not, it may come up as an early question. Well, we'll zoom in just a bit on minerals here, and I will note that every vegetable and every animal (including us) *needs* minerals and that every animal and plant food contains various minerals to various degrees.

One primary distinction among minerals is whether we need them in relatively large or small amounts, these being called macrominerals and microminerals (akin to the way we distinguish between macronutrients and micronutrients). Essential macrominerals include calcium, phosphorus, magnesium, sodium, potassium, and chloride. Essential microminerals (also called "trace" minerals) include chromium, cobalt, copper, iodine, iron, manganese, molybdenum, selenium, and zinc. I imagine you've heard of most of them, and I'm positive you've eaten all of them!

Some of these minerals carry electrical charges vital to cellular functions, including water balance. These are called electrolytes. The most important three are sodium, potassium, and chloride; others include calcium, magnesium, and phosphorous.

In properly tending our temples, we'll want to make sure we give our bodies all the minerals we need. I won't go into detail on the function of each one, but I will make two observations, one relevant to our fundamental principle of eating real foods and another relevant to those who choose to restrict their carbohydrates.

As for real foods, God, in His wisdom, has created all kinds of foods that are highly abundant in minerals. Sadly, some processes of industrial agriculture deplete minerals from the soils to some extent, and some food processing may strip out minerals or even add them in overabundance, back to good old sodium chloride — salt. Still, eating a variety of real foods will increase our chances of getting the minerals we need to build and maintain the sturdiest of temples. And if in doubt, taking a simple multivitamin tablet with minerals would probably not hurt.

As for those adopting very-low-carbohydrate or keto diets, some people, perhaps one out of three by some estimates, experience what is called "keto flu" or "Atkins flu" in the first two weeks or so. These feelings of ill ease may arise from the fact that as the body flushes excess water, important minerals will likely be flushed along with them. Stephen Phinney, M.D., Ph.D., and Jeff Volek, Ph.D, R.D, authors of

The Art and Science of Low Carbohydrate Living, recommend increasing one's intake of salt, and possibly other minerals, when starting a low-carbohydrate eating regimen. One of their recommendations is simply to eat or drink a serving or two of salty bone broth each day.

Although I never experienced keto flu or Atkins flu myself, I have been prone in the past — long before reducing carbohydrates — to muscle cramps, especially in my right hamstring. Such cramps are usually attributed to electrolyte deficiencies or imbalances, including salt, potassium, and magnesium. So, as a precaution since I've lowered my carbohydrates, I've included one small serving of a calorie-free electrolyte powder mixed with sixteen ounces of water before every daily workout, and I've not had a muscle cramp once. I also salt some of my foods, especially eggs.

Okay, so far, we have focused on the value of whole real foods, and we've spent several chapters picking those foods apart, so to speak, by looking at their delicious, nutritious components. We've looked quite a bit at *what* we should eat and *why* we should eat it. Next, we will look at *when* we should eat it, and *why* this makes such a difference.

TEMPLE-TENDING TENET #8

Let's get our vitamins and minerals, as much as possible, from real foods. Some of us might want to consider taking a vitamin-mineral tablet, using an electrolyte powder in water, drinking bone broth, salting some foods, or a combination of these.

9

Fasting and Feasting: Finishing Touches

Fasting gives birth to prophets and strengthens the powerful;
fasting makes lawgivers wise. Fasting is a good safeguard
of the soul, a steadfast companion for the body, a weapon
for the valiant, and a gymnasium for athletes.

— St. Basil the Great[59]

Fasting, Feasting, and Following the Science

When illustrating philosophical and theological principles, St. Thomas Aquinas sometimes used examples from the science of his day. He was quite aware, however, that some scientific understandings of his time might later be found to be wrong. For example, in his commentary on Aristotle's *On the Heavens* (book 11, lecture 17), Thomas cautions against being too certain that the stars revolve around the earth:

The suppositions that these men [Ptolemaic astronomers] have invented need not necessarily be true; for perhaps, while they

[59] As cited in Jay W. Richards, *Eat Fast Feast: Heal Your Body While Feeding Your Soul: A Christian Guide to Fasting* (New York: Harper One, 2020), 1.

save the appearances under these suppositions, they might not be true. For maybe the phenomena of the stars can be explained by some other schema not yet discovered by men.[60]

Well, it seems as if Thomas was onto something with that example, but even more important is the underlying principle. We often hear the phrase "follow the science" regarding certain topics, as if current scientific theories were unquestionable certainties written in stone like the Ten Commandments! Indeed, the very spirit of scientific investigation is not to be too sure of ourselves, to ask ever more penetrating questions, and to devise ever more nuanced methods of getting at underlying causes and principles.

Perhaps the fundamental lesson is that we should not feel too certain about things that are not certain! Ignorance or disregard of this principle may well play a role in our current health pandemics. Experts leapt into dietary recommendations before they carefully looked at (or even gathered) all the pertinent evidence. Once recommendations have spread around the world and became ensconced in our eating practices and even our laws — determining, for example, what kinds of foods can be served in public schools, the military, prisons, and so forth — it can be very difficult for experts to admit they may have been wrong.

Indeed, when I provide my own opinions on scientific findings in these pages, I do not at all claim certainty, but merely that, at this point in time, all the best evidence I have seen seems to point in this direction — and seems to have played out in my own and in others' body compositions and health. We must be willing to admit when we're

---

[60] Edward T. Oakes, "Robert Bellarmine vs. Thomas Aquinas," *First Things*, September 7, 2012, https://www.firstthings.com/blogs/firstthoughts/2012/09/robert-bellarmine-vs-thomas-aquinas. See also *ST*, I, Q. 32, art. 1.

wrong, and something else I've been wrong about in the past is the value of fasting, not only to the soul, but to the body and the mind as well.

Fasting for the Body

As I began to learn about the powerful impact of insulin on the body and on the growing pandemics that insulin resistance and metabolic syndrome leave in their wake, I noticed that in recent years, another method, in addition to restricting carbohydrate, has become more and more popular. This method, however, is about as far from something new as you could possibly get. Fasting has been present around the world for millennia, both for spiritual reasons and for the physical benefits it can provide. Even the ancient Greek Hippocrates of the fifth century BC, "the Father of Western Medicine," included fasting in his arsenal for the treatment of patients with certain diseases. And who among us has not willingly fasted from food when acutely nauseated by a stomach flu?

Well, how might fasting (or the lack thereof) have contributed to our obesity and allied health-disorder pandemics, and how might it be employed to help us cure it? First, I will note that medicinal fasting may connotate the idea of going at least a full day or maybe more without any intake of food, but there are other ways to incorporate fasting into a healthy lifestyle. This method is often called "intermittent fasting," and "time-restricted eating," and it, too, is far from new. (There is a good chance your mom or your grandma knew this well and preached it to you on more than one occasion.)

I refer to the long-cherished homespun wisdom that advised us to eat "three square meals per day" and not to snack between meals. I remember hearing such advice when I was a kid — not that I heeded it much. In Dr. Jason Fung's *The Obesity Code*, chapter 10 is on insulin resistance, which he calls "the major player" in developing obesity. One of his sections is titled "Three Meals a Day. No Snacks" — sounding, perhaps, a lot like Grandma. Dr. Fung shows a very simple graph with three little insulin roller-coaster rides, we might say. In our traditional eating patterns, we started the day with breakfast, noting that it literally *breaks* the mini *fast* we experience every night when we sleep. After a while, our insulin levels drop below baseline, and before long, it is time for lunch. Insulin rises again and then falls before dinner, usually our biggest meal of the day. This causes the largest insulin release, but that is not a problem, because soon after comes our long nighttime fast while we sleep.

This was indeed the most common American eating pattern when I was growing up in the 1960s — not that we didn't sneak in a snack once in a while — and we were a lean nation. Indeed, even in 1977, surveys showed that most Americans ate three times per day when the obesity rate was about 15 percent. By 2003, however, when the obesity rate had risen to about 32 percent, most Americans were eating five or six times per day. Could there possibly be a connection?

Not only did carbohydrate consumption go up and protein and fat consumption go down: people also began to eat more often throughout the day. And that's just what they were told to do. Why? So we would not get too hungry between meals and then proceed to overeat. We were told to eat more of the macronutrient that triggers our insulin and makes us hungry and less of the macronutrients that satiate us and stave off hunger.

Time and again, people who reduce their carbohydrates and increase their fat or protein, or both, report that they no longer feel ravenously hungry between meals and may even skip some meals simply because they get busy and forget. Some people then naturally move toward eating twice or even only once per day. Some set up time-restricted eating patterns, such as a 16:8 fasting-eating pattern in which they only eat meals from perhaps noon until 8:00 p.m. Indeed, it need not even be as restrictive as that, and I'll tell you my own regimen before this chapter is out.

So, there is a great deal of potential physical benefit to fasting if one is careful not to overdo it. Now let's take a peek at its spiritual benefits.

Fasting for the Soul

The Church has always taught that God crafted us as beings with bodies and souls that, together, form our nature. We are ensouled bodies. What affects the body affects the soul, and vice versa. The Church has also always recognized that fasting from food can be a powerful tool in our *spiritual* toolbelts. And here is another neat little body-soul connection.

To make a long story short, I will note that any readers who want to know both the spiritual and physical ins and outs, pros and cons, of fasting and various methods to practice it are directed to Jay Richards's thorough book, *Eat Fast Feast*. Here, I'll simply note a few of the spiritual profundities he brings to center stage. For one thing, he cites numerous Church Fathers who extolled the spiritual value of fasting as we willingly offer our sacrifice to God and discipline our wills. Most Christians are likely quite aware that Jesus Himself practiced fasting — indeed, for up to forty days! Still, some have wondered why Jesus did not explicitly advise or command us to fast, and Jay provides a very good answer.

Consider, for example, that Jesus says the following: "When you fast, do not look dismal, like the hypocrites, for they disfigure their faces that their fasting may be seen by men" (Matt. 6:16). Jesus did not command his disciples to fast because he was pretty sure they were doing it already as a part of the Jewish tradition.

Of course, the Catholic Church, too, has always recommended various kinds of fasting, though in recent times the fasts have been quite a bit more relaxed. During Lent, we still fast from meat on Fridays and on Ash Wednesday, for example, and we are still supposed to fast for at least one hour before we received the Eucharist. And of course, on the flip side, the Church is no stranger to feasting as well as fasting. As Jesus also told us, "I came that they may have life, and have it abundantly" (John 10:10). God wants us to be happy, though not necessarily "fat and happy."

My Experience with Very Fast Fasts

During my childhood and early adolescence, my only experience with fasting was when I was sick and for the one-hour fast before Mass (what I mean by a "very fast fast"). By the time I was a teenager obsessed with lifting big weights and building big muscles, I read somewhere about "juice fasts," and once, for a few weeks, I consumed nothing but fruit juice for one day per week, but that didn't last too long.

In my later teens and my college years, my experience was nearly identical to what I found was the case for Jay Richards. He writes about being a strength-and-fitness trainer in college and advising people to eat according to the complex-carbohydrate food pyramid and to eat multiple small meals throughout the day. Ditto! As I worked as a strength-and-fitness instructor in college, I advised and did just the same. I attended seminars conducted by world-champion bodybuilders who were also advising us to pump fuel and nutrients into our bodies throughout the day. Indeed, I tended to do so myself for the next forty years, right up until the last year or so.[61]

---

[61] Please note that some people can thrive on multiple small meals per day, especially those who exercise rigorously and focus on nourishing foods. Further, my wife, who is no athlete, eats much smaller portions than I do and feels better when she eats more often. When I was younger, I was able to keep lean while eating multiple small meals per day if I was also doing extensive cardiovascular training such as running. Some of our vignette contributors do thrive eating this way. The key is to find the way that works best for *you* — *at this point in your life!*

I recall within the last few years hearing about fasting and "time-restricted eating." I knew a few guys from the gym who were doing it, but I reflexively pooh-poohed the idea, thinking they would fast away the muscle they'd worked so hard to accrue slowly throughout the years. I remember one twenty-something lifter who would occasionally work in some heavy dead lifts with my twenty-something training partner and my fifty-something self around eight o'clock on Friday mornings. When he told us he was lifting in "a fasted state" — that is, before he had any breakfast or even a protein shake — I thought he was off his rocker.

Yet, zoom ahead three or four years, and now I see he was really onto something, but I was too puffed up in prideful disdain to consider that maybe these fasters had good reasons for what they were doing. So, at this point, here is how fasting (or time-restricted eating) has fit into my regimen for the last four months or so. In our next chapter, I'll flesh out the delicious details, but basically, I stop eating at about 5:30 p.m. and don't eat again until after my morning workout at 7:30 a.m., though I do have a cup of black coffee and a few glasses of water before I go to the gym.

Now, I had already lost thirty pounds before I added this method. I did not lose any more weight, but neither did I intend to. My body seems happy to be right where it is now, and I simply enjoy this manner of eating. By eating nothing after 5:30 p.m., I effortlessly crushed my old habit of nighttime snacking, thanks primarily to my increased intake of protein and fat. Further, I have zero regurgitation at night and no longer need to take antacids. As for the morning workout, I always feel fresh and energetic because my body has adjusted to burning a steady stream of fat logs, so I need no carbohydrate kerosene or kindling to keep my fires burning. My strength is as good as ever, and another benefit is that my stomach never feels bloated or queasy when I hit the heavy iron.

Well, there's a fast look at my fast fasts. Now, let's put all this nutritional data together and lay out some simple sample eating plans.

TEMPLE-TENDING TENET #9

Fasting has been known and practiced for its physical and spiritual benefits for millennia, and Jesus Christ Himself fasted. It need not mean going without food for a day or for days at a time. Many people derive physical benefit merely from "time-restricted eating" — in my own case, as simple as not eating between 5:30 p.m. and 7:30 a.m. Only God and your body know what might work best for you.

10

Prudent, Practical, Simple Sample Eating Plans

Since prudence is right reason applied to action, the whole process
of prudence must needs have its source in understanding.

— St. Thomas Aquinas, *Summa Theologica*, II-II, Q. 49, art. 2

Diary of a Daily Diet

It has taken until our tenth chapter for me to get down to business and
give concrete examples of just how we might eat to build, maintain, fuel,
repair, and honor our bodily temples. Since St. Thomas told us that acts
of prudence or practical wisdom must be grounded in understanding,
I felt we really needed to dig into the fundamental principles of nutrition and health before we started shoveling some real foods into our
mouths! Thank you for hanging in there so long.

Now, recalling that we all live our lives at the "n = 1" level, the easiest way for me to illustrate is to start by sharing with you my own. And
note well that many of the elements of my eating plan were culled from
ideas, examples, and recipes of other healthy people I have spoken to
or read about.

Let me make clear that I *never* count calories, and I only loosely
track my protein, fat, and carbohydrate intakes. But for the purposes

of this book, I chose a day at random and calculated protein, fat, carbohydrate, and calorie intake for that entire day:

Time	Foods	Protein grams	Fat grams	Carb grams
4:00 a.m.	black coffee	0	0	0
6:00	16 oz. water/ electrolytes	0	0	0
7:30	mocha protein smoothie	40	22	6
	sugar-free dark chocolate	5	4	1
12:00 p.m.	3 eggs	18	18	2
	3 slices Canadian bacon	12	4	1
	1 tbsp. almond butter	3	9	3
	1 tbsp. cream in decaf coffee	0	5	0
3:00	2 whiskey old-fashioneds[62]	0	0	0
	1 serving pork rinds	7	5	0
	1 oz. cheese	7	9	0
	2 feta-stuffed green olives	0	2	2
	¼ cup pistachios in shells	3	6	4

[62] These are made without sugar or fruit and provide about 210 calories of energy from alcohol.

5:00 p.m.	8 oz. New York strip steak	45	32	0
	1 serving steamed broccoli	3	1	8
	1 serving plain Greek yogurt with vanilla protein powder and a handful of raspberries	20	4	6
Totals		173	121	33
Calories	1,914 total calories (2,124 including alcohol)	692	1089	132

Let's Take a Look at the Numbers

Please note once more that I do not believe it is necessary to track macronutrients carefully (and even less so to track calories) for most people, but I was curious to see what my macronutrient ratios are at a time when my health and fitness results are quite satisfactory. Note too that I have not included the alcohol into my equations so I can compare the three macronutrient ratios.

Anyway, I would say that the sample menu above is pretty typical of how I've been eating for the last nine months or so. The food has been crunched, and now let's crunch the numbers. In my sample above, my daily fare *in terms of calories*, counting protein and carbs at four calories per gram and fat at nine calories per gram, is as follows: 36 percent protein, 57 percent fat, and 7 percent carbohydrate. Current USDA guidelines recommend 10 to 35 percent protein, 20 to 25 percent fat, and 45 to 65 percent carbohydrate. Some call this the standard American diet — sometimes abbreviated, perhaps appropriately, as SAD.

The protein percentage in my sample diet surprised me as being a little higher than I had thought, though maybe that is why I am never hungry between planned meals. The carbs were a little lower than I had expected, and the fat was pretty close to expectations. Some low-carbohydrate proponents call their approach LC–HF, "low carbohy-drate–high fat" diets, recommending that fat supplies 60 to 80 percent of one's daily calories.

Now, am I concerned about "all that fat" lolling about, clogging my arteries? Not really. For one thing, I know my visceral fat has decreased dramatically, judging from the fact that my body is thirty pounds lighter, my waistline is six inches smaller, and my blood pressure is more than twenty points lower. Eating so little carbohydrate, my body obviously used my own body fat as energy during my period of weight loss, and now it uses primarily my daily dietary intake of fat to fuel my activities. Having become a fat-burner, the fat that I consume is not tucked away but is used to keep my temple's fires burning. My most recent labora-tory values showed a high HDL level (perhaps a little too simplistically called "good cholesterol"), with no medical indication for cholesterol medication; though it was prescribed for me once years ago while I was eating a lowfat, high-carbohydrate diet. I have not taken any for several years.

But my lack of concern is also based on more than my own expe-rience. In fact, a massive literature review published in the *Journal of the American College of Cardiology* (yes, cardiology) in 2020 included statements such as the following:

> The recommendation to limit dietary saturated fatty acid (SFA) intake has persisted despite mounting evidence to the contrary.... Whole-fat dairy, unprocessed meat, and dark chocolate are SFA-rich foods with a complex matrix that are not associated with increased risk of CVD (cardiovascular

disease). The totality of available evidence does not support further limiting the intake of such foods.[63]

Next, I'll consider the protein-energy balance recommended by Dr. Ted Naiman. He recommends keeping carbohydrates under 100 grams per day, what the liver can hold in glycogen, to lose body fat, and I'm well under that. As for his protein recommendations, in calculating his recommended ratio, he subtracts fiber grams from carbohydrates. The fiber intake in my sample above was fairly low at about 12 grams, coming from the nuts, vegetables, raspberries, and dark chocolate. Dr. Naiman recommends that we strive for a "P:E ratio" of at least 1:1 in terms of grams, not calories, of protein to energy, energy meaning carbohydrates plus fats. In my sample menu, my protein grams totaled 173 and my fat plus carbs minus fiber totaled 142. This yields a P:E ratio of 1.22:1. How interesting and rewarding, that having never made the calculation on myself until this very minute, my regimen has indeed exceeded that 1:1 P:E ratio goal. Again, no wonder I'm not hungry!

Ah, but what about the two cocktails? I had two drinks with 1½ ounces of whiskey in each. That is a total of 85 grams. Since the whiskey was 80 proof (which means 40 percent alcohol), the drinks did add 34 grams on the energy side of the equation, yielding a total P:E ratio of 173:176 or 0.98, actually a little shy of the 1:1 goal. Shucks! But good to know. My daily diet varies a bit, and my bodyweight has been completely stable for months. If I were to start gaining weight, I could easily shift my P:E ratio higher through a variety of means. Simply omitting one cocktail, for example, would have brought this sample P:E to 173:159 — just a hair shy of 1.1:1.

[63] Arne Astrup, Faidon Magkos, Dennis M. Bier, et al., "Saturated Fats and Health: A Reassessment and Proposal for Food-Based Recommendations," *Journal of the American Academy of Cardiology* 76, no. 7 (August 2020), https://www.jacc.org/doi/10.1016/j.jacc.2020.05.077.

I must note, too, that this simple one-day nutritional analysis did prove helpful to me. One surprise to me was the realization that even though I was still able to maintain low body fat, I was getting just about 10 percent of my daily calories from alcohol (Irish whiskey or Kentucky Bourbon, to be precise); hence, I have reduced my old-fashioned-cocktail afternoon treat to *one* per day.[64]

Perhaps you would like to try tracking your macronutrients for one day, ideally today, and then tracking them again someday if you adopt new eating habits and achieve a new bodyfat level. The changes in your macronutrient ratios might surprise you. You can find out where you feel and function best, and where you have your best laboratory blood values.

Anyway, please recall that all this analysis is simply an exercise based on merely one day of my typical dietary intake, and I have not done it once before today to lose and keep off thirty pounds. Part of the theory behind emphasizing real foods and deemphasizing carbohydrate is that it tends to restore one's natural appetite to a level that maintains a healthy body weight *without overplanning one's diet and having to track nutrients continually.* If I might borrow St. Thomas's terms once more, eating natural, nutritious foods can help us rein in inappropriate concupiscence (desire) and immoderate consumption of what we eat and drink, making it far easier to eat a truly prudent diet — one guided by right reason.

---

[64]   As an interesting coincidence, the new internal medicine doctor I saw just last week informed me that while the USDA guidelines have allowed up to two alcoholic drinks per day for men and one for women, researchers are now suggesting a maximum of *one* drink for either sex on days that they drink. For the latest CDC recommendations, see "Alcohol Use and Your Health," CDC, last reviewed April 14, 2022, https://www.cdc.gov/alcohol/fact-sheets/alcohol-use.htm. (Of course, as we've seen many times, researchers of the day may not always know best!)

Speaking of which, let's not forget perhaps the most important nutritional principle of them all, that of eating real foods versus ultraprocessed foods loaded with salt, sugar, fat, and all kinds of additives and preservatives that may be anything but nice. On the processed-food side, I did have whey protein powder, and although it does not have added salt, sugar, or fat, it does contain some artificial sweetener. That is a trade-off I'm willing to make. I buy the powder from a pharmacist, and it is nearly 100 percent protein with virtually zero fat or carbohydrate. In fact, the pharmacist stocks it because bariatric surgeons in our area prescribe it to patients who have had fat-reduction surgeries. It helps them keep their weight off and ensure they get plenty of the highest-quality protein to maintain their muscle mass. I also sometimes use a different, completely natural protein powder made from milk and egg protein with zero artificial sweeteners. The downside is that it contains seven grams of carbohydrate per serving, but that is an amount I can live with.

So what else? Oh yes, some brands of pork rinds are cooked with vegetable oil instead of lard, and they are a poor source of protein, but I do *not* eat them every day (often substituting ¼ cup of some kind of nuts), and they keep me from craving any other kind of salty, fatty snack. Pretty much everything else in my diet consists of real foods, such as meat, eggs, nuts, vegetables, and berries. I do drink a whole milk that is "ultrafiltered," which reduces the carbohydrate from milk sugars to six grams per cup instead of eleven and increases the protein from eight grams to thirteen. Other food items I eat on other days include bacon, sausage, pork chops, chicken (with skin, on the bone), salmon, tuna, shrimp, scallops, grass-fed butter, extra-virgin olive oil, coconut oil, a variety of vegetables, and a variety of berries. I choose to stay away from all grains and cereals, but high-quality breads and cereals, such as sprouted breads and steel-cut oats or oat groats, can certainly be a part of a healthy diet for those who enjoy them and can tolerate the carbohydrates.

I should not fail to mention two other essentials that provide no nutrients but are extremely important nonetheless. The first is *water*. I listed only the water I had with my pre-workout electrolytes, but I drink several additional glasses throughout the day. It can be even more essential to drink water when one's carbohydrate intake is low, since the body does not hold as much water. The second is coffee. It is essential, at least to me, because I enjoy its flavor, and no dietary regimen will be sustainable for long if is not enjoyable. In addition to what I listed in the table I have one to three additional cups of regular black coffee in the morning while I write.

Different Foods for Different Folks

You might be asking yourself, "What about me?" I certainly do not mean to imply that anyone should eat just like I've been eating this last year. Rather, I would hope you might pick up an idea here or there to craft a HRF (high-real-food) diet for yourself with far less ultraprocessed food; little, if any, processed sugar or industrial oils; a reasonable dose of protein; good amounts of fat from natural food sources; some naturally occurring fiber; and perhaps a more modest measure of carbohydrate. Further, your diet should be based on foods that *you* enjoy and that do not cause digestive or other problems for *you*.

Of course, if you do plan substantial changes in your diet, you should discuss them with your physician or dietician, if you have one. And here is a very important caveat: because such dietary changes can drastically lower things, including blood sugar, insulin, and blood pressure for most people, if you are taking medications for diabetes, hypertension, or other disorders, you should do this under your doctor's care. It may bring your numbers down dangerously low if your medications are not decreased or, in some cases, eliminated. Some of these effects can come into play in merely a matter of hours. I can't help but note, too, that there are many doctors who advocate low carbs and who have produced case studies and empirical research studies showing how they are able to eliminate the need for insulin in many of their diabetic patients. Further, the American Diabetic Association guidelines have recently removed their recommendation to eat at least 130 grams of carbohydrate per day and also noted the following:

> Reducing overall carbohydrate intake for individuals with diabetes has demonstrated the most evidence for improving glycemia and may be applied in a variety of eating patterns that meet individual needs and preferences.[65]

Keeping Ketosis Simple

I suppose it's high time, too, that I defined some important terms. At times I've spoken interchangeably about low-carbohydrate, or *ketogenic*, diets, so I should define "ketones" and "ketosis" (not to be confused with "ketoacidosis"!).

- Ketones are chemicals (I'll spare you their technical formulas), produced in the liver from fat to provide energy when there is not enough glucose in the bloodstream. We all have some ketones at times, and they become more prevalent while we sleep or fast, when we have not eaten for a while, and even more if we exercise while in such a state. Ketones can also cross the blood-brain barrier and supply energy to the brain.
- "Ketosis" refers to a state of elevated ketone production found with fasting and with low-carbohydrate consumption. It facilitates weight loss because, while in a state of ketosis, the body

---

[65] Alison B. Evert, Michelle Dennison, Christopher D. Gardner, et al., "Nutrition Therapy for Adults with Diabetes or Prediabetes: A Consensus Report," *Diabetes Care* 42 (April 18, 2019): 6, https://care.diabetesjournals.org/content/diacare/early/2019/04/10/dci19-0014.full.pdf.

more readily uses its own fat stores to supply energy for the body and brain. The degree to which a person is in ketosis can be measured in a variety of ways, including colored strips that detect it in the urine, specialized blood tests, and specialized tests that can measure it in one's breath.

• "Ketoacidosis" is a term I knew as a disability adjudicator long before I knew the other two terms. Some people with severe, uncontrolled diabetes — especially type 1 — can develop extremely low levels of insulin in their blood that results in hyperglycemia (too much blood sugar) and high blood acidity. It can be life-threatening, requiring emergency medical treatment. In the old "blue book" of medical listings book for social security disability I trained under in the 1980s, diabetes with a required frequency of episodes of ketoacidosis requiring hospitalization was considered disabling.

How are these terms related to healthful eating, and why should they concern us if we are not diabetic? Well, when diets are low enough in carbohydrate, which can vary from person to person but will usually be the case if one takes in perhaps fifty to sixty grams or fewer per day, it will increase one's level of *ketosis* (fat-burning). Calling these diets "ketogenic" simply means they stimulate production of ketones. Sometimes however, people, and even medical doctors, confuse ketosis, which can be a very good thing, with *ketoacidosis*, which is a very bad thing. It is essential to know the difference! Drs. Volek and Phinney point out that the "B-OHB" levels (the major form of ketones) found in advanced diabetics with ketoacidosis due to pancreas or insulin burnout is "5-to-10-fold higher than the levels characteristic of nutritional ketosis."[66]

---

[66] Jeff S. Volek, Ph.D., R.D. and Stephen D. Phinney, M.D., Ph.D., *The Art and Science of Low Carbohydrate Living: An Expert Guide to Making*

So, if you are trying to lose or maintain your weight or to keep your liver nice and lean, ketosis can be your friend and can make you very unlikely to suffer ketoacidosis unless you have a serious case of diabetes and your pancreas is severely damaged. That said, I must note that some books on low-carbohydrate or ketogenic diets recommend that you monitor your ketone levels through urine tests or breath-analysis machines. In the spirit of keeping things simple, I will simply note that I have never done so. Still, if you are a person who likes to track things precisely, it won't bother me at all if you pick up from your local pharmacy some of those keto strips or even one of the newer little blood-sugar and ketone monitoring kits.

TEMPLE-TENDING TENET #10

Consider tracking your nutrient intake, even for merely one day, to examine your macronutrient ratios to see if you find any surprises. You might want to calculate your protein-energy ratio too. If you make significant dietary changes and get good results, consider tracking your nutrients again later to see how your daily eating has changed.

the *Life-Saving Benefits of Carbohydrate Restriction Sustainable and Enjoyable* (n.p.: Beyond Obesity, 2011), 5.

11

Tempting Eating Tips for Your Temple

The food you eat should not have ingredients,
it should be its own ingredient.

— Brett Scher, M.D.[67]

The Simplest, Healthiest Recipes of Them All

Ideally, the recipe and instructions for most of the foods should look something like this: "Rinse, cook, and eat," or perhaps, at its simplest, merely "Eat!" This means that if we eat mostly real foods — such as meats, including chicken and fish; eggs; cheese; vegetables; nuts; and fruits — we can often eat and enjoy them as God made them, on their own. Of course, we can add relish to our foods, and to our lives, by cooking, combining, preparing, and seasoning our foods in nutritious, delicious ways.

In this chapter, I'll begin by giving you some very simple "man recipes," as some call them, simple recipes that ordinary men, like me, might put together. I'll flesh out what I ate in my sample daily fare and provide a few alternatives. Next, I'll provide some guidance on where to go for far fancier and tastier recipes. A section on dining out will

[67]   *Your Best Health Ever! The Cardiologist's Surprisingly Simple Guide to What Really Works* (n.p.: Dr Brett Scher, 2017), 66, emphasis in the original.

follow, and we will end with the two gnawing questions I'm sure have crossed your mind: (1) "What about pizza?" (2) "Does this mean I have to pass up Aunt Doris's delicious homemade desserts?"

Simple Daily Staples

You need never drink a protein smoothie if you don't like them. That said, if you do like them, or might like to give one a try, I'll give you a few of my simple recipes. I like them because they taste good to me and are filling and highly nourishing. They also have nostalgic value because they bring back fond memories of my teenage years when I first drank them to help develop my muscles and strength. I'll never forget an old ad for one of the protein shakes in the muscle magazines: "Tastes like a shake and feeds like a steak!" Please note that I set a target of forty grams of protein, partly for reasons I'll explain in chapter 20, on aging. You might not desire to go so high, though I would suggest shooting for at least twenty grams.

Here they are, with names I've just whipped up for a few of them:

Chocolate Peanut Protein Pleaser: 1 cup water, 32 grams chocolate whey protein, 2 tablespoons natural peanut butter, at least ½ cup crushed ice. *Alternate recipe*: substitute 1 cup ultrafiltered whole milk for the water, reduce the whey protein to 23 grams, and use only one tablespoon of peanut butter.

Mocha Muscle Maker: 1 cup ultrafiltered whole milk, 6 ounces decaf coffee frozen in at least 12 ice-cube-tray sections (for easier mixing), a little extra crushed ice, 27 grams chocolate whey protein, 1 tablespoon extralight olive oil. (Yes, you read that right.) *Alternate recipe*: Substitute water for the milk, and add thirteen more grams of protein powder.

Chocolate Almondine Coconut Dream: 1 cup water, ½ cup or more crushed ice, 38 grams chocolate whey protein powder, 1 tablespoon unsweetened almond butter, and 1 tablespoon virgin, unrefined, cold-pressed coconut oil. (I got this idea from a Doug Brignole video, by the way. We'll meet this Mr. Universe winner and ingenious biomechanic in chapter 14). *Alternate recipe*: Not nuts about coconuts? Still worried about saturated fat? Then skip the coconut and enjoy an extra tablespoon of almond butter.

Cuckoo for Coconuts: 1 cup ultrafiltered milk, 27 grams vanilla protein powder, 1 tablespoon coconut oil, ½ cup or more crushed ice. *Alternate recipes*: Replace the milk with water and bump up the protein powder to 40 grams; or replace the coconut oil with ¼ cup unsweetened coconut flakes; or both.

Smoothie tips: Blend in a blender or use one of those nifty hand-held immersion devices, which require less cleanup. I have scoops that hold 23 and 15 grams, and I estimate from those. Alternatively, one-fourth dry cup yields 32 grams. I'm giving the grams as rough guidelines. I never measure or weigh them too precisely myself. You can also vary these recipes to your heart's (and other muscles') content by using different flavors of protein powder, adding various berries, and so forth. Sometimes I'll do a mixed-nut variety, blending a total of 2 tablespoons of natural, unsweetened peanut, almond, and sometimes even cashew butters. I pretty much rotate through these drinks and some variations every day to keep things tasty and interesting. They typically have from ten to twenty-three grams of fat and ten or fewer grams of carbs.

As for that dark chocolate I mentioned as a favorite little snack after my smoothie, I use a sugar-free brand that is 90 percent cocoa. It says three little squares make a serving, but I always have only one, and it always gets the job done.

Now, when it comes to lunch, I usually incorporate one to four eggs, depending on what other protein sources I eat with them. Kathy and I are fortunate to have access to local brown eggs from free-range chickens. They are absolutely delicious! I may eat the eggs over easy, cooked in a little butter from grass-fed cows, or scrambled with a little cheddar cheese, or hard-boiled. I always salt and pepper them too.

And here is another interesting use for eggs we came across recently. Kathy had a hankering for chicken noodle soup. It turns out that a frozen container of chicken noodle soup she had bought was merely soup starter, with some chicken, broth, and veggies, but nary a noodle in sight! Well, we simply baked a chicken breast, chopped it up, and added it to the soup to boost the protein and make it a meal. Then we fried a few eggs, sliced them, and added them instead of noodles. We thought it was some of the best chicken "noodle" soups we'd ever had. Those are my kind of "egg noodles."

As for snacks, perhaps you noticed that I pooh-poohed them in the chapter on fasting, and then, lo and behold, here I am with cheese, pork rinds, olives, pistachios, and the like at 3:00 in the afternoon. Well, fair enough, but I consider these the appetizers before dinner. In the afternoon, I do indeed include an eating window from 3:00 to 5:30 that has worked for me so far. My snacks — er, *appetizers* — are pretty straightforward, just the foods I mentioned. But as for those cocktails, I'm a fan of the classic old-fashioned, but I now make a "keto" version by omitting cherries and orange slices and replacing the simple sugar syrup with a small packet of monk fruit or stevia or five drops of liquid stevia.

Supper can vary greatly, but the main difference is that Kathy and I used to feel the need to include multiple dishes: meat, chicken, fish or some kind of protein, along with potatoes, bread, and one or more vegetables, or salad. Most of our suppers are far simpler now, being the main animal protein (and fat) dish and one vegetable, especially of the lower-carb green-leafy variety. Sometimes we add sauces. Here is my simple "man recipe" for a sauce we add to steaks and even to hamburger patties sometimes: "Over low heat, melt a few ounces of bleu cheese with a tablespoon or two of heavy cream. Pour on meat. Eat."

Now, how about dessert? Well, we have developed a simple, tasty dessert that we eat in various versions virtually every evening. The simplest version consists of two or three tablespoons of plain whole-fat Greek yogurt, a tablespoon or so (maybe 12 to 14 grams) of vanilla protein powder, a splash of heavy cream or whole milk, and about ¼ cup fresh or frozen berries: raspberries, blueberries, black berries, or strawberries, or a combination of them. We simply stir it all together in small bowls and eat it. One variation is to use ricotta cheese instead of the other dairy ingredients. I also like mine frozen like ice cream and will sometimes pop it into the freezer for an hour or two before I eat it. Sometimes I use chocolate protein instead of vanilla and a tablespoon of peanut or almond butter instead of the berries, though chocolate and raspberry is another nice combo. This one is especially delightful frozen! Kathy and I have both found that by finishing our supper by 5:30 or 6:00 with a dessert like this, we have no desire to eat anything else for the rest of the evening — a far cry from the days, not so long ago, when I would crave alternating rounds of sweet and salty snacks every night. No wonder I'd often reach for the antacids before bedtime!

You may be asking, "So how about some real recipes?" Good question! I am no chef — if you hadn't guessed already — and Kathy is too busy taking care of me, the house, and our dog to write this section for me, so I'll simply make a few suggestions.

First, I imagine that recipe books you already own are full of healthy real-food recipes or could at least be modified in that direction, primarily by reducing processed food ingredients and sugar. If you would care for some recipes both whole and holy, be aware that my publisher, Sophia Institute Press, has produced gorgeous cookbooks, including *The Vatican Cookbook*, *The Vatican Christmas Cookbook*, *Cooking with the*

Saints, and *The Lenten Cookbook.* Further, when we come to appendix 2, I will also guide you to some wonderful recent books on real food and low-carbohydrate eating that include hundreds of chef-tailored recipes.

Dining Out

Many of us enjoy a significant number of our meals dining out, so if we want to best tend our temples, we should consider how we can make healthy food choices at restaurants. In fact, many Americans today spend more than half of their food budget at restaurants. To keep this as simple as possible, one would do well to avoid as much as possible the most obvious potential health-hinderers, such as sugary cola drinks; greasy, deep-fried foods; and copious amounts of breads, sauces, desserts, and the like, and to stick as much as possible to good protein and fat sources, such as meat, chicken, fish, and eggs, along with good, low-starch vegetables, such as lettuce, spinach, broccoli, asparagus, cauliflower, tomatoes, and onions.

At restaurants with a wide variety of American fare, it is usually pretty easy to put together a relatively healthy, wholesome meal. I will often order salads with grilled salmon, chicken, shrimp, or steak on top, asking them to hold the croutons and to serve the dressing on the side. Other times, I'll order steak, chicken, or seafood with a side dish of broccoli or other available vegetables. Sometimes I'll simply order a hamburger, often with cheese and occasionally with bacon or even an egg as well. I'll eat the lettuce, tomato, onion, and pickle that comes on the side but ask them to hold the bun. I skip the condiments too (unless I feel I could use a little more salt or mustard). I skip the fries or chips as a side and go for vegetables or cottage cheese instead. When Kathy and I last ate out last week, I got a grilled-chicken-breast sandwich with Monterey Jack cheese, bacon, lettuce, tomato, and on-ion, served without the bun and with cottage cheese as the side. As for desserts, while we would occasionally split one in the past, since changing our eating patterns we don't even desire dessert anymore when eating out. Happily, we feel satisfied but never overstuffed after our restaurant meals now.

Of course, there are many styles of cuisine out there, and some may be harder to tailor to the real-food, low-sugar guidelines, but you may still want to give it a try. If some of your absolute favorites just can't seem to be made to fit the bill, then consider enjoying them anyway — just not too often or in gigantic portions!

Oh! I almost forgot the question that has certainly crossed most readers' minds. Yes — "What about pizza?" Pizza is one of America's favorite foods for dining out, ordering in, or having at home. Most of us find it quite delicious, and it may contain quite a few nutrients, but the danger lies in its almost irresistible combination of fat, carbohydrate, and salt, not to mention sugar, if you get those cinnamon sticks or chocolate chip cookies to go with it for dessert and wash it all down with a pitcher of soda or beer. If you really enjoy pizza, my general advice is simply not to have it too often and to consider getting the thin-crust variety. If you want to get daring, try using alternative crusts. There are recipes and videos on the Internet that use cauliflower, for example, instead of flour, but try at your own risk! Or, if you want to be as gung-ho as I've been this last year, simply scrape off the cheese, sauce, meats, and veggies from the crust, eat those, and toss out the crust. I've come to enjoy it that way and never feel bloated, as I used to. You can also find various crustless pizza recipes on the Internet.

And Now for Aunt Doris

Dear Aunt Doris is gone, but fond memories of her desserts linger on. When I was first courting Kathy, her Aunt Doris brought a home-baked blackberry pie to a family get-together. I praised her pie lavishly, though honestly, and thanks be to God, to just about every family get-together from that day on, she brought along a blackberry pie!

I don't doubt that you may have aunts, moms, grandmas, or even grandpas who like to bake — late in life, my dad liked to whip up pineapple upside-down cakes for us and the grandkids, who are known for concocting delicious desserts with sugar to spare. Ah, or perhaps you yourself are the guilty party! Of course, I'm pointing no fingers, and my tongue is firmly in my cheek.

What I really mean to say is that, barring some extreme medical condition, such as diabetes unresponsive to treatment, chances are you can indeed enjoy such sugary treats in moderation on special occasions. Since my weight-loss journey this year, I've attended two wedding receptions, a few birthday parties, and a baby shower at which I gladly enjoyed desserts as I celebrated along with everyone else — though sometimes, unless I am handed a plate, I will simply and painlessly abstain.

And speaking of feasting, our local parish just had its fall festival; indeed, they call it a "feast-ival." When Kathy and I got there with our son, daughter-in-law, and grandson, it was time for lunch, but the attendance was so good that no table seats were open. Having purchased from a vendor a juicy bratwurst, I ate it on a white-bread hot-dog bun. This is not the kind of food I eat on a regular basis anymore, but a very limited intake of treats like this has caused me no problems at all. I didn't gain an ounce and felt just fine, and I returned to simple, unprocessed foods at my very next meal. The principles I am sharing are flexible ones. We must still enjoy life and show our loved ones we enjoy their generosity and hospitality. We need to thank them and God for the gifts we receive from them. We don't always have to "just say no" to less than nutritionally ideal foods. The proof is in the pudding (so to speak) of what we routinely eat on a day-to-day basis.

Well, now that we have gathered the building materials we'll need, let's get down to finding out just what we'll need to do to build them up into healthy, holy temples.

TEMPLE-TENDING TENET #11

Give some simple, sample temple-tending recipes a try, or craft your own recipes based on real foods as God made them and on your own tastes, possible food allergies or sensitivities, budget, and food availability in your area.

Part III

--◦❧◦----------------◦❧◦--

Temple-Building Instructions
(Proper Exercise to Build and Maintain Sturdy Temples)

*The LORD is my strength and my song, and he has
become my salvation; this is my God, and I will praise
him, my father's God, and I will exalt him.*

— Exodus 15:2

12

The Barbell Method for Sturdy Columns and Walls

Our strength, more than anything else we possess, determines
the quantity and quality of our time here in these bodies.... A
weak man is not as happy as that same man would be if he were
strong. This reality is offensive to some people who would like the
intellectual or spiritual to take precedence. It is instructive to see
what happens to these very people as their squat strength goes up.

— Mark Rippetoe[68]

He hath shown strength with his arm.

— Luke 1:51

Strength Is Strongest

Mark Rippetoe is one of the world's foremost exponents of barbell-based strength training: as a powerlifting competitor in the past, and as a practitioner, gym owner, trainer, author, and speaker in the present. As he is a very humorous, and powerful, man, I wonder to what degree he is pulling our legs in the last two lines of the quotation above, but I do

---

[68]   Mark Rippetoe with Stef Bradford, *Starting Strength: Basic Barbell Training,* 3rd edition (Wichita Falls, TX: Aasgard, 2017), 1.

see where he is coming from. Even the most intellectual and spiritual among us do derive real joy when our bodies become stronger. And if we set aside the intellectual and spiritual for a moment, in the realm of the physical body, reams of current research show that his first statement above is right on target regarding both the *quantity* and *quality* of our time on earth in these bodies.

Nothing in the physical realm makes our bodily temples as strong as — well, strength. Further, the scientific literature on maintaining healthy body weight and vitality in later life has pointed more and more to the value of strength training, physical activity that was looked on for decades as little more than skin deep compared with cardio, aerobic, or endurance training.

I should note as well that when Mr. Rippetoe talks about the weak and the strong "man," this applies to women too. In fact, his co-author is a woman. Strength training has much to offer both sexes, even decades before maintenance of muscle mass and strength become crucial in maintaining daily functioning in the final years of our lives. Strength training not only builds powerful muscles but builds and strengthens tendons, ligaments, and bones as well, especially important for women who start off with smaller bones and are more prone to osteopenia and osteoporosis over the years. Strength training also perks up our metabolism as muscle requires energy for its upkeep. The more sedentary we are in our daily lives, the more important it is to challenge our muscles regularly and give them something to think about.

As for what some might consider the downside, even the ancient Greek poet Hesiod knew well: "To achieve excellence, we first must sweat." Strength training is not physically easy. It requires that we keep challenging our muscles with heavier loads the stronger they become. The upside, though, is that such challenges and loads always increase incrementally, a little bit at a time, so when properly performed, strength training does not ask our muscles to do anything that will bring us bodily harm. When Joshua ben Sirach advised, "Do not lift a weight beyond your strength" (Sir. 13:2), he was, of course, spot-on, though what you can lift can increase over time.

In ancient Greek legend, the powerful Olympic wrestling champion Milo grew strong by lifting a young calf every day when he was a young lad. As the calf gradually grew larger and heavier, so did Milo, until he become a bull of a man, undefeated in wrestling for decades. For this reason, Milo is known as "the Father of Weightlifting," or "the Father of Progressive Resistance," for the weights lifted — "the resistance" — must increase gradually over time if one is to keep getting stronger. "Resistance training" is synonym for "weightlifting" or "strength training."

Now, turning back to the great biblical strongman, Samson, I invoke once again our attempt to "Keep Things Simple, Samson (or Sarah)." Well, as is the case in the world of nutrition, there are indeed many approaches to building strength, and some of their exponents are quick to point out the flaws in alternative approaches. The happy news here, though, is that most of these methods do, indeed, produce good results, thereby making their practitioners stronger. The keys to choosing which method(s) to use may depend on personal preference and availability of equipment but should also be heavily weighted (so to speak) toward safety and the avoidance of injury for you with your own particular habitus and health history.

Over the next three chapters, I will describe what I have found to be three of the most effective methods in my experience, and in chapter 16, I will mention some methods I don't use myself but that might well interest and benefit you or your loved ones. First up in this chapter is the tried-and-true barbell method, so let's load some bars up and begin.

But I Don't Want to Be a Weightlifter!

As competitive sports, barbells have historically been used in the kind of overhead lifting performed in the modern Olympics, commonly known as *Olympic weightlifting*. Currently contested are two lifts in which the barbell rests on the floor and ends up held overhead, either in one extremely dynamic and explosive movement, called the *snatch*, or in the two-part movement of the *clean* (from floor to shoulders) and *jerk* (from shoulders to overhead). These movements (especially the snatch) require complex neuromotor skills and are rarely performed in most gyms except by the rare Olympic lifting competitor.[69]

The other major form of barbell strength competition is known as *powerlifting*. It gained great popularity in the United States in the 1960s, far eclipsing Olympic-style lifting. It consists of the *squat, bench press*, and *dead lift*. I competed in several of these contests in the early 1980s, squatting 550 pounds, benching 380 pounds, and deadlifting 556 pounds in official competitions while weighing 198 pounds. These lifts are now seen in gyms, basements, and garages all through the United States and the world, and I'll describe them shortly.

I should note, too, that there are some newer competitive sports that include barbells, such as strongman competitions in which massive weights may be squatted, deadlifted, or pressed overhead, and CrossFit competitions, in which impressive but somewhat lighter weights may be lifted in various styles for high repetitions or at great speed. Now, I do bear in mind that probably very few of you, my dear readers, plan to compete in any strength events. Still, barbells may well have a role in tending your own temple if you should decide to start (or continue) using them. Let's see what role they might play.

---

[69] I was in my first Olympic lifting contest at age fifteen. When you get to the Temple Tender Tale of Dan Torpey, you will see that we are honored to have an Olympic lifter's vignette from a man who first took up the sport at age fifty!

A Push, or Pull, and a Leg:
Natural Body-Movement Patterns

Here is Rippetoe's pitch for the primary value of barbells: "Properly performed, full-range-of-motion barbell exercises are essentially the functional expression of human skeletal and muscular anatomy under a load." Rippetoe sometimes describes the exercises he prescribes as focused not on targeting specific individual muscles but on replicating "natural movement patterns."

In *Fit for Eternal Life*, I described the most basic of these natural movement patterns as "a push, a pull, and a leg," meaning that if we do some form of pushing movement, like a bench press or overhead press, some kind of pulling movement, like a chin-up, row, or dead lift, and some kind of major leg exercise, such as some form of a squat (weighted hip and knee bend), we will have trained almost every one of the essential muscles in our body.

Catholic strength coaches Dan John and Pat Flynn usefully distinguish between *pulls*, in which the hands are brought from away from the body toward the body using the various muscles of the upper back, as in chins or rows, and *hinge* exercises, such as dead lifts and kettlebell swings, in which we start bent over and end standing up, hinging from the waist and strongly activating the muscles along the spine. (John and Flynn also discuss *carrying* movements.)[70]

So, if I were to recommend a very simple method of effectively training all the essential movement patterns and muscle groups with as few as four barbell exercises, I would recommend the following:

1. Standing overhead press or bench press
2. Some form of chin, pull-down, or row

[70] For a written example of some of Pat's suggested routines see his *How to Be Better at (Almost) Everything*, (Dallas, TX: Ben Bella Books, 2019), pp. 42-43.

3. Some form of squat, such as the "low-bar" powerlifting squat, the "high-bar" bodybuilding squat, the front squat, or the "safety-bar" squat
4. Some form of dead lift, such as standard, "stiff-leg," "Romanian," or "wide-grip"

Please allow me to briefly explain why.

Pushing or *pressing* movements will strengthen the muscles of the chest, shoulders, and the triceps at the back of the arms. Standing overhead presses will also strengthen, to some extent, virtually all the muscles in the body, including in the legs and the "core," or midsection, which must maintain tension to hold the body in the proper position. If you are going to do only one form of pressing, I recommend overheads over bench presses. I know hardly anyone who has bench-pressed very heavily for decades without also performing heavy overhead work who has not ended up with shoulder problems or pectoral tears as the years have rolled by.

Pulling movements, such as chins and pull-downs — which do not technically involve a barbell, though they use both limbs at once — and bent-over rows all strongly involve the muscles of the upper back, the rear deltoid (shoulder muscles), the biceps, and the muscles of the forearm that are used in gripping.

Squatting movements all involve the powerful muscles of the thighs and hamstrings, the buttocks, the hips, the lower back, and even the calves, though different variations stress these particular muscles to various degrees. Variations in which one is bent more forward with lower-bar placement on the back tend to stress the "posterior chain," muscles — such as the glutes of the buttocks, the hip extensors, the hamstrings, the lower back, and the calves — while higher-bar-placement squats (front squats most of all), done with a more upright posture, place more of a direct demand on the anterior chain muscles (primarily the quadriceps of the frontal thigh).

Hinging movements, such as dead lifts, involve the powerful muscles that run along the spine, the trapezius muscles between the shoulders, the hips and the legs (especially the hamstrings), and the gripping muscles of the forearms. Like overhead presses and squats, dead lifts work almost the entire body as a great many muscles are required to maintain proper body alignment during these lifts.

In a certain sense, these are the big, bad, scary movements of the strength-training world, and yet, for most people — even some of the elderly — they can be done safely. They also provide plenty of stimulation for tendon, ligament, bone mass, and strength. Still, such barbell movements do indeed have potential to cause serious harm if not performed properly. You should never do bench presses or squats, for example, without safety bars set at the bottom of the lift so there is no chance of being crushed by a weight if you misjudge your strength or suffer a muscle or tendon tear mid lift. Sadly, this has happened to even extremely powerful strength athletes who have trained without safety bars in place. Barbell exercises, perhaps even more than most others we'll look at in these pages, need to be executed in proper form for both maximum results and safety.

Those who are new to barbell exercises are advised to obtain live, first-hand supervision from a competent strength trainer, at least until they are thoroughly learned. To my knowledge, the best resource with detailed textual explanations and copious drawings and photographs detailing the precise performance of each of the essential barbell lifts is Mark Rippetoe's *Starting Strength*.

How Much and How Often to Train

The world of strength training is a world of sets and reps, and the different kinds of strength training we'll discuss in these chapters tend to have different "sweet spots" in terms of how many sets and reps we should do for ideal results. Every time you perform a strength exercise from start to finish, from the position in which a muscle is mildly stretched to the position in which it is contracted, and then back, is called a "repetition," or rep for short. A group of repetitions done to some desired number or, in some cases, until one cannot do any more (i.e., "training to failure") is called a "set," that is, a set of repetitions. There are a great number of set and rep schemes out there, but I will merely highlight perhaps the most popular ones for the kinds of big, basic barbell movements we have considered.

Many authorities consider the ideal repetition number to stimulate muscle strength and muscle safely and maximally to be around five. I tend to agree, and I have a "Starting Strength" T-shirt on the back of which is written "Do Your Fives!" As for the number of sets of five that one should do for each exercise, recommendations vary, but a simple program for beginners — and for some old hands too — is to do about five sets of five in each workout, either with the same weight after lighter warm-ups or — my preference — using a progressively heavier weight for each set until only the last one, two, or three are nearly all-out efforts. I'll refer you to Rippetoe's *Starting Strength* books as comprehensive guides to good ways of putting such programs together.

Oh, and I will note, too, that dead lifts can be particularly productive of strength but also particularly demanding and draining. Many strength athletes warm up thoroughly and do only one hard set of them. When I rebuilt my dead lift to nearly five hundred pounds at age fifty-nine, I did one hard working set *once every three weeks*, performing somewhat lighter dead-lift variations, such as "stiff-leg" or "Romanian" dead lifts, on alternate weeks. They are somewhat less draining, as lighter weights are used. They are also especially good at stretching and strengthening the hamstrings.

Another note here: when I work up to heavy dead lifts, I prefer to use a weightlifting belt when I get to my heaviest set, though I do other kinds of dead lifts without one. Also, powerlifters are known for doing dead lifts with one hand in an overhand position and one in an underhand position. This makes one less likely to lose one's grip. Still, unless you are planning to compete in competitions, I recommend keeping both hands in the overhand position and turning to the use of weightlifting straps if your grip starts to give out. Many lifters have torn their biceps on the side with the underhand grip. Keeping both hands in the overhand position also keeps the back and scapulae in symmetrical alignment. I do not use the straps on warm-ups — only on the real set, as I do with a lifting belt.

Finally, while it is customary to train three or four days per week on such barbell-based programs, doing a limited number of exercises each session, busy people may well be able to achieve very nice results training as few as twice or even once weekly. In fact, a thirty-five-year-old friend of my son has been training in our garage gym for three months now. He trains only one day per week, does nothing but presses, squats, dead lifts, and pull-downs, and has grown stronger with every single workout.

TEMPLE-TENDING TENET #12

For some of us, even those with many decades of life under their lifting belts, performing the basic major-muscle-movement patterns of pushing, pulling, hinging, and squatting, under proper guidance, can be a very powerful method for keeping our temples very powerful. Consider it as an option that may, or may not, be the right strength-building method for you.

13

High-Intensity Construction and the Rise of the Machines

The Church, without any doubt whatever, approves of physical culture, if it be in proper proportion.[71]

— Pope Pius XII

Health, Fitness, and Exercise in Proper Proportion

Dr. Doug McGuff, an emergency-room physician and gym owner, has long been one of the major proponents of the many benefits of brief, focused strength training, commonly known as "high-intensity training," or HIT. He defines "health" as a physiological disease-free state in which the body is properly balanced in its catabolic (cellular breakdown) and anabolic (cellular growth and differentiation) metabolic processes. He defines "fitness" as "the bodily state of being physiologically capable of handling challenges that exist above a resting threshold of activity," and "exercise" as a means to promoting both health and fitness — most importantly, in such a way that it

---

[71] Radio message to the Inter-American Congress on Catholic Education, October 6, 1948.

does not enhance fitness (physical capacity) at the expense of health (absence of disease).[72]

An extreme example of enhancing physical fitness to the possible serious detriment of health would be the bodybuilder who takes a combination of anabolic steroids, growth hormone, insulin, thyroxine, and diuretics for maximum muscle size and extremely low levels of fat. In fact, more than a few relatively young world-class bodybuilders have died during or shortly after competitions. Further, some use of performance-enhancing drugs, or PEDs, is found in many competitive sports. Still, one need not look to drugs for ways that excessive or inappropriate exercise can work to the detriment of health, as when people suffer fatigue or stress fractures from too much of activities such as distance running and too little time off for rest. Dr. McGuff is telling us that our exercise must be in proper proportion to maintain both health and fitness.

Pope Pius XII told us in the 1940s that the Church is all in favor of "physical culture," a wonderful older term for fitness activity and sport, implying how bodily exercise and sport can be used to best cultivate and bring forth our God-given natural potentials for health and fitness. He also specifically expressed the need for "proper proportion," but in terms of the proportion between the *physical* and the *spiritual*, between *body* and *soul*. So, what exactly did this very athletic pontiff, who had a gymnasium installed in the Vatican, mean by "proper proportion"? He said that physical culture leads to proper proportion when it:

+ does not lead to worship of the body
+ strengthens and energizes the body rather than draining it (prescient of Dr. McGuff's main point)

---

[72] Doug McGuff, M.D., and John Little, *Body by Science: A Research-Based Program for Strength Training, Bodybuilding, and Complete Fitness in 12 Minutes a Week* (New York: McGraw-Hill, 2009), 3.

• provides refreshment for the spirit
• does not lead to spiritual sloth or crudeness
• provides "new excitements" for study and work
• does not disturb the peace and sanctity of the home

Pope Pius's advice meshes very well with the principles of HIT strength training. Why? Because its sessions are very brief and infrequent. Indeed, the subtitle of Dr. McGuff's *Body by Science* promises "complete fitness in 12 minutes a week," and this is meant quite literally! I've suggested that a more leisurely pace of 20 minutes once per week could be all that a person needs to make dramatic improvements in bodily strength and health. This time factor alone makes these methods far less likely to lead you to obsess about or worship your body, to get overly fatigued, to overlook family responsibilities, or even to miss Mass!

For busy people with many responsibilities, these methods are godsends for keeping fitness activities in line with spiritual priorities. Indeed, as good Pope Pius also said, "The highest merit should not be attributed to him who has the strongest and most agile muscles, but rather to him who shows the most ready ability in keeping them subject to the power of the spirit."[73] With that said, let's quickly revisit high-intensity strength-training methods and why I tied them into "the rise of the machines."

The Rise of the Machines

A man named Arthur Jones (1926–2007) is usually considered "the Father of High-Intensity Training." He was the inventor of the carefully engineered Nautilus machines and of the MedX line of equipment, and his son pioneered the Hammer Strength line of strength-training machines. Well, Jones made a stir in the 1960s when he entered the

---

[73] Quoted in Robert Feeney, *A Catholic Perspective: Physical Exercise and Sports* (San Francisco: Ignatius Press, 1995).

bodybuilding and weightlifting worlds and proclaimed that people did not need to spend hour after hour in pursuit of muscle size and strength according to the false idea that more is better. He argued that, to the contrary, you can work out hard, or long, but not both. He then pioneered intense methods of strength training on machines primarily (though they could also be done with barbells and dumbbells) using only *one* all-out "to muscular failure" set per exercise, training the whole body through twelve exercises or so, in half an hour, three days per week.

Indeed, as the years went by, he found that fewer exercises and fewer days per week were really required. I won't go into great detail here, since I already did in *Fit for Eternal Life* and because I'll also refer you to other sources later on, but, for the record, in terms of sets and reps, HIT methods typically involve only *one set*, and the repetition range is typically from eight to twelve. Once a person can do twelve repetitions with a given weight, he increases it by a few pounds during the next workout and then tries to work up to twelve before raising the weight again. This is the principle of progressive resistance, gradually using heavier weights as one becomes stronger. Also, the repetition speed is emphasized, often taking up to two seconds to lift the weight and up to four seconds to lower it. This reduces momentum, so the muscles are doing all the work, and it captures the great benefit that comes from the "negative," or "eccentric," lowering phases of each movement.

In recent years, a very popular variant of HIT methods is sometimes called the "super-slow" method, pioneered by men such as Dr. Vincent "Ben" Bocchicchio and Ken Hutchins in the 1970s and 1980s. It involves performing repetitions *very* slowly, taking up to ten seconds to raise the weight for each repetition and five or more seconds to lower it.[74] Dr. McGuff's version, and some others, may recommend up to ten

---

[74] Though he has been in the field for several decades, I discovered Dr. Bocchicchio's work only recently. The man has *two* Ph.D.s — in

seconds *in each direction*. Because the reps are so slow and demanding, the typical repetition range is perhaps three to six repetitions per set. This would take one to two minutes to complete. In fact, people who advise slow training tend to focus more on "time under load" or "time under tension" than merely the number of repetitions.

The reason Dr. McGuff can claim benefits from a twelve-minute workout once per week is that his standard routine includes five fundamental compound exercises (similar to Rippetoe's natural-body-movement patterns) but ideally done on exercise machines for ease and safety. His original "Big Five" were a pull-down, a chest press, a row, an overhead press, and a leg press. Taking two minutes or less per set and gradually minimizing the rest time between sets as one's fitness improves, one can indeed complete it in twelve minutes or less; I've done so many times myself. The odd thing about it is that it looks like the exerciser is hardly doing anything, because of the slow motion, but it is just about the most demanding exercise a person can do, since you are working out at near maximum effort during every second of every exercise! Once I put a marathon runner through a ten-minute workout like this, and she decided to skip the cardio workout planned for that day to go home and rest!

Anyway, as daunting as it sounds, it was originally invented as a protocol to be used by elderly people with osteoporosis. Because of the slow speed, it is nontraumatic and joint-friendly and can help thicken bones. Most proponents of the method recommend a series of four to six exercises once or twice a week. As for me, sometimes I spend a few weeks using only super-slow techniques, but most often, I just slip

exercise physiology and in health services. In his *15 Minutes to Fitness* book, which I reference in chapter 19, he explicitly incorporates both a low-carbohydrate diet and slow, intense strength-training methods as essentials in combating metabolic syndrome and maintaining health and fitness across one's life span.

them in for a workout or two, or merely an exercise or two, for a change of pace. I can highly recommend them though as means of tending our temples, keeping the physical and the spiritual in "proper proportion," as Pope Pius XII advises, and with minimal risk of damaging one's health in pursuit of fitness, à la Dr. McGuff.

TEMPLE-TENDING TENET #13

Under qualified supervision, or at least having read detailed books on these methods, people who are physically able to perform high-intensity or super-slow machine training, or both, will find it the most time-efficient method out there for building or maintaining muscle size and strength.

14

Biomechanics to the Rescue of Deteriorating Structures

If you have spent any amount of time performing conventional weight training exercises like barbells squats, dead lifts, overhead presses, incline presses, upright rows, bent-over barbell rows, seated low pulley rows, and hanging leg raises — to name a just a few — I can say with absolute certainty that you have not exercised efficiently.[75]

— Doug Brignole, Mr. Universe

New Ways to Better Build Temples

When one has been intricately involved in some endeavor for nearly all of one's life, it can be easy to become overly skeptical of any new, innovative approaches, figuring one has already "seen 'em all," or "been there, done that." After all, even the Bible tells us: "There is nothing new under the sun" (Eccles. 1:9).

Consider Arthur Jones and the revolutionary Nautilus machines he developed in the 1960s. Sure, there were already a variety of

---

[75] Doug Brignole, *The Physics of Resistance Exercise: An Analysis and Application of Biomechanical Principles in Resistance Exercise* (Monterey, CA: Healthy Learning, 2021), 19.

strength-training machines on the market when his came out, but the complexity and subtlety of Jones's engineering made Nautilus machines stand apart. Still, those interested in strength-training lore, especially as regards the "rise of the machines," might care to do an Internet search on the very complicated-looking and intricately crafted "medico-mechanistic gymnastic machines" developed by Swedish physician Gustav Zander, in the *1860s*, one hundred years before Jones. Again, maybe there *is* nothing new under the sun!

I must admit that I was somewhat skeptical when I first began to learn of Doug Brignole's new biomechanical approach to strength-training, muscle-building, resistance exercise. Of course, what he had in his corner, from my perspective, was that, since he was just a hair older than I, I remember when he was a national teenage sensation in the bodybuilding world, just as I was becoming at least a little bit notable in the tiny world of muscles in my hometown. Further, when I first learned of his newer approach a couple of years ago, he had recently won a Mr. Universe title — at the age of fifty-nine! Finally, the more I heard Doug talk and demonstrate his principles, the more it made complete sense, and I just had to buy his book and incorporate into my routine many new exercises and traditional-exercise modifications he had detailed in extraordinary depth.

So, was there truly something new under the sun? Well, no — and yes. As for the no, we have the same sets of muscles, tendons, ligaments, and bones as we did in the day when Ecclesiastes was written — some say in the tenth century B.C. Our muscles originated in and were attached to the same parts of the body. They used exactly the same leverage systems and had the same ranges of motion. Further, over the next thirty centuries, hundreds upon hundreds of exercises have been invented to make said muscles bigger and stronger.

As for the yes, Doug Brignole, in just the last few years, has done something new by carefully applying a set of sixteen fundamental biomechanical principles to determine a way to rate those hundreds of exercises as to which best serve our goals of building muscle strength and mass. All this without, as Dr. McGuff warned, damaging our health, and as Pope Pius XII warned, wasting our precious time and energy.

Having touched my first barbell at age seven in 1968, I've accrued a few minor injuries over the years. I have a right knee that gets grouchy at times, and I think that came from doing spinning weight-throwing events in Highland Games competitions. I have a mildly painful left wrist, thanks to my doing one-handed barbell dead lifts of 250 pounds while wearing lifting straps about twenty years ago. Still, I pride myself on never having had a musculoskeletal injury that has required any kind of surgery, and none of my minor tweaks and strains limit my functional abilities today in real-life activities, such as moving the occasional piano, sofa, or countless bags of mulch for my wife.

Having acquired many friends over the years in gyms, I am happy to say that most of my men and women friends who were serious into their training forty years ago are still at it, though most of us have acquired various injuries over the years that have caused us to eliminate certain exercises, some of which may have been our very favorites or best lifts in days of yore. Alas, my days of five-hundred-pound squats for eight repetitions are no more. Although the methods I'll describe in this chapter are wonderful for *anyone* who trains, they may be an especial godsend for old, banged-up weight-room warriors who do not want to get banged up any further and, indeed, who may seek to rebuild their temples as strong and sturdy as they were long ago.

Brignole's methods seek out the very best, safest, and most effective exercises for each of the body's main muscles. In a sense, his approach is the opposite of the barbell-based natural body-movement-pattern methods we discussed in chapter 12 because he does not incorporate barbells and he opts to train individual muscles specifically rather than compound movement patterns. Still, as we'll see later, this does not completely rule out the possibility of integrating the two approaches — in fact, the three approaches if we include the HIT/slow-training methods of last chapter.

The Physics of Physical Perfection

In *The Physics of Resistance Exercise*, Brignole lays out his sixteen bio-mechanical principles in great detail, devoting a chapter to each one before providing ideal exercises and critiquing less-than-ideal ones for each of the body's major muscles. I will give just a small appetizer here, and for those whose appetites may be whetted, I direct you to his book (and as we'll see in the appendices, some videos and certification programs). I will begin by describing two exercises that are probably new to most readers and that provide ideal anatomical loading and movement patterns for the muscles involved.

This first exercise is for the *latissimus dorsi* muscles (or "lats"), the big muscles of the back that give bodybuilders their famous V-shaped taper, especially from the rear view, and which help us in daily life whenever we lift things or pull things toward our bodies. Traditional exercises to work them include chin-ups, pull-downs, and a wide variety of barbell, dumbbell, cable, or machine rowing motions. These exercises have undoubtedly built some very impressive latissimus muscles over the years.

Still, Brignole argues that the *one-arm cable lat pull-in* is the ideal and most efficient exercise to build those lats. This holds for several reasons, including that it provides the ideal direction of resistance and range of motion for those back muscles. In a chin-up or a pull-down, for example, the arms begin straight up overhead at about ninety degrees from horizontal of the shoulder joint, which actually exceeds the ideal range of motion of the lats and makes them and the shoulder girdle more vulnerable to injury. Brignole notes that starting the downward pull on a cable with the arm only about thirty degrees above shoulder level provides the safest and most ideal starting point, factoring in the muscle levers involved.

Further, when doing chins or pull-downs with two arms, the lats cannot fully contract by drawing our elbows all the way down until they touch our sides. (Our elbows need not go behind us, as in rowing motions, since that motion is accomplished not by the lats but primarily by the rear deltoids, which have ideal exercises of their own.) Our elbows can be tucked down to our sides when using only one arm at a time for lat pull-ins.

Finally, the ideal body positioning would be to start with one's arm at about a forty-five-degree angle to the front, halfway between having it right at one's side or right out in front. This motion provides for ideal elongation and contraction of the latissimus muscles. Although I do not have space to provide all of the biomechanical principles behind any of these exercises, I can assure you that Brignole spells them out, and I can also assure you that, in my own case, they truly *work*. A main advantage I noticed immediately from all of these biomechanically correct exercises is that they produced no joint pain for me whatsoever — only the gratifying muscle "pump" and "burn" that comes from working muscles thoroughly.

Here's a quick guide to one more exercise, this one to work the front shoulder muscles. Some people have difficulty with overhead pressing motions because of the way they can compress the shoulder capsule and challenge small muscles, such as those of the rotator cuff. Thankfully, I have been able to do them for decades without such problems, but I still very much like this new one!

In the basic version of the *seated anterior deltoid press*, you sit with an adjustable bench set with the back in the upright position, facing outward, with a cable machine behind you. With the cable handles set a bit behind you at around waist height and shoulder width apart, you extend both arms in front of you, keeping your elbows along your sides all the while, rather than flaring them out, which more fully activates the chest muscles, and push forward until your arms are fully extended. This exercise achieves essentially the same or better stimulation of the front shoulder muscles as an overhead press, but without requiring that the arms be raised over the head. I have found it an excellent addition to my routine, and there is even a version that does not require a bench. With cables overhead and slightly behind you, you bend slightly forward and do a similar motion, pushing downward, somewhat like a parallel bar dip. A version can also be done on a flat or slightly declined bench and using a pair of dumbbells.

Although Brignole describes many new exercises, I'll simply note next how applying biomechanical principles can also improve the efficiency of standard strength-training equipment. Leg-extension machines are commonly used to isolate and train the quadriceps muscles of the front of the thighs. Brignole advises that, rather than sitting up almost straight, as is most commonly done, you should set the seat back so you are *leaning backward* when the motion starts. He describes these motions and the rationale behind them most thoroughly in his book, but I will share below the brief explanations he provided me with in a personal communication on November 25, 2021:

> The reason to lean backward on leg extensions is "passive insufficiency" of the hamstrings. In other words, if you are sitting upright (with your hip joint at a ninety-degree angle or so), straightening the knees will overstretch the hamstrings. Overstretching the hamstrings will interfere with optimal quadriceps contraction.
>
> The hamstrings are the "passive" muscles during leg extensions, because they are on the opposite side of the active muscle, which is the quadriceps. It is referred to as "insufficiency" because overstretching the hamstrings inhibits full extension of the knees.

There also seems to be a degree of quadriceps inhibition (by way of the CNS [central nervous system] — a reduction of nerve impulse to the quadriceps — preventing full strength capacity of the quadriceps in order to protect the hamstrings from becoming injured.

Regarding leg curls typically performed for the hamstring muscles on the back of the upper leg, Brignole recommends using a seated rather than a lying, facedown leg-curl machine. He also suggests leaning forward on the seated leg-curl machine. Here, in brief, is why:

Bending the hip joint to ninety degrees (instead of keeping the femur parallel to the torso, or close to it) avoids active insufficiency. Bending the hip joint allows the hamstrings to begin more elongated than if you were lying prone on the leg-curl machine. When your hip is "straight," and you then you bend your knee, the hamstrings will overshorten.

Leaning forward (while on the seated leg-curl machine) just adds a bonus, because it allows the hamstrings to fully elongate, thus causing a bit more muscle stimulation in the "early phase."

I've found Brignole's recommendations for tweaking both leg extensions and leg curls most felicitous in my own training.

Brignole has also described what he calls the "Brig 20" — twenty biomechanically ideal exercises to train the whole body. One could select from only these twenty exercises and build and maintain and very fit and healthy bodily temple, and one could also incorporate some of them and continue to perform other, less-efficient exercises too if they seem to be working well and are enjoyable. In fact, in my own training, I now incorporate two basic barbell movements, the dead lift and the front squat and their variations; I often use low-set,

HIT, or super-slow methods, especially on machines, and I incorporate several of Brignole's Brig 20 movements into most of my workouts.

I'll make a quick note on repetition range too. We saw that the classic repetition number for basic barbell movements tends to be about five per set, that original HIT methods recommended about eight to twelve repetitions per set, and super-slow methods, usually about three to six repetitions per set. The Brignole exercises lend themselves very well to virtually any of these repetition ranges. Doug himself often recommends starting as high as thirty repetitions for a first set that also serves as a warm-up and then doing progressively heavier sets with fewer repetitions per set — for example, twenty, ten, eight, six, and four.

Although I've rarely done high-repetition sets over the decades, I've found that I really enjoy doing higher repetitions with these exercises and sometimes will indeed start with a first set of thirty repetitions. The higher repetition sets are generally performed at a faster pace, while avoiding throwing the weights and generating momentum — perhaps one second up and one down, or you'd be there all day! Still, when pressed for time or when I want a change of pace, I will sometimes employ one set only, after warm-up, HIT, or even super-slow methods with these exercises. Believe me, doing lat pull-ins at a ten-second up/ten-second down pace for even four or five repetitions with a challenging weight will really get those lats burning (and the gripping muscles of the forearms too).

I'd like to note as well that though they are, in a sense, at opposite ends of the strength-building continuum, some prominent powerlifters, who live and breathe barbells, are now also incorporating some of Brignole's exercises as supplementary or "assistance" movements to help make them as strong, and as healthy, as possible.

In sum, if you are aiming at hitting the target of the healthiest, fittest temple you can build, you could entirely fill your quiver with these excellent new exercise movements or pack several in along with some of your favorite rustier old ones and still hit the bull's-eye.

TEMPLE-TENDING TENET #14

If you want to strengthen your temple but don't care for barbell or machine training (or don't have access to them), or, if you have significant persisting joint pains, consider learning about and applying some of Brignole's biomechanically correct movements with cables[76] or dumbbells.

---

[76] My intention is not to endorse any particular brands of equipment, but if you are interested in cable training on machines with selectorized weight stacks, the most versatile machines have two independently operating cable handles that can be arranged at a variety of widths and heights. The commercial gym I use had a wonderfully versatile machine by Free Motion Fitness called Light Commercial XT Dual Cable Cross. For my home gym, I obtained an excellent little Hoist Fitness Mi5 Functional Trainer.

15

Aerobic Exercise Keeps the Temple's Air Flowing

They shall mount up with wings like eagles, they shall run
and not be weary, they shall walk and not faint.

— Isaiah 40:31

Endurance Training

Another category of fitness training is commonly called "aerobic," "cardio," "conditioning," or "endurance training." It is called *aerobic* training in contrast to the *anaerobic* training that characterizes strength training. Deriving from the Greek words *aer*, for "air," and *bios*, for "life," aerobic exercise requires increased uptake of oxygen over a considerable period, while the anaerobic ("without air or oxygen") exercises of strength training are so brief and intense that they draw primarily upon the glycogen stored in the muscle cells for immediate energy. Further, in strength training as commonly performed, the heart rate will elevate during the minute or two it takes to do each set and return to near normal between them, whereas in classic "steady-state" aerobic activities, the heart rate will elevate to around 70 to 80 percent of maximum for an extended time, with a minimum of perhaps twelve minutes or so.

These distinctions are not complete, however, and there are various processes that go on at the cellular levels during both forms of training. Also, if you do intense strength training with little rest between sets, you will be gulping in great drafts of oxygen and your heart rate will stay elevated as well. The same applies to a high-intensity version of aerobic training that we will discuss below.

Okay, it seems that the term "aerobics" for this kind of exercise emphasizes oxygen use within the cells and draws our attention to the huffing and puffing of our lungs while we do it. It is often called "cardio" too. Many gyms will feature a cardio room, where you will find machines such as treadmills, bicycles, climbers, elliptical trainers, and the like that will increase your heart (cardiac) rate. They are also widely perceived as good training for the heart muscle.

I often see the term "conditioning" used by serious lifters who realize that although they might become tremendously powerful, hefting enormous loads, their health might well be less than ideal if they easily get winded from normal daily activities. Hence, they also recommend some kind of activity that also gets the heart and lungs pumping, sometimes through repeated rounds of pushing or pulling weighted sleds, or various lifting and carrying motions, instead of, or in addition to, more traditional aerobic or cardio exercises.

Finally, the term I like to use for this kid of training is "endurance" exercise, contrasting it with "strength" exercise, though there is certainly some overlap here as well. For example, the stronger you become at lifting heavy loads, the more enduring you will become at lifting lighter ones. If you build your dead lift from a maximum of two hundred pounds to four hundred pounds, you will find that you can deadlift two hundred pounds for *many repetitions* and do each repetition much *faster*, to boot!

The distinction between anaerobic (strength) and aerobic (endurance) exercise hinges on the time differential. While a set of strength exercises is usually over in a minute or two, endurance exercises can last from several minutes to several hours for ultra-endurance athletes such as marathon runners, triathletes, long-distance bicyclists, open water swimmers, and cross-country skiers.

Oh, and another reason I like the term "endurance" is because good St. Thomas says "the principal act of fortitude is to endure."[77] As we saw in chapter 3, on the virtues, fortitude is our capacity to overcome or endure difficulties to obtain worthwhile goals, and as overcoming difficult obstacles is what strength training is all about, cardiovascular or aerobic training is also the literal endurance of uncomfortable things, such as huffing, puffing, and sweating over time to achieve the goals of bodily fitness.

As is the case for strength training, thanks to the way God made us and to the ingenuity of trainers and equipment designers, there are a great variety of ways we can train for bodily endurance, and hopefully one or more of these ways will strike a chord with you.

Health Benefits of Endurance Training

A key theme of the first parts of this book has been our growing pandemics: obesity, the insulin-resistant metabolic syndrome, diabetes, fatty livers. It seems natural to wonder if endurance exercise can help us lose weight and help reverse the pandemics. Unfortunately, the answer is rather complicated. Many studies have not shown aerobic exercise alone as particularly helpful in helping people lose weight and keep it off.

Most remarkably, in my opinion, two decades ago, in a Danish study, eighteen sedentary men and nine sedentary women were trained over eighteen months with a goal of running a marathon: 26.2 miles.[78] At

---

[77] *ST*, II-II, Q. 123, art. 8.

[78] G. M. Janssen, C. J. Graef, and W. H. Saris, "Food Intake and Body Composition in Novice Athletes during a Training Period to Run a

the end of the study, the men lost an average of only five pounds of fat, and the women did not lose any fat. Seems rather counterintuitive, no? Well, it seems that high volumes of exercise stimulated their appetites, and they found that both the men and the women had significantly increased the number of calories they were taking in, thereby minimizing or negating significant fat loss.

In my experience, I must say that I attained my lowest bodyweight as an adult (170 pounds) and smallest waistline measurement (32 inches) in my mid-forties while training for 3.1-, 6.2-, 10.0-, and 13.1-mile (half-marathon) running races. I was lifting once per week and doing running or other forms of endurance training every day at that time, while eating a relatively high-carbohydrate and lowfat diet. I was careful, however, not to increase my intake of food as I lost significant amounts of weight (about fifty pounds), but the fat loss did not last — for two primary reasons. First, I found that daily aerobic training of thirty-five minutes or more moved *me* beyond the "proper proportion" Pope Pius XII advised and led to fatigue and overtraining after a period of several months. Second, a diet so low in fat and high in carbohydrates eventually got the best of me. My appetite increased, and the weight came back on.

Still, while endurance training might not help you lose significant weight, like those hardworking Danes, or might help you lose it but not maintain it, like me, there are still a myriad of wonderful reasons to start or keep doing some on a regular basis!

First, regarding weight, exercise physiologist Glenn Gaesser, Ph.D., asserts that while endurance exercise may not lead to significant overall body weight loss, it can be very helpful at targeting the *central* or *visceral* fat that can wreak such metabolic damage. For this kind of fat,

Marathon," *International Journal of Sports Medicine*, suppl. 1 (May 1989): S17–21, National Library of Medicine, https://pubmed.ncbi.nlm.nih.gov/2744924/.

even a few pounds can make a big difference. This may explain why some research suggests that regular exercise may be a more powerful influence on longevity that weight loss alone.[79]

Further, we have long known of benefits of endurance exercise, including the following:

• increased capacity to breathe in large quantities of air
• increased capacity to circulate large volumes of blood throughout the body
• increased ability to deliver oxygen to all parts of the body
• strengthening of the muscles involved in breathing (e.g., the diaphragm and rib-cage muscles)
• increased heart-pumping capacity (delivering more blood with each stroke)
• improvement in endurance of the peripheral muscles (such as the legs) in addition to the heart
• increased total blood volume and increased oxygen-carrying red blood cells

And, if that is not enough, many people find endurance exercise, especially running, it seems, rather enjoyable and stress relieving, with a variety of mental-health benefits that we'll explore in a later chapter.

Now, typical aerobic exercise is done in a relatively "steady state" — that is, between perhaps five minutes or so of gradually warming up and five minutes or so of gradually slowing down, such as walking after a run. People usually do endurance-type activities in sessions as brief as twelve minutes or as long as multiple hours, or anything in between, depending on their goals and interests. In my forty-five years

---

[79] Diet Doctor, "Is Exercise Better Than Weight Loss for Your Health?," Diet Doctor podcast with Glenn Gaesser, Ph.D., YouTube video, 1:00:24, November 16, 2021, https://www.youtube.com/watch?v =eup6npOK71c.

of experience in gyms, cardio-machine users typically exercise between twenty and thirty minutes total for this kind of endurance training. Still, there is another, more-time-efficient method that more and more people are doing instead of — or, at times, in addition to — steady-state aerobic sessions. Let's take a brief but intense look.

From HIT to HIIT

In some ways, these methods are nothing new. Two thousand years ago, the Roman Stoic philosopher Seneca wrote: "Now there are short and simple exercises which tire the body rapidly, and so save our time; and time is something of which we ought to keep strict account. These exercises are running, brandishing weights, and jumping.... But whatever you do, come back quickly from body to mind."[80]

We saw how, in the 1960s, Arthur Jones popularized HIT (high-intensity training): brief, intense, infrequent methods of strength training. A few decades after Jones's work in strength training, we saw a similar development in the realm of intense endurance training that I'm sure would leave Seneca smiling as well. Japanese researcher Dr. Izumi Tabata found that very brief, infrequent episodes of traditional endurance-type, cardiovascular, or aerobic training can produce results superior to easier, but longer, steady-state training.

The original protocol called for five minutes of warm-up on a piece of equipment, such as an exercise bicycle; eight intervals of only twenty seconds of all-out maximum pedaling, followed by ten seconds of rest after each interval; and two minutes of cooldown. If I've done my math right, that's an eleven-minute workout, including both warm-up and cooldown, with four minutes of actual interval training, and one-third of that spent in rest! Dr. Tabata found that VO2 max (a measure of maximum oxygen uptake) improvements in fit college PE majors who

---

[80] Seneca, Epistle 15.

did this protocol five days per week exceeded those of students who did five traditional steady-state sessions lasting sixty minutes each per week.

I will note as well that since that first reported study in 1996, many others have had success with other High-Intensity Interval Training (HIIT) protocols of varying interval and rest durations and frequency of workouts. Most of us should probably *not* work out as intensely as young, fit college PE majors! One method I use myself that is not nearly so demanding is to spend four minutes warming up, gradually increasing the intensity on something such as a stationary bike, and then doing a few one-minute hard (but not all-out) then easy intervals before cooling down for a simple, twelve-minute HIIT workout. If you are new to such exercise, you might start at level 1 instead of level 7, and if you are fitter than I am, you might use higher levels. My latest session, on an upright exercise bike, with my RPMs above eighty, looked like this:

Simple Sample HIIT Workout on a Stationary Bike

Minutes (12 minutes total)	Difficulty Level
0–1	7
1–2	8
2–3	9
3–4	10
4–5	14
5–6	11
6–7	15
7–8	11

Minutes (12 minutes total)	Difficulty Level
8–9	16
9–10	11
10–11	10
11–12	9

Difficulty levels will vary greatly depending on one's leg strength and endurance. If I am doing a particular exercise over a period of weeks, I try to increase the difficulty levels gradually, perhaps just during one or two of the minutes in each subsequent workout. One way to monitor this, if the machine has a calorie-estimating readout, is simply to see if you can burn off at least one more calorie in twelve minutes than you did the time before. The goal here is not to burn calories per se but to use the calorie count to measure how much energy you can expend in a given amount of time and hopefully to see that number grow!

TEMPLE-TENDING TENET #15

Consider including a modest measure of steady-state or timed-interval aerobic, cardio, or endurance training into your fitness regimen. You will know you are doing too much if your strength declines or if you end up feeling drained rather than energized.

16

Real Work Builds Real Temples

In all toil there is profit.

— Proverbs 14:23

Ora et labora: Pray and work.

— Monastic motto

*I began to look at household chores in a whole new light.... I'd become
a veritable white tornado — something between Mr. Universe and
Mr. Clean — and my wife and neighbors much preferred me for it.*

— Bryant Stamford, Ph.D.

Lean, Healthy Temples Long before the
Gym and Aerobics Revolutions

Having gyms and fitness centers of all sorts on almost every street
corner, with many millions of adult men and women doing some kind
of strength training, is a somewhat recent thing. Strength training
was very unusual in the late 1970s. Indeed, my Catholic high school's
newspaper once ran a comical story about my small group of weightlifting buddies and me: we had been arrested after we had broken into a

local stone company's lot at night so we could lift their rocks! Aided by the popularity of people such as movie star and later California governor Arnold Schwarzenegger, lifting weights, or "pumping iron," soon became quite mainstream.

A good decade or more before that, we saw the beginnings of an "aerobics revolution," thanks, in part, to Kenneth Cooper, M.D.'s best-selling book *Aerobics* (1968), with many later books to follow. As people began to get wind of the health-giving benefits of aerobic exercise, they really breathed his message in. A great many of them hit the roads as distance running exploded as a fitness activity and a competitive sport.

We should consider the fact, however, that long before Schwarzenegger's and Cooper's messages hit the masses and people started lacing up their running shoes and tightening their lifting belts, as we saw in chapter 1, we were a pretty lean nation, and since their arrival on the scene, we have become fatter and sicker!

Of course, we must remember that valid and valuable principle that correlation does not prove causation. I'm not blaming Arnold or Dr. Cooper! As I argued before, it seems that the causal variables for our pandemics may be traced primarily to changes in our nutritional habits during this time, trading real foods for processed foods, naturally occurring fats in foods for industrially manufactured seed oils, fats in general for carbohydrates, proteins for fats and carbs, and eating far more often than we used to for countless generations in the past.

Might anything else help account for the fact of relatively low levels of obesity in decades past? Well, in recent decades, we have certainly become more sedentary at home due to a myriad of energy-saving automatic devices. Further, a greater number of us have sedentary desk jobs as well. Also, as noted in previous chapters, nutrition habits that produce an insulin roller coaster can make us hungrier and more tired, feeling like eating more and moving less. One benefit of bringing one's insulin under control and unlocking the energy from one's fat stores is that it gives you more energy. You naturally feel like getting up and moving — as people did to a greater extent before our obesity epidemic and before the rising popularity of aerobic and strength training.

The human body was around for many moons before anyone invented the elliptical trainer, or even the humble barbell, and it functioned pretty well. The average person had to put out significant physical effort merely to earn and produce his daily bread. Further, traditional tales of great heroes throughout all cultures have included the performance of incredible feats of strength or endurance. We have long known all kinds of ways to become lean, strong, and physically fit through natural bodily activities such as work and play.

What I mean to say is that if you do not care for formal aerobic training, you may well be on your way to staying lean and healthy through vigorous normal daily activities if you get up, move around, do, build, arrange, or clean things quite a bit on a daily basis. Next, let's consider this fascinating example from scientific literature.

They Didn't Know They Had It "Maid"

The research subjects were eighty-four roomkeepers working at seven hotels, and the researchers divided them into two groups.[81] Before the experiment, two-thirds of the roomkeepers reported that they did not exercise at all. About half of the workers were told before the experiment that the researchers had determined that their housekeeping duties of cleaning, making beds, and so forth, being on their feet and moving virtually all day long, exceeded the U.S. surgeon general's recommended thirty minutes of daily exercise. The other half was not

---

[81] Alia J. Crum and Ellen J. Langer, "Mind-Set Matters: Exercise and the Placebo Effect," *Psychological Science* 18, no. 2 (2007): 165–171, Digital Access to Scholarship at Harvard, https://dash.harvard.edu/bitstream/handle/1/3196007/Langer_ExcersisePlaceboEffect.pdf.

told this, and all the roomkeepers working in the same hotels were in the same group, so the word would not spread and contaminate the findings.

After only four weeks, the group that was told their work was actually exercise showed statistically significant — that is, not likely due to chance — decreases in weight, blood pressure, body fat, waist-to-hip ratio and BMI! Further, they were not observed to have changed their habits on the job. How is this explained? The Harvard researchers believed the measurable bodily improvements arose from a change in their mindset, a positive manifestation of the placebo effect! A popular saying among motivational writers and speakers goes, "What the mind can conceive, and believe, it can achieve!" Maybe they are onto something. Come to think of it, even old Arnold used to talk about how he would make his muscles grow before a contest through powerful visualization techniques — seeing his biceps, for example, as mountains.

Perhaps another simple lesson here for all of us is that normal semi-vigorous daily activities can indeed help keep us lean and healthy if we perform them with gusto on a regular basis.

House and Yard Aerobics

My eyes were opened to the health and fitness benefits of normal physical activities in a book by an exercise physiologist, Brant Stamford, Ph.D., and a long-distance runner, Porter Shimer, provocatively titled: *Fitness without Exercise: The Scientifically Proven Method for Achieving Maximum Health with Minimum Effort.*

Part of their own "Aha!" about the value of normal physical activity came after they exceeded that "proper proportion" of exercise that Pope Pius XII had warned us about. Stamford, for example, a daily distance runner and serious weightlifter, came to realize as he aged that he expended so much energy in his workouts that he had little left for the normal activities of daily life. Further, his ten-mile runs helped him rationalize the consumption of copious quantities of junky, processed foods.

A deeper look at the research on exercise, health, and longevity revealed that many of the studies showed benefits not from miles run or cycled but from simply walking or engaging in jobs that required one to stand about or move about. Before long, he and Shimer were no longer scoffing at fit elderly neighbors who worked hours in their garden as they jogged by or stared at them while peddling their stationary exercise bikes. I must admit that I have gardening neighbors just like them, and I can hardly keep up with my own wife as she tirelessly works in the yard! I believe it was Stamford who called his new approach "house aerobics," purposefully turning simple chores into opportunities for exercise, much as the maids would do years after his book came out.

So, what is our lesson here? Well, I would hope that, if medically cleared, you do incorporate some strength training into your routine, even if but once per week — unless you have a very physically demanding job or hobby. You can haul only so many bags of mulch or rearrange your furniture only so many times. It is hard to stimulate maximum muscle strength with only normal work and play activities, unless perhaps you live on a farm or a ranch. Stamford himself reported that he continued to lift weights once per week. Further, if you enjoy and benefit from running or some kind of endurance training, do it as often as you'd like without overtraining to the point of producing fatigue or overuse injury.

We should view both strength training and endurance training as powerful medicines. We want to take enough but not to overdose. Rest, too, is vital for recovery and growth, and the ultimate form of rest is healthy sleep at night, with perhaps a very brief nap in the daytime, if it is feasible and if you feel the need. In sum, if your formal exercise regimen is tiring you out, leaving you little energy for normal physical activities, you may well want to rein in the formal exercise a bit and let loose on house or yard aerobics! If you are married, your spouse will not complain. Oh, and if you're still hungry for some real food, consider adding some vegetable gardening or wild-game hunting to your "workout" regimen.

TEMPLE-TENDING TENET #16

Real work works! Don't underestimate the value of keeping physically active in the normal activities of taking care of your house, lawn, garden, or even your pets. Bear in mind, too, that if you are doing formal exercise and find yourself too tired to do these normal activities, you might be over-training and need to ease up a bit on your formal training.

17

How Tending Our Temples Magnifies Our Minds

*The real reason we feel so good when we get our blood pumping
is that it makes the brain function at its best, and in my view,
this benefit of physical activity is far more important — and
fascinating — than what it does for the body.*[82]

— John J. Ratey, M.D.

Exercise Brings the Intellectual Life to Life

The Dominican priest A. D. Sertillanges (1863–1948), inspired by the
wisdom of St. Thomas Aquinas, penned a wonderful book on the intellectual life. In an early section on the discipline of the body, Fr. Sertillanges
was very explicit in his *physical* exercise recommendations to any person
who would seek to perfect his *intellect*. "First then," he wrote, "do not
be ashamed to endeavour to keep well.... Every day you should take
exercise."[83] He said we should always strive to stay healthy, and he particularly recommended walking after the fashion of the ancient Greeks.

[82]   John J. Ratey, M.D., with Eric Hagerman, *Spark: The Revolutionary New
       Science of Exercise and the Brain* (New York: Little, Brown, 2008), 3.
[83]   A. D. Sertillanges, O.P., *The Intellectual Life* (Fort Collins, CO: Roman
       Catholic Books, n.d.), 34–35.

You Are That Temple!

Of course, St. Thomas Aquinas honored one of those ancient Greeks (Aristotle) with the title "the Philosopher," and his ancient school happened to be known as the Peripatetics, those who walk about, because of the colonnaded walkways of his school, the Lyceum, where the students would walk around. According to some legends, Aristotle himself lectured as he walked. Further, Dominicans in Thomas's day generally traversed Europe on foot, and Thomas himself was known to walk while immersed in deep thought. Indeed, when Thomas's great teacher, St. Albert the Great, became a bishop, he hung on to his sturdy Dominican hiking footwear, which earned him the nickname "Bishop Boots"!

In any event, seven centuries after Thomas and Albert, Fr. Sertillanges recommended daily walking, stretching, and moving in the open air, if possible. Further, for those who could not get out, he recommended some "excellent substitute methods," calling those of J. P. Müller some of "the most intelligent." Jørgen Peter Müller (1866–1938) was a gymnastics instructor and health educator who advocated brief (fifteen-minute) daily sessions of bodyweight exercises and stretching movements, perhaps a forerunner of the brief HIT and HIIT methods that grew popular in the late twentieth century. Another case of "nothing new under the sun"?

So then, these important mind-body connections were well known to the Greeks of the fourth century B.C., to Sts. Thomas and Albert in the thirteenth century, and to Fr. Sertillanges of the nineteenth and early twentieth centuries. Still, it has been only since the end of the twentieth and the beginning of the twenty-first century that scientific data showing just how and why exercise enhances our ability to think has steadily mounted. I don't know about you, but it has definitely sparked my interest.

Exercise Ignites the Sparks in Your Brain's Engine

Modern psychiatrist John J. Ratey, M.D., the author of the book *Spark: The Revolutionary New Science of Exercise and the Brain,* has boldly declared, "Exercise is the single most powerful tool you have to optimize your brain function."[84] He bases his claim upon a vast, growing body of experimental research studies in recent decades from around the world, using both animal and human subjects, that links various forms of aerobic and strength-training regimens to enhanced levels of a variety of neurotransmitters, such as dopamine, gamma-aminobutyric acid (GABA), glutamate, norepinephrine, and serotonin, and proteins and hormones such as brain-derived neurotrophic factor (BDNF), fibroblast growth factor (FGF-2), human growth hormone (HGH), insulin growth factor (IGF-1), and vascular endothelial growth factor (VEGF), which help form and grow synaptic connections between brain cells and promote growth and regeneration of the brain cells themselves.

Elaborating just a bit on a hormone quite dear to every aging weightlifter, human growth hormone has been found to be stimulated most strongly by intense exercises using the body's biggest muscles, so that, for example, short, intense sprints stimulate more than walking or jogging. To my pleasant surprise — though it really should not have been surprising — Dr. Ratey notes that the greatest HGH response has been found in response to intense barbell squats that involve several of the body's biggest and strongest muscles in unison. Weightlifters have been aware for decades that exercises such as squats and dead lifts stimulate overall muscle growth and size, some even calling them the "King and Queen of Exercises," albeit without understanding the biochemical mechanisms behind them.

Some studies have also shown measurable growth in brain structures in response to exercise — for example, growth in the hippocampus in schizophrenics who rode exercise bikes and growth in brain volume

---

84 Marie Snyder, "Miracle-Gro for Brains," *Exercise Revolution* (blog), March 2008, https://johnratey.typepad.com/blog/2008/03/miracle-gro-for.html.

in the frontal and temporal lobes (ah, the brain stuff of my own doctoral dissertation) in sixty-to-seventy-nine-year-olds who walked on a treadmill thrice weekly for six months.

Further, many studies have found, in addition to positive changes in body *chemicals* and *structures*, significant changes in response to regular exercise in actual *cognitive functioning* in terms of outcomes such as improved standardized-testing scores among high school students who underwent regulated, progressive aerobic conditioning during PE classes and 20 percent improvement in vocabulary learning among adults immediately following an exercise session.

Although it is difficult to think clearly and learn new information while performing demanding exercise because of the increased demand of blood flow to working muscles, the hormonal and other chemical changes stimulated by exercise produce both short-term and long-term benefits in thinking capacities afterward because of the positive changes in the neurological and cardiovascular systems that feed needed nutrients to the brain. Further, milder forms of exercise, such as walking at a leisurely pace, often enhance our thinking abilities even while we are doing them.

There are yet other ways in which exercise can help improve our thinking that highlight Aristotle's and St. Thomas's insights into the parallels between bodily health and virtues of the soul. Thomas emphasized something that perhaps we have all experienced: the clouding of clear thought by uncontrolled passions such as lust or anger. That is why, although prudence directs moral virtues such as temperance, fortitude, and patience, it also depends on them to control the kinds of passions that distract us and impair our practical reasoning abilities. Exercise can operate in a similar way to regulate some emotions that can impair our ability to think effectively. Dr. Ratey includes chapters on depression, attention deficit disorder, and addictions — because of the cascade of positive chemical changes that exercise can stimulate in the brain and other parts of the body, thereby impacting the mind. And indeed, more than one of the authors of our own Temple Tender Tales has emphasized that exercise provides a powerful antidote to life's stresses.

Food for Thought

As you might have surmised from our earlier chapters, not only how we *exercise* but how we *eat* can play a vital role in our cognitive and emotional functioning. A growing number of psychiatrists, such as Chris Palmer, M.D., and Georgia Ede, M.D., are finding that real-food-based diets low in carbohydrate can positively impact some patients with disorders as severe as schizophrenia. Dr. Palmer has some empirical research studies underway,[85] and Dr. Ede has provided many lectures, available online, in which she discusses results with her patients.[86]

Neurologist David Perlmutter, M.D., has also written about the impact of our diet on a variety of neurological and psychiatric diseases. Last, but not least, the prestigious Johns Hopkins Hospital has provided a ketogenic dietary approach to treating successfully some cases of epilepsy and other neurological disorders in children and adults.

Type 3 Diabetes?

There is another disorder of the brain and mind of special interest to me that may have surprising connections with improper eating in general and carbohydrate overloading in particular. In chapter 1, we looked at type 1 diabetes (formerly called juvenile diabetes) and type 2 diabetes

---

[85] Diet Doctor, "Ketogenic Diets and Mental Health with Dr. Chris Palmer," Diet Doctor Podcast, YouTube video, 1:04:17, October 20, 2021, https://www.youtube.com/watch?v=p_fj6L5tvvc.

[86] For example, see Low Carb Down Under, "Dr. Georgia Ede — 'Our Descent into Madness: Modern Diets and the Global Mental Health Crisis,'" YouTube video, April 21, 2018, https://www.youtube.com/watch?v=TXlVfwJ6RQU.

(formerly called adult-onset diabetes). We looked at the close ties between obesity and diabetes — so closely linked, in fact, that I forgot to mention that some researchers and clinicians now speak of "diabesity" as a syndrome in its own right.[87] Okay, but what about "type 3 diabetes"?

Well, some researchers and clinicians have given this perhaps unfamiliar new name to a well-known and long-dreaded disorder — Alzheimer's disease.[88] They also call it "diabetes of the brain," and abbreviate it as T3D. This is because it has been found that poorly controlled blood sugar may also increase the risk of developing Alzheimer's disease with its associated dementia, since insulin resistance may contribute to the production of the abnormal protein called amyloid, found in high concentrations of people with Alzheimer's. Not only our livers, muscles, and fat cells may become insulin resistant but our *brains* as well.

The causes of and treatments of Alzheimer's disease have baffled doctors and psychologists long before my dissertation in 1997. I looked not at causation or treatment but focused on early diagnosis and assessment by determining how early in the course of the disease higher, frontal-lobe, problem-solving, and "executive functioning" became significantly impaired along with memory.[89] The disease was named after German psychiatrist Alois Alzheimer, who, in 1906, first published

---

[87] Sanjay Kalra, "Diabesity," *Journal of the Pakistan Medical Association* 63, no. 4 (April 2013): 532–534, National Library of Medicine, https://pubmed.ncbi.nlm.nih.gov/23905459/.

[88] Thuy Trang Nguyen, Qui Thanh Hoai Ta, Thi Kim Oanh Nguyen, Thi Thuy Dung Nguyen, and Vo Van Giau, "Type 3 Diabetes and Its Role Implications in Alzheimer's Disease," *International Journal of Molecular Science* 21, no. 9 (May 2020): 3165, National Library of Medicine, https://www.ncbi.nlm.nih.gov/pmc/articles/PMC7246646/.

[89] To make a long dissertation short, we found that when we administered a battery of neurological tests focused on these "executive functions," we obtained 92.8 percent accuracy in differentiating patients diagnosed with early (mild) Alzheimer dementia from age-matched

a case study on a condition he called "pre-senile dementia" that we now call by his name. Because its diagnosis is strongly correlated with age, as our population ages, its incidence will also rise in the years ahead. The Alzheimer Organization reports that whereas about six million Americans suffer with Alzheimer's now, by 2050 the number could more than double, to thirteen million.

Researchers now believe that the changes in the brain Alzheimer's brings may begin even twenty years before it is diagnosed. Indeed, even those I tested in my dissertation research who were "early" in the course of their dementia may have been suffering subtle damage to their brain tissue for many years before they were presented to our clinic.

Of special interest for our purposes is the emerging theory of the relationship between insulin resistance, diabetes, and Alzheimer's disease. If these links are found to hold firm, it may well suggest that the very same kind of dietary changes we employ to reduce our waistlines, to clear our bloodstreams of too much sugar, and to defatten our livers may be doing an enormous favor to our brains as well.[90]

TEMPLE-TENDING TENET #17

Bear in mind that by properly feeding and training our bodily temples, we are not only building muscles, tendons, ligaments, bones, hearts, and lungs, but our very brains as well. Surely, that's something worth thinking about — and acting upon.

---

elderly control subjects. Kevin Vost, "Executive Functioning in Early Alzheimer Disease" (Psy.D. diss., Adler School of Professional Psychology, 1997).

[90] For those who would care to dig deeper, please see the articles provided in the footnotes and also see Dr. Bikman's book *Why We Get Sick* and Dr. Perlmutter's book *Grain Brain*, referenced in our appendices.

Part IV

—◆◇◆—————————◆◇◆—

From Steeple to People
(Special Concerns for Special Groups)

*The glory of young men is their strength, but the
beauty of old men is their gray hair.*

— Proverbs 20:29

18

Women and Children First!

Strength and dignity are her clothing, and she laughs
at the time to come.... Her children rise up and call her
blessed; her husband, also, and he praises her.

— Proverbs 31:25, 28

Before I formed you in the womb I knew you.

— Jeremiah 1:5

Protecting and Perfecting the Feminine Temple

"Male and female he created them.... And God saw everything that
he had made, and behold, it was very good" (Gen. 1:27, 31). Thanks
be to God for creating male and female bodily temples to house His
Holy Spirit! To cite Pope Pius XII once more: "The human body is in
its own right, God's masterpiece in the order of visible creation." We
show God our most sincere gratitude when we honor these bodily
temples, be they male or female. Thankfully too, there is so much com-
monality between male and female anatomy and physiology that the
fundamental principles of nutrition and exercise we've discussed so
far do indeed apply to both sexes.

Still, there are, of course, some physical differences that make all the difference, and since justice is the virtue that gives each person his or her rightful due, we should address some concerns that uniquely impact the health of women. Some of the foundational studies that influenced modern dietary guidelines for men and women were performed only on men, such as Key's six- and seven-countries studies, though I cited two small studies, the "A to Z diet study" in chapter 6 and the hotel roomkeeper study in chapter 16, that used women as subjects. Next, I will briefly describe a very big study performed exclusively with women as subjects.

Part of the reason Ancel Keys' studies targeting saturated fat created such an impact in the middle of the twentieth century was the rising concern with heart attacks *in men* (actually, in retrospect, probably influenced most strongly by the high cigarette-smoking rates of that time). Well, in the mid-1990s, the U.S. government granted researchers an astounding $725 million to conduct the Women's Health Initiative, a long-term, controlled clinical trial of the *lowfat* diet on nearly 49,000 postmenopausal *women*. Indeed, over the course of the fifteen-year study, more than 160,000 women would participate, including participation in intervention groups investigating such treatments as hormone replacement therapy.

At the study's start, nearly 20,000 women in the *lowfat group* "were instructed to cut back on meat, eggs, butter, cream, salad dressings, and other fatty foods" and "were also urged to eat more fruits, vegetables, and whole grains,"[91] in keeping with the USDA and American Heart Association dietary guidelines of that time and our current day, while

---

[91] Per summary in Nina Tiecholz's *The Big Fat Surprise: Why Butter, Meat and Cheese Belong in a Healthy Diet* (New York: Simon & Schuster, 2014), 169. The instructions came over a course of training sessions, meetings, and consultations.

a control group of about the same size had no dietary interventions except direction to the USDA dietary guidelines.

As for the findings published after the first nine years, the women in the lowfat group had successfully reduced overall fat intake from 37 percent to 29 percent of daily calories and saturated fat from 12.4 percent to 9.5 percent. Yet they had lost slightly less than one pound more than the control group. Further, the reduction of dietary fat had no significant impact on the risk of fatal or nonfatal coronary artery disease, stroke, cerebrovascular disease, breast cancer, or colorectal cancer — all of the primary outcome measures of the dietary study.

The results may be worth pondering for women who may needlessly fear dietary fat and believe they need more carbohydrate.

And one last thing on this topic. In January 2021, the results of the Women's Health Study were published. The researchers looked at a total of 50 possible coronary risk factors in a sample of 28,024 American women ages forty-five and over, followed up after 21.4 years. The greatest risk factors for coronary heart disease were type 2 diabetes mellitus, metabolic syndrome, hypertension, obesity, smoking, and family history of heart disease (in that order).[92] Do any of those conditions sound familiar? For those who would care to dig deeper, Tim Noakes, M.D., has provided a recent detailed evaluation of key findings of both the Women's Health Initiative and the Women's Health Study.[93]

---

[92] Sagar B. Dugani, M. Vinayaga Moorthy, Chunying Li, et al., "Association of Lipid, Inflammatory, and Metabolic Biomarkers with Age at Onset for Incident Coronary Heart Disease in Women," JAMA Cardiology 4, no. 4 (2021): 437-447, https://jamanetwork.com/journals/jamacardiology/article-abstract/2775559.

[93] Low Carb Down Under, "Prof. Tim Noakes — 'Hiding Unhealthy Heart Outcomes in Low Fat Diet Trials,'" YouTube video, 1:00:42, November 13, 2021, https://www.youtube.com/watch?v=n-wjEnsEXI0.

Next, let's take a quick look at a medical condition unique to women that may also be impacted by excessive carbohydrates and insulin resistance. Polycystic ovary syndrome (PCOS) is among the most common causes of female infertility, affecting from 6 to 12 percent — up to five million — of American women of reproductive age. The syndrome is believed to be caused by "hyperandrogenism," an overabundance of masculinizing hormone in the bloodstream that prevents the ovaries from the normal release of hormones and eggs. It is believed to be influenced by genetic factors, inflammation, and also by insulin resistance, and it is becoming increasingly prevalent.[94]

I won't go into the complicated details, but bioenergetics expert Benjamin Bikman, Ph.D., has succinctly described how excess insulin is intimately involved in preventing the transformation of masculinizing androgen hormones, such as testosterone, into feminizing hormones, such as estrogen, in a woman's body, thereby negatively impacting other hormones, such as luteinizing hormone (LH), essential to ovulation and fertility.[95] Again, PCOS is a complicated issue but a serious one — and perhaps another reason to consider decreasing one's intake of sugar and excess carbohydrates.

This should also give rise to a consideration of the nutritional needs of pregnant women. Gestational diabetes can happen to any woman, affecting about 2 to 10 percent of pregnancies in the U.S. each year. The CDC notes it is a condition of insulin resistance.[96] All women

[94] Erin K. Barthelmess and Rajesh K. Naz, "Polycystic Ovary Syndrome: Current Status and Future Perspective," *Frontiers in Bioscience-Elite* 6 (2014): 104–119, https://www.ncbi.nlm.nih.gov/pmc/articles/PMC4341818/.

[95] Benjamin Bikman, *Why We Get Sick: The Hidden Epidemic at the Root of Most Chronic Disease — And How to Fight It* (Dallas: BenBella Books, 2020).

[96] "Gestational Diabetes," CDC, last reviewed August 10, 2021, https://www.cdc.gov/diabetes/basics/gestational.html.

have some insulin deficiency late in their pregnancies, but women who display insulin resistance before pregnancy are more likely to develop gestational diabetes. This is a condition that may produce no symptoms, which speaks to the importance of ongoing prenatal care with healthcare professionals during pregnancy. The CDC also notes that about half of women who develop gestational diabetes will also develop type 2 diabetes later in life, though steps can be taken to reduce the risk. Perhaps among the greatest risk reducer of them all is to eat and exercise in such a way that minimizes the chances of insulin resistance and metabolic syndrome long before pregnancy, throughout life, starting as early as possible.

One other factor every pregnant mother should consider is the powerful impact her dietary habits can have on the little girl or boy who is growing in her womb.

Tending the Portiuncula Within

I've always enjoyed the story of St. Francis of Assisi's Portiuncula, and I got to see it for myself in 2005. "Portiuncula" comes from Latin words meaning "small portion." The one in Assisi at the foot of its mountain is a wee but beautiful ninth-century chapel the Benedictines gave to Francis in the thirteenth century. It was there he had received his calling from God, and when he neared his death, he asked to return there, dying in a cell not fifteen yards away from it. One of the most amazing things about this beautiful little church is that it now sits *inside* the gorgeous, enormous Basilica of Santa Maria degli Angeli — Church of St. Mary of the Angels.

In the Vatican II document *Lumen Gentium* (Light of the Nations), the family is called the "domestic church," for it is within the family that children come to be baptized and grow in their Faith. The parents' primary duty is to foster a family life that is centered on Christ and will help lead their children to Heaven.

Consider, too, that every child's first "house" within the "domestic church" is his mother's womb. Within the mother's bodily temple grows her child's own holy temple. Every unborn child is a *portiuncula*, a small portion of the mother and father, housed within the protective basilica of the mother's womb. And indeed, as the great church in Assisi is called St. Mary of the Angels, Church Fathers such as St. Jerome and St. Thomas Aquinas have opined that while the unborn child grows within that first domestic church, the mother's guardian angel also guards over the child.[97]

A woman's capacity to bring forth new life is a marvelous gift from God, among the most marvelous in all of creation. It underlies the very fact that you are here to read these words and I am here to write them, sitting here in our bodily temples. Since every loving mother wants all that is best for her child, it is also of great importance how a mother tends her temple during her pregnancy. Thankfully, most pregnant mothers today know that regular medical prenatal care is essential. We have also come to know that how the mother feeds herself can have a great impact on the child in her womb. Sadly, however, recent statistics have shown that fetal alcohol syndrome has risen in the United States over the last several years.[98]

While avoidance of alcohol during pregnancy is perhaps the most obvious way to honor the child's temple growing within, the child can also be honored, nurtured, and nourished by the mother's eating predominantly real foods during pregnancy, while nursing, and even before becoming pregnant.

And here is another little dietary tidbit that surprised me when I first learned it. For decades, we have been warned about the possible

---

[97] *ST*, I, Q. 113, art. 5.
[98] "Fetal Alcohol Spectrum Disorders (FASDs)," CDC, last reviewed January 26, 2022, https://www.cdc.gov/ncbddd/fasd/data.html.

health hazards of consuming dairy products and from exposing our skin to the sun — two primary sources of essential vitamin D. That advice, I knew. What I did not know is that women who breastfeed are advised by the American Academy of Pediatrics to give their babies 400 International Units of vitamin D in supplement form beginning in the first days of life.[99] Dr. Ken Berry has pointed out, however, that such drops in vitamin D levels have existed for less than a hundred years, and mothers have successfully breastfed their infants for quite a bit longer than that! Research started showing about seventy years ago that breastmilk has almost no vitamin D, and Dr. Berry cites new research indicating that this may simply be the case because modern women are not getting enough vitamin D. When pregnant women were given 6,400 IU of vitamin D per day, their breastmilk contained so much vitamin D that there was no need give their babies a vitamin D supplement! Dr. Berry recommends plenty of sun and high-fat diets for women, especially if they plan to breastfeed.

As for obesity, while we have briefly looked at growing childhood obesity rates and the fact that children and teens in the United States are now consuming more than two-thirds of their daily food intake through ultraprocessed food products, I have not yet mentioned the obesity epidemic — in infants and toddlers. Consider these few points from a recent research review:

> The most recent national estimates indicate that 8.1 percent of infants and toddlers have a weight-for-length greater than the 95th percentile, with sociodemographic disparities detectable by age 2 years. Most obesity intervention trials in childhood have focused on school-age children. However,

[99] "Breastfeeding," CDC, last reviewed July 2, 2021, https://www.cdc.gov/breastfeeding/breastfeeding-special-circumstances/diet-and-micronutrients/vitamin-d.html.

given that once obesity develops it is likely to persist, there has been an increasing focus on prevention at earlier stages of the life course.... Associations between rapid weight gain in infancy and subsequent obesity are well established, but the underlying mechanisms and any causal associations remain unclear.[100]

So obesity is rising in children who cannot yet even walk, talk, or feed themselves, making it highly unlikely that gluttony or physical sloth are to blame! While a detailed analysis of the proper nutrition for expectant mothers and for children from zygotes to teens would take another book of its own, I can provide a few basic tips and recommended resources.

As for the nature of the problem with childhood obesity, one good source is Dr. Robert Lustig's *Fat Chance: Beating the Odds against Sugar, Processed Food, Obesity, and Disease*. Dr. Lustig is a clinical endocrinologist who has treated obese children for decades, and most of his chapters begin with a real-case scenario involving young boys and girls who have been his patients. One of the many life stories I recall from his book is the story of a four-hundred-pound teenager who had drunk at least one-half gallon of cola "every day since he was old enough to open the refrigerator."[101] At age fifteen, he underwent a liver transplant for advanced cirrhosis. Dr. Lustig summarizes a one-year follow-up

---

[100] Julie C. Lumeng, Elsie M. Taveras, Leann Birch, and Susan Z. Yanovski, "Prevention of Obesity in Infancy and Early Childhood: A National Institutes of Health Workshop," *JAMA Pediatrics* 169, no. 5 (May 2015): 484–490, National Library of Medicine, https://www.ncbi.nlm.nih.gov/pmc/articles/PMC6800095/.

[101] Robert Lustig, M.D., M.S.L., *Fat Chance: Beating the Odds against Sugar, Processed Food, Obesity, and Disease* (New York: Penguin Books, 2012), 150.

visit like this: "His diet hasn't changed, the soft drinks continue, his weight has not declined, and an ultrasound shows fatty deposits in his new liver."[102]

Cases like this are extreme, but less extreme cases are out there in the millions. As parents, we would do well to buy and serve the kind of foods that will establish healthy eating patterns in our children, especially while they are very young and we can play a significant role in determining the kinds of eating habits they will form. For those who might care to do so, I can highly recommend Professor Tim Noakes and colleagues' *Super Food for Super Children* (a complete reference is provided in our appendix).[103] It is full of colorful pictures of complete recipes compiled by a chef and a registered pediatric dietician. For now, I certainly have the space to share their three "golden rules" for raising "superchildren" all the way to adulthood:

1. No added sugar
2. No refined carbs
3. Keep it real!

We've talked quite a bit about all three of their rules already, but I will note that in our concluding chapter, I will elaborate further on rule 3 and precisely what it means to eat real foods as God made them.

---

[102] Ibid.

[103] I will note as well that a vignette provider recently brought to my attention a diet for children pioneered by dentist Weston A Price, D.D.S., who had studied children's dentition and overall health in multiple nations throughout the world in the 1930s. The vast majority of the recommendations he provides are in keeping with the lessons I've learned and presented in these pages. See, for example, Jill Nienhiser, "Dietary Guidelines," The Weston A. Price Foundation, January 1, 2000, https://www.westonaprice.org/health-topics/abcs-of-nutrition/dietary-guidelines/. His book is also recommended in our appendix.

You Are That Temple!

For an excellent resource not only on nutrition but on safe slow-speed strength training for teens and even for prepubescent children, I highly recommend Fredrick Hahn's *Strong Kids, Healthy Kids*.

Temple-Tending Tenet 18

One of the most loving things a woman can do is to properly nourish her own body and that of her unborn or already born children — and when they get a little older, to introduce them to safe strength training too.

19

Old Temples, but Good Ones

Thus all the days of Methuselah were nine hundred
and sixty-nine years; and he died.

— Genesis 5:27

Life Span and Health Span

Though we all look forward to eternal life in Heaven, we probably also hope to enjoy a long life as wayfarers here on earth. And while we are unlikely to break old Methuselah's record, the pursuit of longevity can indeed honor the Spirit who resides in our bodily temples. For many decades, the average lifespan in the United States and throughout most of the industrialized modern world has risen fairly steadily. For example, in 1919, the U.S. life expectancy was 53.5 years for men and 56 years for women; in 2019, it was 76.3 years for men and 80.5 years for women. Most of the advances were due to improved medical treatments, especially those that curtailed infant mortality, which drastically brought down the averages in the past. There have indeed been a fair number of fairly old people throughout history, Methuselah being but the extreme example!

Now, will eating right and exercising regularly improve my life span or yours? Possibly, maybe even probably, but we cannot say for sure when our own personal judgment day will come, or by how many days, months, or years proper eating and exercise habits might extend our lives. If we shift our focus, however, from quantity to quality of life, proper eating and exercise habits can almost undoubtedly provide substantial improvements for virtually all of us. I'm sure that most of us hope that regardless of how long we might live on earth, we might do so while maintaining as much of our mental and physical capacities as possible. Alas, this can become harder and harder as our bodies age — but there is no cause for despair.

We've addressed the growing threats of insulin resistance and metabolic syndrome in previous pages, but advancing age may pile on new threats of its own. Jonathan Sullivan, M.D., author of *The Barbell Prescription* and owner of the "Greysteel" website and training facility for older adults, writes about what he calls "the Sick Aging Phenotype," "phenotype" being the outward expression of one's "genotype" — an individual's genetic profile.

The wobbly temple of the Sick Aging Phenotype is built upon the foundation of the all-too-familiar *metabolic syndrome* with its cornerstones of visceral obesity, insulin resistance and high blood sugar, high blood pressure, dyslipidemia (triglyceride and cholesterol abnormalities), and, unique to Dr. Sullivan's description, inflammation, "the chronic over-activation of cellular and biological defense mechanisms that cause pain and damage to tissues."[104]

But as the years rolls by, stacked upon this increasingly shaky foundation are sarcopenia (loss of muscle mass) and osteopenia (loss of bone density). Indeed, sarcopenia can further worsen the metabolic syndrome with less lean tissue available to store excess blood sugar as

---

[104] Jonathan Sullivan, M.D., and Andy Baker, *The Barbell Prescription: Strength Training for Life after 40* (Aasgard, 2016), 7–8.

glycogen and to use it up through exercise. Further, as muscles weaken significantly later in life, a person who missteps and brings his body out of alignment will more likely be unable to restore his balance due to lack of muscle strength, resulting in a fall. Unfortunately, his weakened bones will then be more likely to break. Hip fractures in particular are very common in the elderly and are associated with shortened life span. To further compound matters, if an elderly person with sarcopenia and osteopenia breaks a hip and is immobilized for a time, without proper rehabilitative exercise, sarcopenia and osteopenia may grow yet worse. Indeed, Dr. Sullivan lists frailty as another component of the Sick Aging Phenotype. The aging individual has likely become beset by bodily pain and is more prone to bone breaks.

A last component the good doctor notes, is *polypharmacy*, meaning "lots of drugs." As particular body systems break down, the older patient is often prescribed a wide variety of medications, one or more each for diabetes, hypertension, joint pain, depression, leg swelling, breathing problems, and more (which for the most part treat *symptoms* and *laboratory values* and not underlying disease).

It's a sad, scary, and common state of affairs, but there is indeed a great deal that we can do to slow down or reverse the Sick Aging Phenotype and turn a long *life*-span into a long *health*-span as well. Let's take a quick look at just a few ways.

The Biomarker Olympics

Back in 1991, when even I was fairly young, William Evans, Ph.D., and Irwin Rosenberg, M.D., created a bit of a stir with their book *Biomarkers: The 10 Keys to Prolonging Vitality*. Based on the analysis of findings from the USDA Human Nutrition Research Center on Aging at Tufts University, they laid out ten essential "biomarkers": key physiological factors that have been associated with the maintenance of high levels of health and fitness as one ages. They are:

- Lean body (muscle) mass
- Strength
- Basal metabolic rate
- Low body fat percentage
- High aerobic capacity
- Normal blood pressure
- Insulin sensitivity
- Healthy cholesterol/HDL ratio
- Bone density
- Body temperature regulation

We've come across most of these already, haven't we? Well, among these ten markers, which do you think they found to be the most important? (Drum roll please.) The gold-medal winner was muscle mass, and muscle strength took home the silver. They noted that these two are so essential because, to some extent, the other markers depend on them.

As for metabolic rate, for example, the more muscle you carry, the higher your metabolism, because muscles are more metabolically active than fat. Of course, the more muscle you have in comparison with fat, the leaner your body composition. To do aerobic exercise, you need strong muscles, and even strength training alone provides aerobic benefits at the cellular level. Such exercise can help regulate blood pressure. Insulin sensitivity, as we've seen time and again, is also improved when we have a lot of muscle and keep it there by using it. The metabolic activity of muscle can also impact the fats in our bloodstream. The kind of strength exercise and intake of protein that builds muscles also thickens bone. And finally, those metabolically active muscles also help us regulate our internal body temperature. When it comes to biomarkers, muscle rules!

Most interestingly too, among measures of physical capacity that predict longevity, a test as simple as grip strength has been called "an indispensable biomarker for older adults,"[105] and this has been known and corroborated by reams of research for decades. Grip strength correlates with strength in other bodily muscles, and people with higher grip strength tend to live longer. Indeed, as a recent research reviewer concludes, "the routine use of grip strength can be recommended as a stand-alone measurement or as a component of a small battery of measurements for identifying older adults at risk of poor health status."[106] Ready to go and grab a firm hold on those barbells, dumbbells, or kettlebells now?

I've already preached on the power of various kinds of strength training aplenty in these pages. One resource I've mentioned but have not emphasized yet is *The First Program Fighting Insulin Resistance with Strength Training* by William Y. Shang, M.D. Although the home exercise program he provides is pretty straightforward and simple compared with the barbell, HIT machine, and biomechanical approaches I detailed, Dr. Shang goes into great detail about why and how strength training can help reverse the metabolic syndrome and Sick Aging Phenotype problems we've studied. One nice chart he provides shows how weight-trained men at even eighty years of age can match the physical strength of untrained thirty-year-olds. Unless a person has a certain medical condition, old muscles respond pretty much like young ones to strength training.

Ideally, a person will start strength training in the early teens and persist at it throughout life, getting as strong as possible as an adult and hanging on to as much muscle size and strength as possible in the later years. Still, a person starting late can still get stronger and enjoy real-life

[105] Richard W Bohannon, "Grip Strength: An Indispensable Biomarker for Older Adults," *Clinical Interventions in Aging* 14 (2019): 1681–1691, National Library of Medicine, https://www.ncbi.nlm.nih.gov/pmc/articles/PMC6778477/.

[106] Ibid.

benefits in improved health, fitness, and daily function. Dr. Sullivan, for example, routinely starts elderly clients on carefully monitored barbell training — yes, even great-grandmas and great-grandpas doing dead lifts and squats! He calls them "Athletes of Aging." Also, people who start such training later in life may have an added advantage of sorts if they have not suffered injuries from poor training methods earlier in life.

Further, do you recall that the super-slow methods were precisely designed with elderly, osteopenic individuals in mind to stimulate the muscles and bones without harrowing the joints? In my opinion, Doug Brignole's biomechanically friendly cable and dumbbell exercises are also a perfect match for elderly trainees.

Protein: Yes, Whey!

So far, so good. But what about nutrition for maintaining aging temples? Well, the fundamental principles of eating predominantly real foods, avoiding excess sugars and processed foods, and getting adequate fat, protein, vitamins, minerals, and water all apply — but with a couple of important distinctions.

Sarcopenia, muscle loss, has taken center stage in research on health functioning in the elderly. In the field of spiritual warfare, St. Joseph has been called "the terror of demons," and in the field of nutrition, protein may well be called "the terror of sarcopenia." In my world of strength training and muscle building, protein has been a controversial subject for many decades. Knowing that muscle consists partly of protein, about 80 percent dry weight, though more than two-thirds of muscle is water, lifters and bodybuilders long believed that, within limits, "the more, the better." Still, some in the field argued that you cannot force your muscles to grow by simply eating more protein and that those who want to build muscle would need just a little bit of extra protein for the body to gradually build small amounts of muscle tissue in response to the damage that comes from training.

Well, in recent years, more has become known about how protein and particular amino acids may actually trigger protein synthesis and muscle growth. It involves chemicals, including the *mammalian target of rapamycin*, or m-TOR. While I will not go into its complex potential relationship with a variety of variables, including longevity and cancer growth, I will simply highlight that increased protein intake is now widely recommended for the elderly due to a growing body of sound research.

Modern research shows that aging adults tend to become not only insulin resistant but to develop *anabolic resistance*. This means that, as we age, it can take greater amounts of protein in our diets to stimulate muscle maintenance or growth. Therefore, as we get older, we may need to take in more protein than we needed when we were younger. Some evidence has suggested that forty grams of protein in a single meal may maximally stimulate protein synthesis in older adults.[107] This is why I have targeted forty grams in my post-workout protein smoothies. Also, the essential amino acid leucine has been found, in both in vitro and in vivo studies, to enhance protein synthesis.[108] This amino acid is especially high in whey proteins, and that is why I predominantly use whey protein in my smoothies.

In the very recent (2021) academic tome *Clinical Nutrition and Aging: Sarcopenia and Muscle Metabolism,* five chapters focus on the research studies and reviews of the effects of protein and exercise on

[107] I refer you to the many videos available online from protein research scientists Donald Layman, Ph.D., of the University of Illinois and Stuart Phillips, Ph.D., of McMaster University, as well as the "Muscle Centric Medicine" of osteopathic physician Gabrielle Lyon, D.O.

[108] Peter J. Garlick, "The Role of Leucine in the Regulation of Protein Metabolism," *Journal of Nutrition* 135, no. 6 (June 2005): 1553S–1556S, National Library of Medicine, https://pubmed.ncbi.nlm.nih.gov/15930468/.

sarcopenia in older adults. All point to the effectiveness of increased protein in stimulating protein synthesis and muscle hypertrophy in the elderly, and one study showed that while both forms of protein stimulated muscle protein synthesis in the elderly, whey protein did so more than soy protein, probably due to its higher leucine content. The ideal situation for protein synthesis and muscle-mass stimulation is found when elderly subjects eat more protein and do strength training — which may come as no surprise!

One Last Nod to Old Milo

Ah, but perhaps you recall that I mentioned another possible exception regarding nutrition and the elderly, and here I refer to creatine. In the past, I've expressed caution about its use, especially for teenager lifters. It is a natural food substance that provides energy for muscles. Perhaps it is because it is especially abundant in meat, along with the protein, that even the ancient Greeks believed in "meat for strength." In fact, in describing his theory of the "golden mean," and just-right proportions for virtue, Aristotle used the example of determining just how much meat Milo should eat, noting that six pounds per day might not be enough! (Indeed, it tickled me pink when I first found that in his *Commentary on Aristotle's* Nichomachean Ethics, good St. Thomas Aquinas himself tell his readers about Milo!)[109]

Anyway, creatine has been found to stimulate some degree of strength and muscle size gains, but myself, and almost everyone in my acquaintance, has also noted significant body-weight gain and bloating with it. I have taken it off and on for years, but I stopped in July

---

[109] "This would indeed be little for a man called Milo who, according to Solinus, ate a whole beef in a day." St. Thomas Aquinas, *Commentary on Aristotle's* Nichomachean Ethics (Notre Dame, IN: Dumb Ox Books, 1993), 105.

2020 while rebuilding my dead lifts. My body weight had climbed to 230 pounds, and I suffered the most severe nighttime leg cramp in my life. When I dead lifted 410 pounds for five repetitions on my sixtieth birthday, I had taken no creatine for six months.

While researching this book, however, I came across some research on the elderly that suggests creatine may indeed help combat sarcopenia later in life. In *Clinical Nutrition and Aging,* twenty-seven research articles were noted to have investigated creatine and sarcopenia, and they suggested that modest amounts of creatine supplementation, up to about five grams per day, especially when combined with strength training, could help ward off sarcopenia in some people.

Hence, I've been conducting a little mini experiment of my own. Sixty-seven days ago, I started supplementing with creatine again — but with a twist. Knowing I take in a fair amount of creatine in the meat-based proteins I eat, instead of taking five grams of powdered creatine per day I take only three grams in capsule form.

Further, it occurred to me that while I had massive water retention and weight gain from creatine in the past, I was also eating large amounts of carbohydrates, probably two hundred to three hundred grams or more (which also hold water), at the time. This is the first time I have taken creatine while eating very few carbohydrates, and this would be the first time I would feel its positive effects on strength without any weight gain. It is certainly not essential, but for some with aging temples, it might prove worth giving a try.

TEMPLE-TENDING TENET #19

For those who would protect their bodily temples from the ravages of Sick Aging Phenotype, consider buttressing your buttresses with plenty of protein and the right kind and amount of strength training.

20

Physically Disabled, Perhaps:
Spiritually Strong, for Sure!

*What is sown is perishable, what is raised is imperishable. It is sown
in dishonor, it is raised in glory. It is sown in weakness, it is raised
in power. It is sown a physical body, it is raised a spiritual body.*

— 1 Corinthians 15:42–44

The Small, Crooked, Temple That Reached to Heaven

I was moved as a child by the story of Helen Keller (1880–1968). Before the age of two, she became both blind and deaf, due to an illness, possibly meningitis. Her parents were well off and did all they could to care for and educate her, but she described March 15, 1887, as her "soul's birthday." That day, one Anne Sullivan came to the family home and taught her how to communicate by handing her objects and spelling their names in the palm of her hand. Though it was rough going at first, Helen would later become so proficient at communication that she would travel the world giving lectures and became a great advocate for the rights of people with disabilities.

Many decades later, I became aware of a story, in our own Catholic tradition, with some striking similarities and crucial differences — a story that predates Ms. Keller's by about six hundred years. I learned about it myself when asked to speak earlier this year at a Dominican conference named in her honor.

Well, to make a thirty-three-year-long story short: in 1287, when a noble couple in Perugia, Italy, awaited the arrival of what they hoped to be a healthy son, a baby girl was born — a little girl with dwarfism, a hunched back, and blindness. Her parents, shocked and ashamed, hid their daughter in a secluded section of their castle until she was accidentally seen by a guest when she was six years old.

Her parents then constructed and walled her into a small room next to the parish church, where she remained for the next ten years. She was provided food and necessities through a small window, and another window gave her access to Mass and Holy Communion. She was befriended and taught by the parish priest, who found her amazingly open to learning, humble, loving, and without resentment toward her parents.

At the age of sixteen, her parents took her to a shrine in a Franciscan church in Castello, in hopes of a miraculous healing. When, after two days, they saw that God had not healed her, they abandoned their daughter on the streets, where she begged food and was later taken in and cared for by a group of Dominican nuns. She would later join them as a Third Order member of the Order of Preachers and would don the distinctive black and white Dominican religious habit.

As she grew in age and in faith, this young woman would be far from only on the *receiving* end of care. She was noted for her remarkably cheerful demeanor, and she actively ministered to the needs of the sick, the dying, and incarcerated prisoners. She died on April 13, 1320, at the age of thirty-three.

When her body was exhumed two hundred years later, she was all of four feet tall, with a large head; small, serrated teeth; and a right leg an inch and a half shorter than her left (explaining her pronounced limp). More than two hundred miracles have been credited to her intercession since her death,[110] and 701 years after her death, on April 24, 2021, Margaret of Castello was officially canonized by the Catholic Church. She is the patron saint of the disabled, the blind, and the pro-life cause. St. Margaret's four-foot-tall temple has indeed reached all the way to Heaven.

St. Margaret's Lesson for Us All

St. Margaret of Castello's short but amazing life should make clear to us all the lesson that every single person's temple, regardless of how small, how large, how misshapen, how shaky its foundation, or how crooked its steeple, is literally a *magnificent* work of God (for "magnificent" comes from the Latin *magnus*, "great," and *facere*, "to make"). We are all wondrously made since it is through our bodies that we exercise our intellects and wills, by which we were made in God's image and likeness. God loves us all with infinite love regardless of what our bodies look like.

For those of us physically capable, sure, we are called to perfect and maintain our bodily temples, as much as we possibly can, but even a person who is bedfast can honor God through his or her body, by nourishing it as healthily as possible, by thanking God for every day of life, and by chatting with, praying with, sharing smiles with, and even simply maintaining eye contact with visitors, if possible. Further, if we are too advanced of age or too hampered by chronic injuries to exercise vigorously, maybe we can cheerfully help educate others, perhaps our grandchildren, to better appreciate the bodies God gave them and to develop habits to grow healthy, holy bodily temples. Still, for all of us

---

[110] "St. Margaret of Castello," Dominican Sisters of Saint Cecilia, https://www.nashvilledominican.org/community/our-dominican-heritage/our-saints-and-blesseds/bl-margaret-castello/.

who *believe in* Christ and who *believe* Christ, when it comes to our bodily temples, the best is yet to come!

All Saints Are Athletes for Christ

Every one of us is called to be a saint, for that is what we call the souls who have made it to Heaven. Only a relative handful of Heaven's inhabitants have been officially canonized by the Church. The Church teaches that when each of us dies, we receive an individual, *private judgment* that determines whether our *souls* will be sent to Heaven, Hell, or Purgatory, depending on the stains of sin left on them.[111]

Still, a most fascinating and everlasting thing will occur when Jesus returns at the Second Coming and we all face a *general judgment* as members of the human race. After this judgment, God and the angels will gather our ashes, and our bodies will be reunited with our souls. For those of us already in Heaven or soon to be there, God will provide us with *glorified* bodies.

Guided by St. Paul's revelations (see our opening quotation), Church Fathers and Doctors, including St. Thomas Aquinas, have taught that our glorified bodies will be blessed with *impassibility* (Paul's "imperishable"), *clarity*, or radiance ("glory"), *agility* ("power"), and *subtlety*, or spirit-like qualities ("spiritual"). Our glorified bodies will not suffer injury or decay, will perfectly obey the commands of our wills, will literally glow with beauty, and will move with near instantaneous swiftness throughout a glorified universe. Indeed, in Heaven we

---

[111] For a modern, straightforward catechetical treatment of such issues I refer you to Fr. Wade Menezes's *The Four Last Things: A Catechetical Guide to Death, Judgment, Heaven, and Hell* (Manchester, NH: Sophia Institute Press, 2017). For a summary of St. Thomas Aquinas's treatment of such issues, I refer you to my *Aquinas on the Four Last Things: Everything You Need to Know about Death, Judgment, Heaven, and Hell* (Manchester, NH: Sophia Institute Press, 2021).

will be like great athletes for Christ — as strong as Samson and Milo and fleeter of foot than the Flash!

Our great theologians speculate, too, that our bodies will appear at about the human peak of physical age, around thirty-three, the age at which Jesus Christ was transfigured and then received His glorified body — and, come to think of it, the age at which St. Margaret's soul rose to meet Him. In other words, even those with significant disabilities will receive perfected bodies restored in Heaven, so that they, too, may fly like eagles and walk without getting weary.

In a certain sense, tending our temples as best we can on earth can help us prepare for our glorified bodies in Heaven. Consider these words of our Angelic Doctor on the glorified body in Heaven:

> The glorified body will be altogether subject to the glorified soul, so that not only will there be nothing in it to resist the will of the spirit, for it was even so in the case of Adam's body, but also from the glorified soul there will flow into the body a certain perfection, whereby it will become adapted to that subjection; and this perfection is called the gift of the glorified body.[112]

In our glorified state, our bodies will fully obey the dictates of our spirits, unlike in our present state, in which, all too often, the spirit is willing, but the flesh is weak. Without this interior conflict, our very bodily movements will become fluid, agile, effortless.

But we don't have to wait for Heaven in order to enjoy greater harmony between body and soul. St. Thomas also writes that "those in whom the motive power is stronger, and those who through exercise have the body more adapted to obey the moving spirit, labor less in being moved."[113]

---

[112] *ST*, Supplement, Q. 84, art. 1.
[113] Ibid.

As followers of Christ, we are not like St. Thomas's great nemesis the Manichees, who taught that the flesh itself is evil. Jesus Himself took on human flesh in the Incarnation and thereby glorified it, and, Mary, the Mother of God, rests with the Trinity and the souls of the Communion of Saints and the angels even now in body and soul. Jesus came not to destroy the bodily temple, if you will, but to fulfill it. He showed us the way to perfection of our entire being, heart, soul, mind, and strength, which includes our physical bodies — bones, sinews, and all.

Temple-Tending Tenet #20

Every one of us was magnificently made. As physically able or disabled as we might be right now, let us thank God for these bodily temples as we rest in the hope of new glorified ones.

Conclusion

All for the Glory of the God within *and beyond* Our Bodily Temples

And God blessed them, and God said to them, "Be fruitful
and multiply, and fill the earth and subdue it."

— Genesis 1:28

Destroy this temple, and in three days I will raise it up.

—John 2:19

Body and Mind, Temple and Soul

God crafted us as integrated beings of mind, body, and soul to serve as temples for His Holy Spirit. Contemplate, if you will, the meaning of the word "contemplation." Latin word *contemplari* means "to observe carefully" and was based on the ancient pagan practice of augury: looking for signs and omens. The word referred to marking off a *templum*, or "place for observation," in which the augurs would carefully observe what they interpreted as signs before making their predictions. The Latin word *templum* became the Old English word *tempel* and modern English word "temple," which refer to the consecrated ground and the building constructed for the worship of a god.

You Are That Temple!

The modern word "contemplate" has clear intellectual connotations, meaning "to ponder or consider thoughtfully" according to one definition in the *American Heritage Dictionary*. In our Catholic tradition, it has spiritual connotations as well (and even more so). Consider the words of St. Albert the Great, patron saint of scientists and Thomas Aquinas's teacher:

> One should bear in mind the difference between the contemplation of faithful Catholics and that of pagan philosophers, for the contemplation of the philosophers is for the perfection of the contemplator himself, and consequently it is confined to the intellect and their aim in it is intellectual knowledge. But the contemplation of the Saints, and of Catholics, is for the love of him, that is of the God they are contemplating.[114]

So then, when we *contemplate*, we use our *mind* in service of our *spirit* to show God our deep love for Him, and we do so from within the *temple* that is our *body*. But we should be sure to realize as well that our holy bodily temples exist within consecrated ground as vast as the universe itself.

It All Goes Back to Genesis:
The World Is the Temple Ground

God commanded us not only to love Him, our neighbors, and ourselves, but to serve as His good stewards over all of creation. Many people today argue that the kind of food we produce and eat has not only nutritional, but ecological and ethical implications as well, and in this I believe they are quite correct. We certainly should try to learn about and practice methods of feeding ourselves that show good

---

[114] St. Albert the Great, *On Cleaving to God* (Indianapolis, IN: Lamp Post Books, 2008), 32–33.

stewardship of the animals and plants on planet Earth and indeed of the planet itself. Here too, though, we should contemplate the impact of our dietary habits with careful thought, cautiously calling the virtues of science, understanding, and wisdom to our aid, before we jump to conclusions based on insufficient or stilted evidence.

There is a good deal of debate today about the environmental and ethical implications of largely animal-based or plant-based diets, for example, and one should be careful to denounce either practice without careful consideration of the actual evidence with a mind toward grasping the big picture. Surely, we should not want any animals to suffer inhumane living conditions or treatment, not only because the meat of healthy, happy, naturally fed and exercised animals provides us with better nutrition but because we have concern for the animals themselves.

Indeed, in one of my favorite stories about St. Thomas Aquinas, a rich man insists that he allow him to give Thomas a great present. After contemplating the situation for a while, Thomas asks him for all the caged birds sold on a particular street in Paris, which he proceeds to purchase — and set free! In a story of another favorite saint, while lying upon his deathbed, St. Martin de Porres, a great lover of animals and possessor of great medical and pharmaceutical knowledge, said to bring him no medications that had been developed by the suffering of animals.

Does this mean I argue for veganism? No, not for myself, anyway, though I have no qualms if you should conclude that such a diet is best for you. Still, human beings have long been *omnivores,* eating both animal and plant foods since the days of Cain, the farmer, and Abel, the shepherd (Gen. 4).[115] Further, the animals killed for our food do

---

[115] Indeed, a good deal of modern nutritional theory examines and compares and contrasts anthropological evidence of earlier cultures that

not suffer the fate of many animals out in the wild, and indeed, even in my own backyard sometimes, that are eaten alive by other animals or die from painful injuries or diseases.

There are certainly opportunities for the abuse of both animals and of the land in the production of both animal and plant products. Indeed, large tracks of the Amazon forests are converted into not only pastureland, but into agriculture cropland each year, fueled largely by the world's increased demand for soy products.

Whether one is a carnivore, a vegan, or like most of us, somewhere in between, one simple way we can address environmental and ethical concerns is to stick to the primary nutritional tenet of eating, as much as possible, real foods as God made them. This reduces the need for the industrialization of food production, even of plant-based foods, not to mention the pollution from plastic and other forms of packaging.

An important related idea is to become a "locovore" — that is, as much as possible, to eat foods produced locally. This reduces all of the environmental costs involved in shipping, flying, railroading, or trucking foods around the world. If possible, get to know a good farmer, farmers' market, or food co-op in your area; grow a garden; take up deer or small-gaming hunting or fishing, or perhaps pick up a few chickens or goats for your backyard. (Kathy has not yet okayed that for me.)

There may be another benefit to the "locovore" thing. Though I've given plenty of reasons for my personal preference for a diet low in carbohydrates, many native cultures around the world have produced healthy men and women for thousands of years on all kinds of diets, some of them quite high in carbohydrate-rich foods such as fruit, rice, or sweet potatoes. Throughout most of human history, we have only been able to eat, for the most part, the kinds of real foods that are

---

were primarily hunter-gathers or based upon agriculture, giving rise to diets such as the "Paleo" or "Primal" diets.

produced where we live and in their proper season. This might be a lesson well worth relearning.[116]

You Are That Temple!

To cross our final *T*s, as in "temple," and to honor Christ's sacrifice for us of His own bodily temple upon the Cross, I hope and pray that we will all find ways to keep healthy and holy, while exercising great care and gratitude for all of God's green earth: "For God's temple is holy, and that temple you are" (1 Cor. 3:17).

---

[116] One might contemplate the possible connections between such "lo-covorism," so to speak, and Catholic principles of distributism and subsidiarity.

Appendix 1

Simple Sample Workouts
(for Samson or for Sarah)

But they who wait for the LORD *shall renew their strength.*

—Isaiah 40:31

More Than Five Ways to Build a Temple

To sum up just a bit, we have looked at five main ways to build and maintain our temples: (1) barbell training; (2) high-intensity or super-slow machine-based training, or both; (3) biomechanical cable and dumbbell training; (4) aerobic/cardio/conditioning/endurance training; and (5) normal physical work and play. Further (as I'll give my own example in the last section), we can mix and match these methods in a vast variety of ways.

And yet there are many more ways still! While I cannot detail them all here (and they lie outside my areas of expertise, to boot), excellent methods to use in addition to, or instead of, the methods I've detailed include: kettlebell training, formal group exercise classes, bodyweight calisthenic-type exercises, flexibility training, wrestling and other martial arts training, and even trampolining. Indeed, some of these are detailed by practicing experts who have provided vignettes, as you shall see at the end of this book.

The main point I want to make is that God made us all unique individuals with different genetic makeups, skeletal frames, athletic abilities, and personal likes and dislikes in exercise as well as in food. This being said, there is some form of exercise or physical activity out there that should work well for just about every healthy person. It may be a matter of trying a variety of approaches to find what works for you. Further, although we are all unique, we all share in a common humanity too, and our bodies were all made for using in one way or another.

What I'll do next is flesh out three extremely simple examples of what could constitute a weekly workout regimen employing one of our three main strength-training methods. Please note that I will suggest written and online resources for digging deeper into these methods when we get to chapter 19, but here I will provide examples of *barebones minimum* approaches to the three strength-training methods I've discussed.

Simple Sample Barbell Routine

If you are not familiar with the performance of basic barbell exercises but are interested in trying them, I encourage you either to seek out a personal trainer or strength coach for one-on-one instruction; to read illustrated manuals such as *Starting Strength* or *The Barbell Prescription*, detailed in our appendix; or to watch quality Internet videos on the performance of these movements from Starting Strength, Greysteel, or Barbell Logic. With that said, here is how simple such workout regimens can be.

Day 1 Workout
- *Overhead press* — five sets of five to six repetitions. The first three sets are gradually heavier warm-ups, and the last two

sets are the difficult work sets. When you achieve six repetitions for both sets, jump up five pounds the next week and try to work back to two sets of six before going heavier again.

- *Dead lift* — five sets of five to six repetitions. The first four sets are gradually heavier warm-ups, and only the last set is all-out (or close to it). When you can do six repetitions in your work set, add five pounds to it the next week.

Day 2 Workout (ideally, two or three days later)

- *Squat* (low bar, high bar, front, or safety) — five sets of five to six repetitions. The first three sets are gradually heavier warm-ups, and the last two sets are the difficult work sets. When you achieve six repetitions for both sets, jump up five pounds the next week and try to work back to two sets of six before going heavier again.
- *Barbell row* — same progression as for squat with the appropriate weight for this movement.

I'll note that I've done variations of a routine for many years, and my thirty-five-year-old son is making gains on it right now. If you don't insist on sticking to barbells, chin-ups or pull-downs can be done instead of barbell rows. You could also add bicep, tricep, forearm, side and rear shoulder, abdominal, or calf exercises to either workout.

Simple Sample HIT/Super-Slow Routine

There are many ways to incorporate HIT and super-slow methods into super-time-efficient workouts. I'm going to start with Dr. McGuff's "big five" super-slow workout, which hits virtually all of the body's major muscles in as few machine-based movements as possible.

- *Pull-down from overhead* (if the machine allows a neutral, hands-facing-each-other, grip, this is ideal for less strain on the biceps and forearms) — one set of three to six repetitions, taking about ten seconds to bring your arms down and another ten to raise them up each repetition. When you achieve all six, it is time to add a little weight to the next workout.

• *Seated chest-press machine* — one set of three to six repetitions at the ten-ten pace. When you achieve six, add a little weight the next time.

• *Rowing machine* — same method and progression.

• *Seated overhead-press machine* — same.

• *Leg press* — same.

If you take little time between sets, this workout can be completed in ten to fifteen minutes and is a rather amazing experience! Some people who train this way like to work out twice per week or even more often, using different exercises in any additional workouts. I should also note that it is essential not to hold your breath during slow repetitions but to breath naturally as often as is necessary. Further, please do not grip the handles hard while doing leg presses since this can really elevate your blood pressure. Instead, get firmly set within the machine and gently rest your hands on top or beside the handles.

Simple Sample Biomechanically Correct Routine

If you are unfamiliar with these exercises, they can be found in the books and videos from Doug Brignole, as detailed in our appendix. Since the focus now is on individual muscles, rather than on general body-movement patterns, I will specify the muscles of focus within each workout. Note, too, that this is simply a sample routine and that you can group together different muscles depending on your preference.

Day 1: Chest, back, and front shoulders

• *Seated cable-chest press* (or flat or slightly declined dumbbell chest press) — four sets of thirty, twenty, ten, and six repetitions with increasingly heavier weights. When you get all of the reps for the ten and six repetition sets, add a little weight to one or the other next time. The first two sets should not be all-out, and you'll just creep those weights up quite gradually.

• *Lat (latissimus dorsi muscles of the back) pull-ins* — Same set and repetition scheme and progression as above.

• *Seated (or standing bent) anterior shoulder cable press* (or flat or slightly declined dumbbell shoulder press) — Same set and repetition scheme and progression.

• *Seated cable scapular retractions* (a rowing-type motion described by Brignole that extends and contracts the scapula using the lower trapezius muscles and that stops when the elbows hit the sides — an alternative would be machine or dumbbell rowing) — Same.

• *Cable or dumbbell shrugs* — Same.

Day 2: Legs and midsection (two or three days later)

• *Leg-extension machine* — (leaning back) — four sets of thirty, twenty, ten, and six, as above.

• *Seated leg-curl machine* — (leaning forward) — same.

• *Calf raise* (standing or on leg press machine) — same.

• *Abdominal-crunch machine* — same.

• *Torso-twisting machine or cable side bends* — same.

Day 3: Side and rear shoulders and arms (two or three days later)

• *One-arm cable side (or lateral) raise with cable at hip height* (or side shoulder machine) — four sets of thirty, twenty, ten, and six.

• *One-arm cable rear-deltoid exercise* — same. Hand starts above head level on the opposite side of the body and pulls down and to the rear across the body. By the way, both cable movements can be done best by purchasing cheap D-ring wrist cuffs, which remove the need to grip the handles with the weaker muscles of the forearm.

• *Cable, dumbbell, or seated machine biceps curl* — same.
• *Cable pushdown, lying dumbbell triceps extension, or triceps-extension machine* — same.

The Current Plans for My Own Old Temple

There are so many ways to put strength and cardio routines together, and mine changes regularly. After providing a little background, I will simply give you a look at what mine looks like right at the moment, as I approach age sixty-one. When I first started eating real foods consistently many months ago, I was lifting every day and doing no formal aerobic activity for the first forty days or so as I lost the first fourteen pounds from 220 to 206. I then started adding twenty-minute cardio sessions, mostly inclined treadmill walking or recumbent or upright bicycling, at the end of my strength workouts for a few months until I hit my low of 190 pounds body weight on day 160. For a while after that, I did cardio only every other day and then switched back to daily. Three weeks ago, I took a break from any form of cardio training, and my weight has stayed the same.

Anyway, here's a peek at my current routine — for now, that is, because I change it at will. I have recorded most of my workouts in dated appointment books since 1982. Here is what I recorded for last week's workouts. Please note that typically every set but the last is done as a warm-up to prepare for the last working set, performed at near-maximum intensity. The poundage is listed first and then the number of repetitions performed. Note, too, that the weights I use are what's appropriate for me, at this point in my life. Everyone needs to determine the right weights for themselves, ensuring proper form and erring on the side of going too light, especially when one is just getting started.

Day 1 (Monday)

- *Front squat* (pausing at bottom with safety catch at depth well below parallel) — 45 x 5 reps, 95 x 3, 135 x 2, 165 x 1, 190 x 1, 225 x 2.
- *Standing calf raise* (one leg at a time) — one set of body weight x 20 reps.

Day 2 (Wednesday)

- *Seated overhead-press machine* — 90 x 5, 140 x 3, 180 x 2, 200 x 1, 230 x 1, 250 x 1, 270 x 2, 205 x 11.
- *Side deltoid lateral raise machine* (one arm at a time) — 130 x 6, 160 x 6, 200 x 10.

Day 3 (Friday)

- *Dead lift* — 45 x 5, 135 x 5, 225 x 5, 315 x 1, 365 x 1, 405 x 4.
- *Abdominal machine* — 160 x 5, 190 x 3, 225 x 20.

Day 4 (Saturday)

- *One-arm lat pull-in with cable machine* — 67.5 x 6, 87.5 x 6, 99 x 7.
- *Seated biceps machine* (one arm at a time) — 50 x 6, 65 x 6, 80 x 6, 95 x 4.

Sunday

- Whew! Rest, grow, go to Mass!

So this is but one way of laying out a formal weekly exercise routine. You will note that I included two basic barbell motions (front squats and dead lifts) along with machines and cables. I also mix things up freely, and every other week, I alternate overhead-pressing or straight-across bench-pressing-type movements. I have an alternate side shoulder and arm day that uses only dumbbells or cables, rather than machines. Also, I vary the extent to which I include super-slow (ten-second-up and ten-second-down) methods and will sometimes even do "just plain slow," we might say, taking about five seconds in each direction for sets of eight to ten or so.

Although I'm retired, I'm usually awake by around 4:00 a.m. and at the gym by 6:00 or 6:30 six days per week. When I was younger, most of my workouts were done after work and sometimes during work hours. Any time of day that works for your body rhythms and your schedule can get the job done, as long as you try to avoid working out on a full stomach or too soon before bedtime, which may make it difficult to fall asleep.

Hopefully this will inspire you to craft some kind of routine that works for you! Now, though, it is time to look at what kind of benefits we may reap by keeping our *minds* focused on properly feeding and training our *bodies*.

Temple-Tending Tenet #21

Experiment with different enjoyable fitness routines that fit into your schedule, to keep you feeling strong and enduring without wearing you out or robbing time from your other responsibilities in life.

Appendix 2

How to Keep Learning to Care for Our Temples

He said to me, "Son of man, eat this scroll that I
give you and fill your stomach with it." Then I ate it;
and it was in my mouth as sweet as honey.

— Ezekiel 3:3

Eating the book is the starting-point of reading and of
basic history. When, by diligent meditation, we store
away the book of the Lord in our memorial treasury, our
belly is filled spiritually and our guts are satisfied.

— St. Jerome, *Commentary on Ezekiel*[117]

Eat Books, Learn More

Study after study and personal experience after personal experience show that, all too often, when people clean up their eating habits, take up regular exercise, lose fat, and improve their health and fitness, they backslide over time to drop their new habits and turn back to their old

---

[117] As cited in Mary Carruthers, *The Book of Memory: A Study of Memory in Medieval Culture* (Cambridge, MA: Cambridge University Press, 1990), 44.

ones, only to regain the lost fat and forfeit the health benefits. Many reasons contribute to this all-too-common phenomenon, as I can attest from personal experience. (Though I have always exercised, my eating habits have varied quite widely over the years.) Still, I think that our new mantra or motto can go very far to help us keep our temples sturdy and firm once we have built them up properly.

People often go back to ultraprocessed foods, to sugary, starchy foods and drinks, because they have grown bored with their new ways of eating and perhaps because after a period of intensified interest in nutrition and exercise, their focus may change to a myriad of other things in life. This may be most appropriate indeed, for we do not want to obsess constantly about what we eat, knocking on spiritual gluttony's door, or get so absorbed in physical exercise that we ignore spiritual exercise too. We must strive to keep that "proper proportion," as you'll recall, a motto that comes courtesy of Pope Pius XII.

In endorsing Zoë Harcombe's book *The Obesity Epidemic,* Julie Hurst, director of the Work Life Balance Centre, wrote, "For those bombarded by the weight loss message of 'eat — move more,' this book is an opportunity to espouse a different mantra: read more — learn more. Then do it all differently." As for the "read more — learn more" idea, I believe it may well be key to maintaining proper care of our bodily temples throughout our lives here on earth. Things of the body, such as nutrition and exercise, are indeed worth studying and learning for the rest of our lives. Hopefully, we have all developed the habit of regular spiritual reading from Scripture, lives and works of the saints, devotional books, modern Catholic books, and more. Indeed, Ezekiel has informed us that we will find them as sweet as honey (without all the fructose, I might add), and St. Jerome has added that if we meditate on them diligently, "our belly is filled spiritually and our guts are satisfied." I hope, too, you will set aside some time to keep gobbling up good books on bodily health as well, books that address our literal bellies and guts! After all, St. Thomas Aquinas did tell us that charity demands that we love our own bodies.

If we do keep reading and learning about our bodies, it will likely increase our motivation to keep tending our temples as we gain an understanding of the myriad of benefits that can come to us from doing so. It can also help stave off boredom in our diets or exercise regimens, as we learn about new methods — and new recipes! Further, harking back to good old Pope Pius XII again, it can provide us with "new excitements" for study and work. It can and should be fun to learn more about these wonderful bodies God gave us — and what we can do to show Him our gratitude.

In chapter 17 we learned how good nutrition and bodily exercise can benefit our minds. In this appendix we will zoom in on good sources to "feed" our minds that will further inspire us to tend to our bodies properly. I have personally been absorbed in the "new excitements" of learning about nutrition and exercise in the last year or so, and I'm excited to share with you some of the very best books and videos I've consumed to feed both body and mind.

Many of these books are not exactly mainstream, though research findings and convinced adherents are rapidly on the rise. We should read them in the spirit of St. Thomas Aquinas, ferreting out truth wherever it might be found, while striving to separate carefully the wheat from the chaff; and the more we read and learn, the better equipped we will be to know the difference! I can't say that I agree with every statement in every one of these books, but I have found every one of them thought-provoking and useful, and I hope you might find the same for at least a few of them.

Oh, and some of these books were written by contributors to this book. I will identify those authors with an asterisk (*). You certainly need not read them all, but hopefully a title or two will speak to your special interests or needs and you will eat them up. I will group them by topics, pretty much in the order they are addressed in this book. *Bon appetit!*

Catholic Approaches to Health, Faith, and Fitness

*Peggy Bowes, *The Rosary Workout* (Bezalel Books, 2010).

Robert Feeney, *A Catholic Perspective: Physical Exercise and Sports* (Ignatius Press, 1995).

Melody Lyons, *The Sunshine Principle: A Radically Simple Guide to Natural Catholic Healing* (Intinction Press, 2019).

Bishop Thomas John Paprocki, *Running for a Higher Purpose: 8 Steps to Spiritual and Physical Fitness* (Ave Maria Press, 2021).

*Kevin Vost, Psy.D., *Fit for Eternal Life: A Christian Approach to Working Out, Eating Right, and Building the Virtues of Fitness in Your Soul* (Sophia Institute Press, 2007).

*Kevin Vost, Psy.D., Peggy Bowes, and Shane Kapler, *Tending the Temple: 365 Days of Spiritual and Physical Devotions* (Bezalel Books, 2011).

*Jared Zimmerer, *Ten Commandments of Lifting Weights* (Bezalel Books, 2012).

General Health

Ken Berry, M.D., *Lies My Doctor Told Me: Medical Myths That Can Harm Your Health* (Victory Belt Publishing, 2019).

Bret Scher, M.D., *Your Best Health Ever! The Cardiologist's Surprisingly Simple Guide to What Really Works* (Scher, 2017).

On UltraProcessed Foods (and Real Foods)

Robert Lustig, M.D., M.S.L., *Metabolical: The Lure and Lies of Processed Food, Nutrition, and Modern Medicine* (Harper Wave, 2021).

Michael Moss, *Salt Sugar Fat: How Giant Foods Hooked Us* (Random House, 2014) and *Hooked: How Processed Foods Became Addictive* (W. H. Allen, 2021).

Weston A. Price, D.D.S., *Nutrition and Physical Degeneration*, 8th ed. (1939; Price-Pottenger Nutrition Foundation, 2009).

The Obesity Epidemic

Jason Fung, M.D., *The Obesity Code: Unlocking the Secrets of Weight Loss* (Greystone, 2016).

Zoë Harcombe, Ph.D., *The Obesity Epidemic: What Causes It? How Can We Stop It?* (Columbus Publishing, 2010).

Gary Taubes, *Why We Get Fat: And What to Do about It* (Knopf, 2011).

The Insulin Resistance, Metabolic Syndrome, and Diabetes Pandemics

Benjamin Bikman, Ph.D., *Why We Get Sick: The Hidden Epidemic at the Root of Most Chronic Disease — And How to Fight It* (BenBella Books, 2020).

Jason Fung, M.D., *The Diabetes Code: Prevent and Reverse Type 2 Diabetes Naturally* (Greystone, 2018).

William Y. Shang, M.D., *The FIRST Program: Fighting Insulin Resistance with Strength Training* (Shang Publishing, 2021).

Low-Carbohydrate and Ketogenic Eating Rationales and Plans

Robert C. Atkins, M.D., *Dr. Atkins' New Diet Revolution* (M. Evans, 2002).

Ivor Cummins and Jeffry Gerber, M.D., *Eat Rich, Live Long: Use the Power of Low-Carb and Keto for Weight Loss and Great Health* (Victory Belt, 2018).

David Ludwig, M.D., Ph.D., *Always Hungry? Conquer Cravings, Retrain Your Fat Cells, and Lose Weight Permanently* (Grand Central Life & Style, 2016).

Jimmy Moore with Eric Westman, M.D., *Keto Clarity: Your Definitive Guide to the Benefits of a Low-Carb, High-Fat Diet* (Victory Belt, 2014).

Timothy Noakes, M.D., Jonno Proudfoot, and Sally-Ann Creed, *The Real Meal Revolution: The Radical, Sustainable Approach to Healthy Eating* (Robinson Books, 2015).

Gary Taubes, *The Case for Keto: Rethinking Weight Control and the Science and Practice of Low-Carb/High-Fat Eating* (Knopf, 2020) and *Good Calories, Bad Calories: Fats, Carbs, and the Controversial Science of Diet and Health* (Anchor Books, 2008).

Jeff S. Volek, Ph.D., R.D., and Stephen D. Phinney, M.D., Ph.D., *The Art and Science of Low Carbohydrate Living* (Beyond Obesity, 2011) and *The Art and Science of Low Carbohydrate Performance* (Beyond Obesity, 2012).

Eric Westman, M.D., Stephen D. Phinney, M.D., and Jeff S. Volek, Ph.D., *The New Atkins for a New You: The Ultimate Diet for Shedding Weight and Feeling Great* (Simon & Schuster, 2010).

Eric Westman, M.D. with Amy Berger, C.N.S, *End Your Carb Confusion: A Simple Guide to Customize Your Carb Intake for Optimal Health* (Victory Belt, 2021).

Sugar

Robert Lustig, M.D., M.S.L. *Fat Chance: Beating the Odds against Sugar, Processed Food, Obesity, and Disease* (Penguin Books, 2012).

Gary Taubes, *The Case against Sugar* (Anchor Books, 2017).

John Yudkin, Ph.D. *Pure, White, and Deadly: How Sugar Is Killing Us and What We Can Do to Stop It* (Penguin Books, 2013).

Modern Wheat

William Davis, M.D., *Wheat Belly (Revised and Expanded): Lose the Wheat, Lose the Weight, and Find Your Path Back to Health* (Rodale Books, 2019).

Fats and Cholesterol

Paul J. Rosch, M.D. FACP, ed., *Fat and Cholesterol Don't Cause Heart Attacks and Statins Are Not the Solution* (Columbus Publishing, 2016).

Nina Teicholz, *The Big Fat Surprise: Why Butter, Meat & Cheese Belong in a Healthy Diet* (Simon and Schuster, 2014).

The Nature and History of Ketones and Ketosis

Travis Christofferson, *Ketones, the Fourth Fuel: Warburg to Krebs to Veech — the 250 Year Journey to Find the Fountain of Youth* (Christofferson, 2020).

The Primacy of Protein

Michael Eades, M.D., and Mary Dan Eades, M.D., *Protein Power: The High-Protein/Low Carbohydrate Way to Lose Weight, Feel Fit, and Boost Your Health — In Just Weeks!* (Bantam Books, 1996).

Brooks D. Kubik, *Knife, Fork, Muscle* (Kubik, 2014).

Ted Naiman, M.D., and William Shewfelt, *The P:E Diet:Leverage Your Biology to Achieve Optimal Health* (Naiman, 2020).

David Raubenheimer, Ph.D., and Stephen J. Simpson, Ph.D., *Eat Like the Animals: What Nature Tells Us about the Science of Healthy Eating* (Mariner Books, 2020).

Meat

Shawn Baker, M.D., *The Carnivore Diet* (Victory Belt, 2019).

Diana Rodgers, R.D., and Robb Wolf, *Sacred Cow: The Case for (Better) Meat: Why Well-Raised Meat Is Good for You and Good for the Planet* (BenBella Books, 2020).

Paul Saladino, M.D., *The Carnivore Code: Unlocking the Secrets to Optimal Health by Returning to Our Ancestral Diet* (Fundamental Press, 2020).

Salt

James DiNicolantonio, Pharm.D., *The Salt Fix: Why the Experts Got It All Wrong — and How Eating More Might Save Your Life* (Harmony Books, 2017).

Fasting (and Feasting)

Jay W. Richards, Ph.D., *Eat Fast Feast: Heal Your Body While Feeding Your Soul — A Christian Guide to Fasting* (Harper One, 2020).

Basic Barbell Training

Mark Rippetoe with Stef Bradford, *Starting Strength: Basic Barbell Training*, 3rd ed. (Aasgard, 2017).

High-Intensity and Super-Slow Machine Training

Vincent "Ben" Bocchicchio, Ph.D., *15 Minutes to FITNESS. Dr. Ben's SMaRT Plan for Diet and Total Health* (Select Books, 2017).

Fredrick Hahn, Michael R. Eades, M.D., and Mary Dan Eades, M.D., *The Slow Burn Fitness Revolution: The Slow-Motion Exercise That Will Change Your Body in 30 Minutes a Week* (Broadway Books, 2003).

Doug McGuff, M.D., and John Little, *Body by Science: A Research-Based Program for Strength Training, Bodybuilding, and Complete Fitness in 12 Minutes a Week* (McGraw-Hill, 2009) and *The Body by Science Question and Answer Book* (Doug McGuff and Northern River Productions, 2009).

Adam Zickerman and Bill Schley, *The Power of 10: The Once-a-Week Slow Motion Fitness Revolution* (Quill, 2003).

The Biomechanical Approach to Muscle Development

Doug Brignole, *The Physics of Resistance Exercise: An Analysis and Application of Biomechanical Principles in Resistance Exercise* (Healthy Learning, 2021).

Kettlebell Training

*Pat Flynn, *Introduction to Kettlebells: A Minimalist's Guide to Blasting Fat and Boosting Muscle* (Pat Flynn, 2018).

How Nutrition Affects the Brain

Eric H. Kossoff, M.D., Zahava Turner, R.D., C.S.P., L.D.N, MacKenzie C. Cervenka, M.D., and Bobbie J. Barron, R.D., L.D.N., *Ketogenic Diet Therapies for Epilepsy and Other Conditions*, 7th ed. (Demos Health, 2021).

David Perlmutter, M.D., *Grain Brain: The Surprising Truth about Wheat, Carbs, and Sugar — Your Brain's Silent Killers* (Little, Brown Spark, 2013).

How Training the Body Benefits the Mind

Clarence Bass, *Take Charge: Fitness at the Edge of Science* (Ripped Enterprises, 2013).

John J. Ratey, M.D., with Eric Hagerman, *Spark: The Revolutionary New Science of Exercise and the Brain* (Little, Brown, 2008).

How the Mind Impacts Athletic Performance

*Gene Zannetti, M.S., M.A., *Develop the Predator Mindset: Win in Sports and Life* (Gene Zannetti, 2020).

Healthy Exercise and Nutrition for Children and Teens

Fredrick Hahn, *Strong Kids, Healthy Kids: The Revolutionary Program for Increasing Your Child's Fitness in 30 Minutes a Week* (New York: AMACOM Books, 2008).

Tim Noakes, M.D., Jonno Proudfoot, and Bridget Surtees, *Super Food for Superchildren: Delicious, Low-Sugar Recipes for Healthy, Happy Meals, From Toddlers to Teens* (Constable & Robinson, 2016).

Tending the Feminine Temple

Roger Schwab, *Strength of a Woman: The Truth about Training the Female Body* (Main Line Publications, 1997).

Keeping Aging Temples Strong

Chad Cox, Ph.D., ed., *Clinical Nutrition and Aging: Sarcopenia and Muscle Metabolism* (Apple Academic Press, 2021).

Brooks D. Kubik, *Gray Hair and Black Iron: Secrets of Successful Strength Training for Older Lifters* (Kubik, 2009).

Jonathan Sullivan, M.D., and Andy Baker, *The Barbell Prescription: Strength Training for Life after 40* (Aasgard, 2016).

Videos, Websites, and More

Websites that post videos of interviews and lectures from many of the authors cited above (along with dozens or hundreds of other health professionals) on popular social media sites include these:

- https://lowcarbdownunder.com.au/
- www.lowcarbusa.org
- www.dietdoctor.com

Several of the doctors and nutrition scientists cited in the books above also have their own websites and videos with vast amounts of information. They include Shawn Baker, Ken Berry, Jason Fung, and Eric Westman. They can easily be found on the Internet. An excellent documentary that includes many of these prominent researchers and clinicians is called *Fat Fiction* (see https://fatfiction.movie/). I'll note as well, regarding the ketogenic diet for children with epilepsy, that it was the subject of the 1997 made-for-TV movie *First Do No Harm*, starring Meryl Streep.

The most prominent exponents of strength training, including Mr. Universe Doug Brignole, Doug McGuff, powerlifting champion Mark Rippetoe, and Jonathan Sullivan, can also easily be found online at their own websites and on various sites that show videos. Doug Brignole's complete training certification programs can be found at https:// smarttraining365.com/.

Hopefully I served up a hearty enough menu to keep your minds satisfied for a while. And remember, we are *not* counting calories!

Appendix 3

Temple-Tender Tales

HIGH AND LOW NOTES OF A MUSICAL COMEDIAN'S WEIGHT-LOSS JOURNEY

For as long as I could remember, I had struggled with my weight. Eating properly and exercising were often pushed aside as I pursued balancing my work, my home life, and my evolving national ministry. Things came to a head when, on an eventful Valentine's Day, my wife (then pregnant) took photos of me across the dinner table from her, and looking at them, I felt repulsed. I had let my bad habits get out of control.

A change was needed.

I knew for this change to stick, it had to be linked to my love of God. For far too often, I had heard professional faith speakers mock those who hawked exercise programs, as if desiring a healthy body was akin to idolatry and was somehow in conflict with pursuing God. Instead, I strove to come up with a mindset that united the two.

After much thought, I came up with this mindset: if God were to use me on earth, I needed to be alive and healthy, first and foremost. There is no way I could be used employing my particular talents if I were too sick and immobile to do so; considering what I had looked like at the time, this was not a distant possibility. Furthermore, being a public entertainer invites instant judgment. Past appearances on television invited incendiary anonymous comments directed at me on various blogs. Being visibly unhealthy had worked against my evangelical witness. Lastly, I was about to become a father, and I needed to live in such a manner that would increase the likelihood that I would be there for my children as they grew up.

For starters, I had to get my diet in order. I had definitely tried many approaches and fads to accomplish the weight loss, from Weight Watchers, to Rocco DiSpirito's Negative Calorie Diet (recipes using low-calorie/nutrient-dense whole foods), to where I am at today: keto, plus intermittent fasting once a week (twice during Lent). Each time I tried a different approach, I had learned something about myself along the way. The key is to keep trying different approaches until you find the diet you can live with.

Secondly, I needed to focus on exercise. I found that my lunch hour was a great way to sneak in exercise without interfering with my routine. The neighborhood my office resides in has many walkways, and if I hustle, I can make it to a nearby beach and back, during my lunch hour. Furthermore, I learned how to use some workout machines (treadmills and rowing machines) while listening to music and reading books on my Kindle, providing myself with the maximum amount of diversion while exerting myself. For instance, I would focus on listening to a specific musical artist while reading a biography of that artist — a truly immersive experience.

Once I got into the rhythm of diet, exercise, and fasting, the pounds melted off. One year, my company offered a weight-loss competition, which spurred me to even greater motivation. Imagine my surprise when, after the end of the thirteen weeks, I had lost the greatest percentage of weight in my category: roughly forty pounds. It was thrilling!

I'm not perfect. There have been times when I lost sight of my goal and the weight began creeping up again. That said, one of my goals in the next few years is to learn to incorporate more strength training into my regimen. I have never returned to my heaviest weight, and my children have only photos to see how obese I once was. Best of all, my self-discipline has seeped into my faith-walk as well, allowing me to love God sacrificially in specific areas in my life (and conversely, celebrate extravagantly in other areas).

Nick Alexander is a computer programmer, a public speaker, a worship leader, and a musical comedian in the vein of "Weird Al" Yankovic. He has performed at World Youth Day and at national youth conferences and has appeared on EWTN, CatholicTV, and The Dr. Demento Show. He is married and is the dad of two teenagers. His website is www.nickalexander.com, and his motivational parody, "Salad Bowl," is available on most streaming sites.

AUTHORS ENJOY ABUNDANT LIFE AFTER DEARTH OF CARBOHYDRATES

When I look at photos from five or more years ago, one thing really jumps out. It's what I now know to be our "carb face." Both Art and I have it in those older photos: big, overstuffed cheeks, no sign of underlying cheek bones. We look very well fed. Disguised by our clothing were our chubby tummies. I thought the bloated belly was something inevitable, due to age — or, in my case, menopause.

It was a shock to both of us, as we dropped weight after dropping carbs, that we also lost our belly fat, something that never decreased on any other diet. And neither of us was "fat" really. We were both active. I trained for and ran a marathon with about ten extra stubborn pounds. I used to joke that I was probably the only person in the world who *gained* weight while training for a marathon. Now I realize that it was the entirely unnecessary addition of "Gu," or highly concentrated carbs, that I was constantly using for energy during long runs, plus the famed traditional "carb loading" prior to a big race. I now do all my runs with no additions other than water and electrolytes with no sugar. It took a while to switch over from running on glucose to running on fat stores. During that time before I was "fat adapted," running felt like moving through quicksand, but eventually my body adapted.

Art had been sidelined from running due to arthritis. He switched to riding a stationary bike at the gym and walking. Nonetheless, even his arthritis pain dramatically improved on a low-carb diet, which dramatically reduces inflammation all around. He still needed knee-replacement surgery because the damage had already been done. But his orthopedic surgeon was shocked that, prior to his surgery, when X-rays showed that his knees were bone on bone, he was able to walk five miles without pain! Art credits this to the anti-inflammatory nature of the low-carb diet.

I used to run three to four miles every day and ice my knees after every run longer than six miles. I now know that the extra ten or fifteen pounds I used to carry on my body made long runs so difficult. I now have increased my mileage to an average of seven miles per run, with a total of about thirty miles per week, running and walking together with Art without icing my knees afterward.

Art has lost approximately thirty pounds (he is six foot two), and I have lost ten or fifteen pounds (I am five foot one). More dramatic for me than the weight loss is the fact that I went from a size 6 or 8 to a size 2. And the horrid muffin top that always spilled out over my pants — ladies, you know what I am talking about! — is completely gone. Our blood glucose is excellent. All of our blood work is excellent, with the exception of cholesterol, which went up on the keto diet. We are in the process of trying to decrease the amount of dairy we use (we love whipping cream in our coffee!) as a way to decrease the cholesterol numbers. My theory is that doctors will eventually discover that cholesterol is a more complex situation than can be handled on a case-by-case basis, rather than just looking at the numbers and prescribing a statin. In fact, some recent studies have shown that higher cholesterol is protective in older women. Hedging our bets, we gave up drinking whipping cream in every cup of coffee and now use it only on Sundays. If I could go back to the cream every day without alarming my doctor, I would.

Even though Art loves pizza, pasta, and bread, the low-carb diet has eliminated the cravings he used to experience. Before, he would eat a tortilla and cheese for breakfast and be starving an hour later. I used to love oatmeal and granola, but again, an entire bowl with nuts and raisins wasn't as satiating as eating a single egg. Because we now feel satiated after eating, we rarely crave those other things as much. A diet for me used to be lots of salads, very little protein, and rarely red meat. I had assumed that red meat was the culprit in all cardiovascular disease, but I now realize that the situation is probably more nuanced. Most of the studies were based on self-reports and may not have differentiated between those people who ate a highly processed food diet along with red meat, like a cheeseburger and fries from McDonald's every day for lunch, and those who ate sustainably farmed red meat without the addition of processed seed oils and fast foods. We now eat local farm-raised beef and chicken, as well as fish, preferably wild-caught. We eat fewer meals because we aren't constantly starving due to lack of protein, and we use whatever is in our fridge, as opposed to buying inordinate amounts of greens, fruits, and veggies and then tossing them when they go bad. We have been following this low-carb diet now for nearly four years. Our diet in the past had not been outrageously poor; we rarely ate at restaurants or indulged in fast foods. We would have called our former diet a "Mediterranean" diet, with pasta, olive oil, vegetables, fish, and chicken, but higher on the carb side.

Now we occasionally splurge and eat pizza or drink beer or have cake at a party. We are not rigid with this diet; I am nearly incapable of passing up a burger with fries! But we have found that, as long as we immediately resume the low-carb way of eating, we seem to be able to maintain our weights.

Another point that is less objective than weight loss is a greater sense of calmness with this diet that includes healthy fats, protein, and very few carbohydrates other than certain vegetables. We credit the lack of blood-sugar spikes that likely occurred on a regular basis when we were eating mostly carbohydrates.

Current diet: We eat a diet high in healthy fats, which, for us, means olive oil, butter, and the fats that come from nuts, avocados, red meat, and salmon and cod. We eat protein daily, alternating among fish, chicken, eggs, cheese, and red meat. We eat salads daily and veggies such as cauliflower, cooked cabbage, and asparagus. I use carrots and celery in soups and bone broth. We eat fruit: tomatoes, avocados, and berries — and peaches from the farmers' market in the summer. We use intermittent fasting but are not zealous about it; generally, we eat one big meal and snack on nuts, such as macadamias, brazil nuts, or walnuts (though we try to keep this sort of snacking to a minimum); an egg or some cheese; or homemade bone broth.

We feel stronger, fitter, lighter, and capable of much longer endurance activities than previously. I even started playing tennis at age sixty-six. I hadn't played since I was in high school! And we are hiking the Camino de Santiago in 2022 with all our energy.

Laraine (and Art) Bennett *are prolific book authors, with many excellent titles, from their bestselling* The Temperament God Gave You *(Sophia Institute Press, 2005) to Laraine's latest book,* A Little Way of Living with Less: Learning to Let Go with the Little Flower *(Sophia Institute Press, 2022).*

FORMER CIRCUS PERFORMER DISCOVERS REAL FOODS AS GOD MADE THEM

At age fifty-five, I still haven't decided what I want to be when I grow up. I've been a circus performer, Air Force pilot, aerobics instructor, personal trainer, small-business owner, full-time RVing homeschool mom, Catholic author, waitress, and travel nurse in the operating room — in that order. I love being active, and I'm not afraid of change. That's important because just over a year ago, I discovered that nearly everything I had learned about nutrition was a lie.

During the initial Covid-19 lockdown, I was unemployed due to the cancellation of elective surgeries nationwide. At the recommendation of my son, I read a book called *Deep Nutrition* by Dr. Catherine Shanahan. Skeptical at first, I researched her claims and was shocked to discover that one of the primary causes of our current health problems is vegetable and seed oils. These harmful oils are in nearly everything! Packaged foods, salad dressing, mayonnaise, restaurant meals ... I started making my own salad dressing and using butter, olive oil, and avocado oils when cooking or baking.

A second startling revelation from "Dr. Cate" is the importance of eating organ meats and meat on the bone. I vividly remember my delight in tearing a drumstick off a freshly roasted free-range chicken and biting into the buttery skin and juicy, tender meat. All those years of eating bland, boring, boneless, skinless chicken breasts would now be in my past. Hallelujah!

"Every moving thing that lives shall be food for you; and as I gave you the green plants, I give you everything" (Gen. 9:3–4).

Other changes I've made to my eating habits as a result of this newfound knowledge are eliminating snacking and thereby drastically reducing carbohydrates and sugars. I eat a modified keto diet most days, drinking raw milk, eating tons of vegetables with very little fruit, and intermittently fasting. I now buy more food at the local farmers' market than at the supermarket. When dining out, I try to patronize local-farm-to-table restaurants and request that my food be cooked in olive oil or butter. My husband and I started raising chickens and planted a garden to grow vegetables.

The results of these changes have been nothing short of life changing. I can outwork twenty-somethings and run the hospital stairs on my breaks, and the pesky post-menopause pounds literally melted off my body. Food has never tasted more delicious! More importantly, my body has become a fat-burning machine.

My spiritual life has benefited as well. I offer up my fasts for various intercessions and find that the mind-clearing effect deepens my prayer routine. I believe that God has shown me the importance of eating the food He has provided from the earth, and I am grateful for the blessings this revelation has brought to my life and the lives of my family.

"Do not labor for the food which perishes, but for the food which endures to eternal life, which the Son of man will give to you; for on him has God the Father set his seal" (John 6:27).

Peggy Bowes is a wife, mother, nurse, author of The Rosary Workout *and co-author of* Tending the Temple.

"This Is My Body" Says Christ — and His Priest

I am thirty-seven years old and a native of Brooklyn, New York. In 2001, at the discerning age of sixteen, I converted to the Catholic Faith after discovering the mystery of the Real Presence of Christ in the Eucharist. I enlisted in the navy after high school, at the age of seventeen. As an enlisted sailor in the navy, I served as information systems technician for nine years in various assignments overseas before entering the seminary to become a Catholic priest. I was ordained a priest for the Diocese of Brooklyn in 2016 and was commissioned an active-duty navy chaplain in 2019. Currently I am assigned to the chapel at Naval Station Rota, Spain, attending the spiritual and emotional needs of more than five thousand service members and their families.

My occupation requires a certain level of physical fitness. Navy chaplains are military officers; therefore, they are held to the same physical fitness standard as any other navy officer. Twice a year, navy personnel are given a physical fitness assessment, including a body composition assessment (BCA) and a physical fitness test (PRT). The BCA involves evaluating your height and weight according to the preferred body mass index for your age group. The PRT measures the strength of your upper body, core, and cardiovascular health by having you complete a certain number of push-ups in two minutes, hold your body in a plank position for a period of time, and completing a 1.5-mile run or 500-yard swim in a certain amount of time based on your age. To pass the navy physical fitness assessment, you must pass both the BCA and the PRT; the failure of either will result in a negative mark on your evaluation record and in your placement in a mandatory remedial program to get you back into shape.

In my nineteen years of naval service, I never failed my fitness assessment, but I have come close. My wake-up call occurred during the COVID pandemic. I was stationed onboard the USS *Theodore Roosevelt* in 2020, and when I returned home from the deployment, I noticed I had gained more than thirty pounds. I felt sluggish every day after work, and my blood pressure was at hypertension levels. My doctors were ready to put me on medication.

Things began to change when I changed my eating habits and my lifestyle. I realized I was consuming more calories than I was burning, due to lack of physical activity. Many gyms were closed, so I was not working out regularly. I needed to reduce my calorie intake. Instead of eating three large meals, I began to have six small meals over the course of the day. The meals included lean protein and green vegetables adding up to 1,500 calories a day. At first, I was worried I would get hungry and not have any energy, but with the help of protein bars and drinking at least half a gallon of water a day, I had enough energy throughout the day and didn't get any headaches. Eating smaller meals taught me to slow down when I eat and really enjoy my food instead of rushing through it to get to the next activity. In addition to my diet, I incorporated some strength training and cardio to my daily routine. My favorite cardio exercise is cycling. I enrolled in a local spin class; I enjoy it because it makes exercise feel like dancing. After six weeks of eating smaller portions of lean protein and green vegetables, I lost thirty pounds and my blood pressure returned to normal.

I believe my physical fitness is strongly related to my spiritual fitness. When I made physical fitness a priority in my life, I discovered that the virtues of temperance, justice, and prudence apply not only to the moral life but also to what we do with and put into our bodies. Many times, I needed to exercise the virtue of temperance and prudence to eat a few almonds instead of eating a bag of potato chips. I have even had to pray for the grace to overcome the temptation of eating the wrong thing at the wrong time. Knowing what is right for my body has given me power to exercise the virtue of justice — to eat what I ought to eat instead of what I want. Making healthy habits a lifestyle, eating healthy, exercising, and getting proper sleep has enriched my spiritual health. I don't find myself falling asleep during my Holy Hour or when it's time for me to pray the Liturgy of the Hours. I noticed I am more alert and attentive to the needs of others when I serve them as a priest and a chaplain. Moreover, I feel more united to Christ in the Holy Sacrifice of the Mass.

If you are baptized, no matter what your vocation is — if you're a parent, a military officer, or a priest — your body is a temple of the Holy Spirit, where God Himself dwells. In the Holy Sacrifice of the Mass, the priest unites himself with the People of God to Christ, the one High Priest, as a living sacrifice to God the Father. When the priest speaks *in persona Christi* the words of consecration: "This is my Body," it is not only Christ who is speaking but the priest also. At every Mass, I am reminded that I am called to offer my own body as an offering to God. It is only right and just that I give God my best, which is a healthy body, mind, and soul. We are all reminded to give God our best when the priest says, "Pray, brothers and sisters, that my sacrifice and yours [*meum ac vestrum sacrificium*] may be acceptable to God the Almighty Father." No matter our vocation, we each share in a unique way in the one sacrifice of Jesus Christ. This sacrifice does not end when we walk out the doors of the church. It continues, when we say a prayer of thanksgiving for that tiny protein bar we had for a meal. Or when a puddle of my sweat gathers in the gym after a high-intensity spin class. Our whole life is shaped by Christ, who offered His entire body to God the Father as a living sacrifice. It was the Eucharist, the Holy Sacrifice of the Mass, that inspired me to become Roman Catholic, a priest, and a navy chaplain, and it is the Eucharist that encourages me to be a healthy one.

Father Mark C. Bristol is a lieutenant in the United States Navy Chaplain Corps.

THE PRO-LIFE SCIENTIST WHO RUNS FOR CHRIST!

We are what we eat (see John 6). LIFE Runners, an organization whose members run in more than two thousand cities in more than forty nations, delivers to the world this message on its jerseys: "Remember the Unborn." The root of "discipleship" is "discipline." Distance running requires great discipline to follow a training schedule that is difficult. As the LIFE Runners creed states, "We run to build endurance, for the race is long and we must keep our eyes fixed on You, Lord." Tough training miles afford for powerful prayers. Our creed continues, "We run as a prayer, to defend children in the womb, so they may be born and united with our Christian community."

As for nutrition, as an Air Force Academy cadet, I took a class on physical fitness methods. Based on how the body works, I learned the value of a balanced diet and the importance of how much to eat and when to eat. I began to eat what my body needs rather than what I want to eat. Dairy causes me bloating and acid reflux, so I use coconut milk. I also drink a full glass of water before each meal. As the guide said on the way up Mount Kilimanjaro, water is life. (We put a "Remember the Unborn" flag on top of Mount Kilimanjaro on July 13, 2021, for the least of our brothers and sisters [see Matt. 25:40]). The full glass of water before each meal is a simple way to lose weight — to stay at your "fit to fight the good fight" weight, your "tending the temple" weight.

As for my health and exercise routine, I run six days per week: four easy days, one speed day, one long day, and one day off. I do stretching and strengthening four days per week: pull-ups, push-ups, sit-ups. I eat right, as described above, and get enough rest. Staying free of injury is based on smart training methods such as the following: Don't increase intensity or distance more than 10 percent per week. Don't take more than two days off in a row. Something is better than nothing for a workout. Don't skip out of stretching and strengthening. It's best to do exercise first thing in the morning. Make it a priority.

Mind, body, and soul are all connected. All areas influence the other areas. All areas need exercise to remain strong and ready to serve God. While running, I have some of my most creative thoughts. I often race home to write them down.

Exercise affords redemptive suffering for an end to abortion. My opening prayer is "Lord, please help me run as fast or as slow as You need me to today." I always pray the LIFE Runners Creed, which you can find at liferunners.org/creed. I finish with a prayer of gratitude, thanking God for everything. I am thankful that God gave us bodies to worship Him and love one another (see Heb. 12:1–2).

Pat Castle has a Ph.D. in nano-analytical chemistry, was a lieutenant colonel and professor in the U.S. Air Force, and is a board member at the Institute for Theological Encounter with Science and Technology. Pat, now age fifty, works as a full-time pro-life missionary and is the editor of LIFE Runners Daily Devotions: All in Christ for Pro-Life! *(En Route Books and Media, 2021). Learn more at liferunners.org/leaders.*

THE FAMILY THAT BENCH-PRESSES TOGETHER STAYS TOGETHER

I grew up in 1980s America. Sylvester Stallone and Arnold Schwarzenegger were my heroes. But if I were to tell anyone that when I was growing up, they might have laughed because I was physically the opposite of those two muscular men.

In first grade, I was the smallest child in my class, by far. In fact, most of the girls in my class could lift me off the ground (which, if I remember correctly, they seemed to do a lot). When I was fifteen, I was five feet tall and weighed 117 pounds. It was then that I started to lift weights.

Over the years, I have written down my physical goals for various programs. I remember that my first goal was to gain four pounds in six weeks. All I had to work out with was a set of plastic-coated cement weights from K-Mart. I think I had 110 pounds of weights, which was plenty for me, because I could bench press only 60 pounds. But there was another problem: I couldn't afford a weight bench. My first "weight bench" was an old wooden chair. I guess it worked well enough. I remember advancing to the point at which I could bench press 90 pounds, and I was so happy with that progress.

After saving my money for a few months, I finally bought a Weider weight bench. To this day, I don't think I've ever been happier with a purchase. Finally, I felt like an honest-to-goodness weightlifter! I converted a little room in my basement to my official workout room, complete with posters of Stallone and Schwarzenegger. And every day after my homeschooling, I would work out with weights for about an hour.

Though I was too young to express it this way at the time, weightlifting was my solace and refuge. It was very hard for me to be the smallest kid on the football field with the neighborhood kids. Needless to say, when team members were chosen, I was picked last every time. But when I lifted weights, I was competing only with myself. No one was looking (except for Stallone), and I realized that I could make myself stronger and more muscular. The psychological benefits were tremendous, although again, I had no way of knowing this at the time.

By the time I started college at age seventeen, I had grown to nearly six feet in height and had gained about fifty lean pounds. During college, I lifted weights only during the summer, but it certainly helped shape me, literally, as a teenager.

In the ensuing years, until I was about thirty-five, I lifted weights only off and on. Around that age, I weighed 243 pounds, drank six or seven Cokes a day, and ate at McDonald's almost every day at lunch. One night, I climbed the stairs and noticed that I was out of breath. I realized that I had to change my ways. I quit eating at McDonald's and started eating healthy food. I began doing cardio — a lot of cardio. My cardio regimen was walking. Every day for weeks, I watched a movie and walked on a treadmill for two hours. Three months later, I weighed 193. I lost 50 pounds in ninety days.

I stayed on a weight regimen for several years following that, but I dropped off, and in my early forties, I again weighed about 240. This time, my heart rate was an issue. My blood pressure was 143/98. I realized again that I had to change — and change my entire approach this time. Within the next two years, I lost about 30 pounds and got my blood pressure down to 118/72.

In 2020, when COVID hit the scene, the gyms closed. I frantically tried to find home gym equipment so I could work out in my basement. Other people were trying to hoard toilet paper; I wanted weights! In July of that year, my family moved to Florida, which was much more "open" than the other states, so I immediately joined a gym. Happily, it's the best gym I've ever belonged to. Now, at fifty years old, I'm setting new gains. In December 2021, I weigh 195 and am probably in the best shape of my life relative to my age. In fact, I feel better — and, in many ways, *younger* — than I did twenty years ago.

As a weightlifter who is mostly concerned with muscle mass, as opposed to simply being trim and fit, I opt for proteins. I eat beef at least five times a week, eggs nearly every day, and bacon at least three times a week. I eat chicken and turkey quite a bit. I don't ever eat gluten. Four of my daughters are allergic to or intolerant of gluten, so even though I don't have a gluten problem, I simply adopted their diet. A turkey "sandwich" for me means no bread, except for occasional gluten-free bread.

I have protein shakes with Fairlife milk quite a bit. In fact, I rarely drink any other milk these days. I also try to eat fruits and vegetables every day. In Florida, I can pick my own oranges. I try to eat plenty of blueberries. I limit my carbs, but I do eat oatmeal and even low-sugar oatmeal cookies. I very rarely eat desserts.

I have come to realize that different foods have different effects on people. My wife and I work out together, but certain foods have a different impact on her. I doubt most people find a workout benefit to cinnamon, but I do. For whatever reason, cinnamon before a workout makes me stronger.

If people are looking to get in shape, they should keep records. Most people keep records of repairs and maintenance on their cars but not on their bodies. That's a shame, because if they did, they would learn a lot. On my phone, I keep a record of my workouts, weight, and daily food intake. When you keep such records, you learn plenty about your body! For instance, I have found the foods and workout regimen that complement each other to achieve my goals.

Going forward, my goal over the coming year is to incorporate fish into my diet. I'm aware of the health benefits, and frankly, I like the idea of eating the same diet as Jesus and the apostles. Living in Florida, I'm surrounded by bodies of water, so it's time to make fish a protein-rich staple of nutrition.

My goal is to work out with weights six days a week. I rarely work out fewer than four times a week. Typically, my workouts run an hour. I have done ninety-minute workouts for weeks at a time, but I think it takes too great a toll. At some point, training becomes overtraining.

I change my workouts pretty regularly. Sometimes, I work on my chest, triceps, and shoulders on day 1 and my back, biceps, and legs on day 2. But over the past year or two, I have gone to one body part per day. That is, on bicep day for instance, I do thirty sets of biceps: barbell curls, dumbbell curls, preacher curls, cable curls, 1/9 curls (which is an 18-rep set that changes position nine times during the set), and so forth. For chest day, I do decline presses, dips, incline presses, cable crossovers, and so forth. I change the sets regularly.

At my age, I have also begun stretching before weightlifting. I probably should have been stretching my whole life, but at fifty, it's no longer optional. So before I even pick up a dumbbell, I've already stretched that body part. I have my chiropractor to thank for that. She was getting my shoulder back in alignment one day and asked, "Do you ever stretch?" I told her I didn't, and she responded, "No kidding!"

Another important part of the process is recovery. When you lift weights, your muscles undergo trauma, and they need to recover. Thirty sets for biceps is brutal, but I know that I'm not going to work them out again for about seven days.

I am also blessed that my gym has several water massage chairs, and I try to get in a ten-minute massage after every workout. After a really intense workout, I also try to spend time in my hot tub for twenty minutes.

I know that some people reading this might think that this sounds expensive: beef, protein shakes, gym memberships, and hot tubs. And you can throw in athletic footwear and gym clothes. Yes, I guess this can all be expensive. But you know what's really expensive in America? Health care. When you spend money on your gym membership and a new pair of Asics, you are really spending money on your heart and lungs. By any rational standard, you should be *searching* for ways to spend money on your workout regimen. If a new workout outfit gets you in the gym more often, please go buy it!

My cousin is a former powerlifting champion. She says that your mood and mentality on the way home from the gym are much different from on the way *to* the gym. I agree. After a really stressful day, I go the gym and work it all out. I'll sometimes tell my wife, Lisa, "I need to lift heavy today."

There is a certain amount of self-confidence that we all need. I have found that weightlifting is a source of that confidence. But being in shape puts me in a better mood, and I'm sure that numerous studies confirm that fact.

The body is a temple of the Holy Spirit. We have a moral duty to care for our bodies. That fact should both inspire and challenge us as Christians. We humans are a body-soul-mind composite. I would guess that any competitive athlete considers that fact to be intuitive. I remember Arnold Schwarzenegger writing that "the mind always fails before the body." Whichever fails first, there is clearly a relation between the two.

Saint Paul's athletic imagery is no accident. The athlete must make his body conform to his mind and soul. The body often wants to quit, and so we force it to go further. Many of the temptations in life are material (sloth, gluttony, lust). But weightlifting tells the body that the mind and soul are in charge. The body wants comfort, but the soul makes the body conform. Weightlifting is warfare against concupiscence. I think prayer is the difference between perseverance and giving up. It might sound funny, but I say a little prayer before I step on the scale every morning. If the body is a temple of the Holy Spirit, I want to make that temple strong.

One other point I'd like to make is that weightlifting is something that can be done as a family. Once my children turn sixteen, I automatically buy them a gym membership. In fact, my son Athanasius had a gym membership at twelve. When we go to the gym, Lisa and I usually take several of our children. Four of us walked into the gym one day, and someone asked, "Where are the rest of you?"

It seems to have paid off. Two of my daughters are now on athletic scholarships: one for swimming and another for basketball. One of our daughters can leg-press well over five hundred pounds. As it turns out, the family that bench-presses together stays together.

John Francis Clark is a full-time writer: a writer of homeschool courses, a speechwriter, a blogger, a columnist, and foremost, a Catholic apologist.

A Time for Every Activity
under Heaven

"I have never seen anyone with more natural athletic ability." I heard my high school tennis coach utter these words about me at our sports' awards ceremony. I had gone to state and played tennis on the national circuit, broken numerous track records, and started varsity basketball my freshman year, but my sports career had ended due to a torn ACL (anterior cruciate ligament). Those kind words cut deeply, and I could not hold back the tears! I would continue to enjoy sports at a less competitive level, but my racket was a painful reminder of what might have been, and so it was put away.

About thirty years passed, and I stood in front of a mirror at Tae Kwon Do with my husband and five of our eight children. I did not look like the athlete I once was. It was time to get in shape! The year was 2017, and my chiropractor, Dr. John Sullivan, gave me the method that would help me achieve and maintain a healthy weight and virtue through intermittent fasting (IF).

So, after losing weight and tearing my other ACL, I underwent double knee reconstruction; thankfully it was successfully achieved just before the COVID quarantine. I earned my black belt at age fifty, and the tennis racket came back out of the closet. I thought of Gandalf's words: "Your fingers would remember their old strength better if they grasped your sword." Since then I've been back out on the court with my husband and kids — it's good to do recreational activities with family, when possible — and I am now coaching high school tennis. I love sharing my favorite sport with others!

I felt God had helped me avoid placing sports as an idol. When we were expecting our first child, my husband and I started taking golf lessons together, and the instructor said to me, "In less than two years, I can get you into the LPGA as a professional golfer." It would be my last chance at a sports career, and I didn't even flinch. In giving top priority to doing God's will and attending first to my vocation as wife and mother, God has given me back more than I could have ever achieved if I had chosen another route in an attempt to gain fame.

That being my background, it wasn't a loss to have strength and agility in raising eight children! I had no time for the gym during those early days, but I knew that being active with our children and trying to teach them and care for them was where I was supposed to be. My faith and understanding grew along with my efforts to homeschool.

An amazing thing happened when our eighth child was born: the short version is that the midwife said she was going to have to take me to the hospital if the baby didn't appear with the next push. In one of those grace-filled, adrenaline-rush moments, I exerted strength that was truly beyond me, and Andrew John Paul Matthias was born. My instant muscle growth was crazy (and painful for a while). When I finally lost weight, I was pleasantly surprised at the serious muscle tone still evident from that moment.

God gives strength when needed; in our weakness, He is strong. The strength was much needed when that baby turned three because I was carrying his older sister through airports and hospitals, trying to find a way to save her from the chronic illness that threatened her life. That was over eight years ago, and she is doing much better. But that leg of our journey required physical, mental, and spiritual strength. During the most challenging of times, I began reading the *Summa Theologica* to occupy my mind. What happened is that it occupied my heart and strengthened my faith as well. I began attending daily Mass. Around the same time we started Tae Kwon Do, the Angelic Doctor also inspired me to strengthen "my temple."

I was once asked by a priest to write an essay about having balance in life. I went to Adoration and lay prostrate in a cruciform pose before our Lord and asked, "So, about balance?" I felt Him answer in that moment, "This [total gift of self] is how I did it."

Cheryl Drozda, O.P., has been married to Jeff Drozda, O.P., for more than twenty-eight years, and they have eight children. They reside in Lafayette, Louisiana, but Cheryl considers herself a Buckeye that bleeds Hoosier (having been born and raised in Ohio and having lived a decade in Indiana). She continues to do IF, coaches high school tennis at John Paul the Great Academy, plays tennis on a team at Oakbourne (neighborhood club), and works out in her garage/gym. She is a lay Dominican, loves to read and meet with her Well-Read Moms group, and teaches high school to homeschoolers at a Catholic Schoolhouse co-op.

FROM EXISTENTIAL DREAD TO GRATITUDE TO GOD

They say philosophy starts in wonder. For me, it started in existential dread, which, as it happens, is how my fitness journey began as well.

Growing up, I was never athletic, and most of my activity consisted in sitting, resting, and playing video games. And with no nutritional boundaries in place, these conditions quickly caused me to become overweight. I was, to put it one way, a slob.

In late middle school, while hanging around with some of my band buddies, we challenged each other (all guys) to a "wet T-shirt contest." Unfortunately, I won. And though I laughed, pretending to enjoy my "victory," it was deeply embarrassing. I didn't know how I would escape my woes. I only knew that something — anything — had to be done. So I walked into the kitchen and peeled and ate an orange. My fitness journey had begun.

I knew I had to get started exercising as well. Lifting weights, however, was a definite no-go. My athletic friends occupied the high school weight room, and I already knew I would generate nothing but mockery walking in there — not something I wanted to deal with. So I began by working out at home, dusting off fitness tapes from the basement and drinking my mom's never-ending supply of Slim Fast. Incredibly, things started to change, and my confidence grew. I was looking trimmer, even without having any well-thought-out plan. At some point, my mother, a lifelong diet hopper, noticed a change and asked what I had been doing. "Well, I'm basically just doing all the stuff *you* bought."

My biggest change came after venturing into a martial arts studio, which started as something unserious. I was driving around with a friend, bored, just looking for something to do, when we passed by a roadside advertisement for a free Tae Kwon Do lesson. That seemed as entertaining as anything, so we walked in.

I loved it. Finally, I had found a sport I enjoyed playing and that allowed me to form a competitive spirit. I had also discovered an inspiring, intelligent coach — a man who taught me important things about eating and lifting and life. Master Scott was his name.

By the time I went to college, I was seriously into martial arts and lifting weights. I went from being an insipid, fat person to earning money as a personal trainer to pay for room and board. Eventually, my Tae Kwon Do coach in college — Master Som — introduced me to a new training tool: kettlebells. Their versatility and efficiency so impressed me that I decided to get certified in them, becoming the youngest person (at the time) to pass the Russian Kettlebell Challenge. It was around that time that I began blogging, including about my fitness routines, and that eventually picked up enough steam to land me my first book deal: *Paleo Workouts for Dummies.*

Looking back, this journey of mine still seems as much fantasy as reality. Had you told my middle school self that I would sooner or later publish books on strength training and nutrition, I don't know what I would have done. Probably I would have gone to sleep with a petrified diaphragm from all the laughing. But here I am.

My nutrition is simple: eat foods that are minimally processed (close to nature), consume adequate protein and plenty of vegetables, and fast. If we're using labels, my diet would probably be closest to the Mediterranean or Paleo style of eating. I also take advantage of regular meal replacement shakes — which is just to say protein mixed with berries and healthy fat. I find strategically timed protein shakes go a long way toward blunting hunger, helping me hit my daily protein target, and adequately fueling performance in the gym. They are a seriously useful nutritional tool. I also engage in an extended fast two or three times a week, where I may not have my first meal until around lunchtime. On Fridays, my family abstains from meat.

Lately, my exercise routine has consisted of traditional strength and conditioning routines, three to four times per week, typically done in the form of a circuit, and using mostly barbells, kettlebells, and dumbbells. My strategy is to assemble big, multi-joint lifts (presses, squats, kettlebell swings, etc.) and then work them anywhere between six and twelve reps, for three or four sets, using a relatively high intensity. Performing these exercises in a circuit — that is, back-to-back, with little or no rest between — induces an awesome cardiovascular challenge.

Otherwise, I'm practicing Brazilian jiu-jitsu two or three times per week, which is, for me, the perfect cardio/mobility supplement to the traditional strength training. Oh, and I'm a big fan of extended brisk walking as well: not just for exercise, but as one of my favorite ways to spend time with my wife and children.

Regular exercise has done wonders for my mental health, especially with respect to sleep quality, anxiety, focus, and overall optimism. It's not the only thing that has made a difference, but it's one of the biggest.

Occasionally, I'm able to pray the Rosary between sets. But since coming back to the Faith, my fitness and health routine has taken on far greater spiritual significance. When I was young, it was largely vanity driven. How many looks could I get at the beach? Now I see what happens in the gym (or in the kitchen) as opportunities for virtue: to grow in fortitude ("grit") by pushing through challenging workouts that I know are good for me and to grow in temperance by refraining from indulgences I know (at certain times) really aren't good for me. Of course, Catholicism teaches that we aren't just ghosts in a machine but are embodied souls. We're physical beings by nature, and our bodies are great goods — goods we should be eager to care for and, by doing so, to express our gratitude to God.

Pat Flynn is an award-winning writer, author of six books, and trainer of special-forces and professional athletes. He has a background in economics and philosophy and records music on the weekends. He's also the host of The Pat Flynn Show *on iTunes.*

You Can't Set the World on Fire if You Don't Take Care of Yourself

I did not enter the world of physical fitness until I was thirty-eight or thirty-nine years old. I had looked upon gyms as "Satan's church," where people went to worship their bodies — not God. But eventually, God told me to go to the gym, to take better care of my body and soul, and to help others to do the same. As I began to work out in the gym, I found there were many sincere Christians working out there with the right motivation, and we helped each other along.

As I grew in my Catholic Faith in the early years of marriage, I was very into modesty. I had not given it enough concern in the past, and now the pendulum swung too far in the other direction. As my physical condition improved, friends urged me to compete in women's bodybuilding, but I felt very uncomfortable about appearing before an audience in a woman's posing suit. I was attending a very conservative Catholic church, was strongly pro-life, and was a homeschool mother of nine! It was one of those nine children, my son, who urged me to compete, as a positive example, to show that it is possible for a busy mother of nine to tend to her bodily temple and to keep it healthy and fit.

I recall, too, on the way to adoration one day, hearing Jared Zimmerer on Johnnette Benkovic's *Women of Grace* program talking about training the body as a means of honoring and glorifying God. I knew that Christ told us that He came so that we should have abundant life in Him. Further, our Lady helped me to more clearly see people as not mere bodies but souls as well, as temples of the Holy Spirit. I came to see that the proper kind of display of the human physique could be done in keeping with modesty and while honoring the Holy Spirit within.

When I first turned to physical training, I also found that it helped me cope with anxiety and with traumatic events in my life. I've found that it can greatly help others too.

I now run a nonprofit that helps clients in mind, body, and even in financial stability. We have gathered together experts to form a physical health team, a mental health team, and a financial health team. I work as a personal fitness trainer, a Flexologist, and a nutrition counselor. For those unfamiliar with the term, a Flexologist has gone through a certification program to assist clients in healthy stretching routines. As a Catholic, I do not endorse yoga with its associated religious principles. The Flexology method of assisted stretching has proven effective not only in improving flexibility but in promoting relaxation, reducing stress, enhancing nerve function, and more.

As for my own workout routine, the Flexology work I do with clients provides a good amount of isometric strength work and core work on its own. I also lift weights two or three times per week and do cardio workouts — such as running or using an elliptical machine — two or three times per week. Sometimes on Sundays I enjoy a long run of five to ten miles.

When it comes to working with clients, I like to keep things simple. It's similar to our Faith. We can go far when we take advantage of the basics, such as going to Mass and praying the Rosary.

As for nutrition, one of the fundamental principles goes like this: "Protein is king! Fiber is queen!" We work to find a client's protein needs and then determine the person's other macronutrient needs. One advantage of putting protein first is that the body burns more calories to process it than it does for fat or carbohydrate. Also, protein increases satiety and decreases food cravings.

I love this quote from St. Catherine of Siena: "Be who you were created to be and you will set the world on fire!" I've come to learn that you can't set the world on fire if you don't take care of yourself.

Samantha LaMar is the founder and CEO of Roundabout Fitness and Produce and is the co-host of Podcast on the Plaza.

HE COMES FROM A LAND DOWN UNDER AND IS SEVENTY-SIX AND FULL OF MUSCLE

I write this vignette as an Australian, a Queenslander, and I am about to turn seventy-six. Do I feel that old? Certainly not in mind. To the contrary, I am very much young at heart." Although by no means an "Arnie," I regard my physique as "above average," particularly for one of my vintage. Quietly, I am proud of my achievements in the world of health and fitness, which despite a start-stop history initially, have now spanned fifty years (1971–2021). You may want to know how it all began and what gave me fifty years of persistence.

The seeds of physique development, of health and fitness, really began way back in 1963, when I was completing my final year of secondary school at a Catholic boys' boarding college in Queensland, but those seeds never saw the light of day till I commenced gym training proper, at thirty-four years of age. You could thus classify me as a late bloomer! Maybe it was that which gave me long-term persistence. I did not participate in many sports, but what caught my eye on the grounds of the college were a few rusty-looking old weights, bars, and dumbbells. Of our class of about twenty-three students, only one boy ever pumped this iron. I can remember his "before" and "after" shapes. He changed markedly from rather slight in build to very much thickset. No doubt at seventeen or eighteen, he was greatly assisted by testosterone supply.

His personality also altered somewhat, for he was transformed into a very self-confident young man. These two results for him were deeply imprinted into my subconscious. Again, it's a matter of persistence.

Those seeds were to lie dormant in my life till about 1971, when I saw advertised a device called a "Bullworker." It was a device that was largely underpinned by the use of isometric exercises. I bought one and used it intermittently for several years. Then, once again, a little dormancy set in.

My next foray into muscular fitness was to come in 1979, when I went to a gym to get some help with training. A very helpful Dutchman rendered me assistance. That interaction was an exciting one for me, and it set the stage for me to commence regular training in gyms right up till when the COVID pandemic struck in 2020. (Since then, it has largely been home workouts minus gym camaraderie.)

In the late seventies and early eighties, muscle magazines were gradually making their appearance on the market. In retrospect, goodness knows what heresy they preached but that was all there was to be found for assistance, and when one is hungry, one will eat anything! I do recall even importing some books from the United States. What a laborious process that was!

Gyms like the YMCA had their own spotters, but personal trainers were not yet on the scene. These spotters were more like "floor walkers," helping anyone who wanted assistance. It never ceases to amaze me how the coming of the World Wide Web and its superhighway of information have revolutionized knowledge in the world of health and fitness. (Some of it, though, needs careful sifting!) I find it interesting nowadays too, to cast a discerning eye over what the Internet provides about "old-school" bodybuilders. Certainly they achieved some wonderful gains and without the use of machines and resistance bands, which have also come into gyms.

I have never called myself a bodybuilder. I prefer to say I was into "physique development," for I never had the intention of going on stage in a bodybuilding contest, though I have attended a couple as a spectator. I have never taken supplements (nor anabolic steroids), save for one vitamin D capsule daily, authorized by a medical doctor. A personal trainer I employed at one stage used to pride himself on all the supplements he took, and each time he added another one, I shuddered a little more as to what some of his internal organs might be like years down the track — if indeed, he had those years! I have always followed the rule that any fitness that could not be achieved naturally would have to be done without.

Since the early eighties I have eaten a lot of healthy foods, probably most closely imitating the Mediterranean diet but also never being afraid once in a while to eat nonsensible items; after all, the only worthwhile rule is one occasionally to be broken — so say some at least! Surely, too, once in a while, the taste buds need a bit of variety!

You Are That Temple!

Gym training over the years has taught me a lot about human behavior and the psychology behind those who pump iron. The explosion in availability of gym equipment has been good, but the downside is that, particularly for the young, it can lead to overglorification of the body but leave the "spiritual tank" empty! A tragedy. I have found that gyms generally are not places where religious belief and practice pervade.

Still, I am deeply grateful to those men who have imparted their knowledge to me both in gyms and out in public. Likewise, I too, have been more than happy to impart what I know to beginners and to more advanced trainees. (To anyone who would wish to contact me, having read this, please seek my e-mail address from Dr. Vost, and I would be only too happy to answer you.)

Others, by their own results, have inspired me to keep on training, but I should also include that I have modified my programs as I aged, and only recently, a younger fellow told me how, because of my age, I had inspired him to keep on training. Over the years, and more so recently, I have had a few compliments passed to me by well-wishers. This adds up to self-confidence and a better self-image, which physique development has done for me and for many — all a great gift from God, and with God. "Nothing is impossible," as the Good Book says (see Matt. 19:26). It also says, "You give me the wild ox's strength" (see Ps. 92:10).

I should not omit to say that I have, in the past forty or so years, been in a road-runners' club, played social tennis and volleyball, did some Muay Thai training, did grappling with a trainer, and am currently doing a weekly thirty-minute session of boxing with a trainer. Plus, I do plenty of walking each week. All this has added up to sound annual blood test results, administered by my doctor, and to two successful bone mineral density tests. They have most likely also contributed to my having a high degree of mental alertness.

Speaking of the bone and blood tests, it is timely here to include recognition of the functionality of the body as a result of gym work and healthy eating. Even though a defined body is a great by-product of pumping iron, it must also be able to perform in everyday life. As one wise head said to me, "Training all starts with physique but ends up with functionality." That man's statement has been true for me with one exception: I think that if one body part in the physique has not been as developed as far as it might have been, then that yearning for completion may linger in the subconscious until fulfilled. It's like a telephone ringing until someone answers!

Muscle development itself is universally hardwired into every male, and those who do not keep a fit body are either in denial or suffer from a degree of inertia! Is there evidence for this being hardwired? I recall once, years ago, the owner of the only gym in a small town telling me that whenever a muscle-bound hulk was the main star of a movie in the town's only movie theatre on a weekend, on Monday his gym would be full of new faces and old ones who had come back!

A long time ago, I made Mary, Mother of God, patroness of my gym activities, and I always pray to her before workouts for no "accidents, illnesses, or injuries," and likewise after each session, I render her thanks. Those three possible negatives have not occurred to date!

As far as God is concerned, it is He who planted my fitness seeds back in 1963 and then enabled me to span the fitness years through to 2022 — even though I was a bit of a late starter.

To the glory of God and in accordance with the title of this book, I conclude by quoting the last (petition-like) stanza of the hymn for Evening Prayer for Week 2 , Thursday, of the psalter, Divine Office:

> Lord, we thy presence seek;
> May ours this blessing be;
> Give us a pure and lowly heart,
> A temple fit for thee.

Barry Lasey, seventy-six years young, resides in Queensland, Australia.

——❦———————❦——

With Padre Pio in His Corner, Busy Family Man Finds Time to Stay Strong

I am a husband and the father of four children. In my early thirties, I stumbled upon Dr. Vost's book *Fit for Eternal Life*, after hearing about it on Catholic Radio. My busy work and life schedule had left my workouts in shambles, and I thought it was impossible to maintain strength and conditioning without one- to two-hour workouts per day.

Fit for Eternal life was a revelation and quickly became one of my all-time favorite books. I was fascinated by how I could easily maintain and even gain strength in as little as twenty minutes a week. Fast-forward ten years: I've maintained my strength level from ages thirty-six to forty-six and have spent only one to two hours a week doing so!

For the last ten years, I have integrated Dr. Vost's strength-training routines and recommendations into my everyday life. My time with the Lord in prayer and my quality time with family are critical to me. I simply didn't have hours each day to exercise.

As for nutrition, to call myself a "sugar" addict would be an understatement. This is the weakest part of my health regimen — and the one I constantly read up on and ask Dr. Vost for advice on. Sugar can give such a feeling of happiness (however brief), alertness, and good vibes that resisting the 24/7 barrage of temptations is tough. I'm hoping more research can be done on this difficult topic, but the low-sugar, low-carb approach seems to be the answer.

I currently do one or two strength-training workouts per week, each lasting no more than thirty minutes. My typical routine is upper body one day and lower body the next. If I have more time to exercise (rare with four kids), I walk twenty to thirty minutes and listen to Catholic podcasts such as Dr. Vost's and Dr. Scott Hahn's. The time flies by! Following a regular exercise routine has helped to maintain my strength and keep anxiety at bay; if I miss a workout or two, I can mentally feel the difference.

When I lift weights in my basement, I have a mirror with a picture of Padre Pio in one corner and a picture of the Divine Mercy image in the other. As I struggle to push and pull each and every single repetition to 100 percent capacity, I look at those images and feel the Lord's strength and joy pushing me past my limitations. Nothing is impossible with God! Ironically, by spending less time in the gym with high-intensity workouts, I've gained more time for spiritual reading, Bible study, and a daily Rosary.

Peter Lawson, age forty-six, works as a business analyst for Little Sisters of the Poor in Baltimore.

Lay Dominican Preaches, Teaches, Publishes — and Runs Marathons

When my father passed into eternal life in the spring of 2004 at the age of fifty-six, my sister, Valerie "the Wolfe" Mahfood (so named because of her professional boxing career), and I decided to take up marathon running to maintain the kind of fitness conditions that would help us avoid dying so young. Since 2005, we have completed twenty-five marathons in almost as many states and have come away with cherished memories of our training and our celebrations of that training at each crossing of a finish line. What began as an effort to maintain our fitness became over the years an excellent bonding experience for us as we came to know each other; we grew spiritually and emotionally closer and became the kind of siblings our parents had hoped we'd be in our youth.

We raced each other and challenged each other, yet we almost always paced ourselves so that we'd cross the finish line together on each of our runs. And these weren't just play courses. Death Valley at a hundred feet below sea level on a rocky, flat plain was an adventure, but it was nothing like the Bataan Memorial Death March, which took us ten hours to complete in seventy-eight-degree weather, with fifty-miles-per-hour winds blowing in our faces, and wearing thirty-five-pound backpacks and treading through three to five inches of sand as we climbed to a mile high over the old missile testing grounds. And the midnight marathon in Rachel, Nevada, on a night clear enough to see Mars and Venus almost as big as our full moon, was magical — like running on the surface of a different planet. We came away from each marathon with not only a stronger bond between us but also as part of a social fabric that included the stories of every other marathoner we had met along the trails.

After the Disney World Marathon in January 2014, I fell into a rather unhealthy work and social routine, spending long hours at my desk, preparing a Catholic college for its reaffirmation of accreditation visit in the fall of 2015 and for our initial accreditation with the Association of Theological Schools the following year. I fell out of the habit of maintaining my training schedule, and I gained thirty-five pounds. Stepping on a scale in the spring of 2017, I realized I was about to step over a weight line that I never thought I'd reach. I began to diet, cutting my calorie intake to something lower than I thought I could sustain, and within seven weeks of healthier eating and outdoor walks, I was back to my pre-accreditation weight. I rejoined a gym and began working out regularly, inviting my thirteen-year-old son to join me. He grew in strength (and can now, at age seventeen, bench 285) — another fitness bonding experience. To anyone who asks, I recommend a healthy diet, regular exercise, and the fullness of a social life with those closest to us to share in those habits. I think of my dad often, and I hope to see him when I, too, pass into eternal life — but just not too soon, given the joy that healthy living brings, both physically and spiritually.

One thing my return to healthy eating and exercise brought me was a realization that everyone has a story, and not just any story — a faith message that has to be shared — and very few of them have a venue or a platform through which to share it. As part of my desk routine in 2014, I founded, with the help of Dr. Ronda Chervin and Shaun McAfee, a publishing house that we called En Route Books and Media, and after sharing our story, I began helping others share theirs. In the years since, I've published two hundred Catholic books and promoted the development of seventy-five Catholic radio programs, six thousand episodes of which have by now been shared on WCAT Radio with downloads at the time of this writing exceeding two hundred thousand. My experience over the past seven years helped shape my understanding of how we really can do everything we set our minds to, with the help of God, family, and friends, but a balanced lifestyle that includes healthy eating, healthy exercise, and healthy work habits is necessary for the running of any race.

What has particularly sustained me through it all is my spiritual life — the life of a lay Dominican, which combines the contemplative nature of prayer with the active life of evangelization. St. Catherine wrote that if we are who we are designed to be, we will set the world on fire. I took her words seriously and have endeavored to be the kind of husband, father, teacher, and friend that God has formed me to be and to share the life I have come to enjoy so much with everyone I meet. There is nothing more profound than the kind of relationship to which Christ has called us, loving God with all our mind, heart, soul, and strength, and loving our neighbors as ourselves. I recommend that, too, and may we live as many decades of that as the good Lord will allow before He calls us home. If we do it right, that home to which He calls us is one that we can live in every day of our lives in preparation for our eternal home.

Sebastian Mahfood, Ph.D., O.P., is a lay Dominican of the Queen of the Holy Rosary chapter in the Province of St. Albert the Great. Among the books he has authored or co-authored are Catholic Realism, Among the

Marvelous Things, *and* Missionary Priests in the Homeland. *He is fifty years old and* counting. *Having retired from his role as vice president of external affairs at Holy Apostles College and Seminary in September 2021, Dr. Mahfood remains an adjunct faculty member, teaching courses in the humanities while investing his time in the growth of his publishing house,* En Route Books and Media *(https://www.enroutebooksandmedia.com), and his radio station,* WCAT Radio *(https://www.wcatradio.com), whose missions are to advance the Catholic spiritual journey in the introduction of first-time Catholic authors and show hosts to our Faith tradition.*

GOD, FAMILY, AND FITNESS

I have lost more than thirty pounds a few times now — in my late twenties, mid-thirties, and early forties. But after many years, several injuries, and lifestyle changes, it is now harder than ever. On my fiftieth birthday, I had an MRI and an ultrasound and X-rays on both of my knees. They showed some damage and a lot of wear and tear going back to high school sports. But my doctor's advice was to change my lifestyle and push surgery off as long as possible.

In the last few years, I have had water on the knee or knee sprains seven times. And prior to that, I was diagnosed with plantar fasciitis. I kept trying to push through the pain and keep working out, as I did when I was younger, and ended up causing some permanent damage to my feet. Now in my early fifties, I need to get back to basics and make changes and stick to them, so I can be here for my children and maybe even grandchildren. And so that I can live and serve God better.

My nutrition is a hard point. My wife keeps the house full of junk: chips, ice cream, candy, and so forth. At one point, we had more than thirty types of pop in the fridge! It is hard to make changes and stick to them. But I know several things that work for me, and I need to be consistent about them. What works well for me is avoiding gluten, juicing, and intermittent fasting with one full-day fast a week. I love vegetables and will juice almost anything.

I try to walk five days a week with one or more of my kids — anywhere from twenty minutes to two hours, depending on the trail we choose and whether my knees cooperate. I try to use the rebounder for five minutes three times a day. And I am trying to get back to three weight workouts a week. Before my knees went wonky, I had great success with the workouts from Team Body Project. They even have a whole week's worth of programs that can be done seated; that is a blessing when my knees are really bad.

I believe it is our responsibility to look after our bodies as long as we keep it in proportion. When I was in college, I heard a talk that explained that our lives are like a tripod or a car with three gas tanks: physical, spiritual, and mental. If any of the tanks is empty or any of the legs unstable, the who thing falls apart. I know that when I am not eating well and moving, the other areas eventually suffer. If I am physically healthy, my spiritual life is easier to engage with.

Steven R. McEvoy, age fifty-one, works in IT full-time but wears several hats, including Tech Lead Servers & Storage worker and freelance writer. He spent the better part of twenty years in college. He started a book-review blog Book Reviews and More *in 2005 mainly as an online archive for reviews that appeared in print. His area of focus in reading is divided between Christianity, classics, fiction, and fitness.*

BLACK-BELTED DEFENDER OF LIFE

I am licensed to practice law in Illinois, but primarily I work for a large legal publisher, offering information and workflow solutions to government and academic lawyers. I sit at my desk a lot, so getting up and out of the chair frequently to get my blood moving helps me stay focused.

One of the benefits of my army service is that those daily exercise routines kept me in good shape and developed in me a fitness habit. My interest in martial arts, outdoor life, and keeping up with seven children motivated me to continue my fitness routines (albeit fit to the domestic life). This routine changed as I coached kids' soccer, worked my farmette, or repaired my rental properties.

I learned martial arts (Goju Ryu karate) basics as a teen and dabbled in karate as a college student, and I wanted my children exposed to the principles of self-defense through karate. As a parent, I attended many classes, sitting on the floor in the dojo (gym) until one of my children asked me to join the karate class with him as a participant. We both received our black belts five years later. Karate is a life journey; the lessons never end: just look at the reboot of *The Karate Kid* and its latest iteration, *Cobra Kai*.

In karate, I studied body kinetics: muscle and bone aligning at the right speed at the right time to deliver the right amount of force. Good kinetics are enhanced by staying limber and stretched — another ancillary benefit of years of karate. Delivering the right kick, punch, or block correctly takes years of practice. You develop reflexive muscle memory and keen response times. Balance and coordination are essential. Accordingly, karate demands whole-body fitness. Even if you remember how to do the moves, if you don't keep up with the demands of those moves, the effect will be limited, and such failure will result in painful injuries.

I still practice my karate workouts — the various moves along with the methodical dances known as *kata*. *Kata* are a series of predetermined moves in a pattern in which the student fights against an imaginary opponent to demonstrate a skill level. The more advanced *kata* are more intricate and difficult, and a successful execution of these moves often determines the student's proficiency. Of course, these days, I am in the dojo less and walk much more, incorporating my karate into my walks without trying to look too weird. I aim to do this twice a day. The space requirement for maintaining my skills is small, and the tools are as available as YouTube.

As for nutrition, I'm a fan of Dave Asprey's Bulletproof diet, which comprises lots of whole foods, high-quality proteins, and limited portions. I start the day with Bulletproof Coffee: 1 tablespoon of butter (or coconut oil) and 1 tablespoon of MCT oil (medium-chain triglyceride oil has many benefits — like WD40 for the brain), blended thoroughly with coffee in the Ninja or blender. This is my breakfast. It's filling and gets my day going. I don't eat lunch until 11:30 or 12:30. In that respect, it's like intermittent fasting, since my previous meal was likely at 6:00 the previous evening. For lunch, I usually take something light, such as a three- or four-ounce meat or fish protein or salad, or both if I meet Kevin, this book's author, for lunch at Core Life. Lately, as I practice more fasting (for religious reasons), I enjoy a bone-broth version of the Bulletproof Coffee mentioned above or two pieces of toasted Ezekiel Bread (raisin), buttered lightly.

As for exercise, I try at *sixty* to take care of my *ninety*-year-old body *now*. So I pursue flexibility, balance, core strength, and I try to stay active into my advanced years.

I walk every day — usually twice a day, for a total of about 1.5 miles. During my walk, I stretch and perform basic karate movements (blocks and punches) or other musculoskeletal exercises, which sometimes looks like a Russian soldier march.

Weight training in karate is unique: the ideal *karateka* (student) should move weights using the intricacies and all the basic movements of the kata. As with kettlebells, the workout involves holding the weight and moving it through the motion of the block, punch, kick, rotation, or extension. Imagine the karateka lifting a half-gallon milk jug filled with sand through a sequence of slow punching motions: drawing the jug back to the hip, moving it forward while turning the weight as the punch rises to its target. The goal is a stronger core, a better grip, wrist strength, and enduring arm and leg muscles. Yes, even toes: they can grip the floor, or your opponent, if you train them to. The goal is a more sinewed body with greater endurance.

There are other practices I have used to varying degrees of success, such as punching bags. Some karate fitness methods involve devices and tools found in the fishing community. Other, more traditional Okinawans use resistance training in which two students square up against each other in fighting drills or body-on-body resistance exercises in which the students square muscle on muscle and bone on bone as the chief means of exercise. "Iron Shirt" and "Sticky Hands" are two examples, both of which require a partner. There are many choices, but these are some of my favorites.

At present, I tend to adopt methods that fit most easily into my lifestyle. For example, for years I liked push-ups, but a shoulder injury makes this painful. So instead, I prefer planks or standing or wall push-ups instead. Similarly, I like exercises that enhance my core, and I adjust them to what my abilities are on a given day with the time available.

My habit is to stay healthy. When I must skip exercising due to travel or illness, I notice that I tire more easily, which, on its face, seems contradictory. Mental sharpness is maintained, if not improved, with the practice of an exercise regimen. Likewise, I look to my diet to keep my mind sharp and clear. The Bullet Coffee helps in the morning, along with a green-tea booster later in the day.

Correspondingly, my alcohol tolerance is very low these days, so if I overindulge, I have poor sleep and reduced cognitive function the next day.

Study after study shows the importance of good sleep habits, especially as we age. Getting a good night's sleep and indulging in an afternoon nap help me stay sharp for the whole day.

I sometimes listen to Fr. Mike Schmitz's *Bible in a Year* or a Bishop Barron homily during my walks. As you've read elsewhere in this book, our bodies are temples of the Holy Spirit. And I like the more traditional-looking churches, so I imagine my temple having the beautiful flying buttresses of strong bones and muscles, a sacred heart in the center of the temple, and a clean and full-throated choir of two healthy lungs. My eyes are clear, like two stained-glass rose windows that have just been washed, letting in the light of God's grace.

On fasting, I look to my spiritual father, Thomas à Kempis. He fasted to imitate Christ, becoming detached from worldly satiations, and to deepen his prayer life. I fast to imitate Thomas. I doubt that he thought about detoxing, but fasting also does that too. Fasting reawakens appetites: in Thomas's day, food was likely bland and of limited quantity. Fasting helped him appreciate the fare in front of him. Dave Asprey's book *Fast This Way* is well researched, well written, and practical. I baptized it to make his methods more Catholic.

Strangely, I look forward to fasting. My weekly fasts are offered to end abortion. Fasting helps me focus because my hunger reminds me to pray — often when I am on the sidewalk in front of the abortion facility. (See Acts 13 and Matt. 17:20–21 on the power of fasting and of prayer.)

So the benefits of fasting are more frequent prayer, self-mastery, detachment, detox, and appreciation.

Another important thing is sleep. Study after study shows the importance of good sleep habits, especially as we age. I mention this because I'm very intentional about this in my overall health awareness.

Tim Moore turned sixty in February 2022. He is married to Donna and is the father of seven children and the author of the book series The Imitation of Christ, by Thomas à Kempis, with Edits and Commentaries and Fictional Narrative. *It's available at www.timothyedmoore.com or from any online bookseller. Tim is president of Springfield Right to Life and Two Hearts Springfield (Sonograms), and he also holds a black belt in Goju Ryu karate.*

••❊••————————••❊••

Father of a Parish (and of Six Children) Runs to Reconcile Soul and Body

All my life, I've struggled with depression, made worse by the fact that I have a difficult time getting in touch with my emotions. This means that I would often drift through a day in a fog, aware I was deeply sad and something wasn't right but not understanding why or how to take time to care for myself mentally and physically.

That was when I discovered long-distance running.

I find that on long bicycle rides or runs — I'm talking hours, here — my mind goes quiet. Thoughts move in and out effortlessly, floating like a gentle breeze, as if a sustained thought would require Herculean effort to break the spell. I never engage in time-killing activities such as counting cars. I prefer to run alone and don't feel the need to talk or gossip. I am never bored. I simply flex my muscles, push forward, feel the sun hot on my skin, and wordlessly observe the universe and my place in it. No great mental efforts are completed, no prodigies of mysticism are infused into my consciousness, but I have space to achieve perfect recollection. I feel it in a mental and emotional relief that is experienced first physically as my muscles loosen up. Then the oxygen in the air hits my lungs, I smile a bit, and I experience freedom. As if released from captivity, my thoughts roll away over the horizon.

It is a gift given by my body, given by the physical suffering of the run. It strikes me, as I reflect upon it, as a beautiful harmony of the physical and intellectual faculties. I'm content with myself, not concerned or anxious about anything at all. I run because that is what I am meant to do. And for that moment, it's enough.

It isn't that exercise makes all my other problems magically disappear, but it offers me breathing space so that I can engage my personal issues constructively and with positivity. Knowing that I'm a Catholic priest and also have young children, people will ask me how I make the time every day to exercise. My response is: How could I not? That time to exercise is precious. Without it, the rest of my day would be far less orderly, far less productive, and far less happy.

I've come to see exercise as an act of love. My exercise isn't a means to physical power or health; it's a way of engaging in voluntary suffering to reconcile soul and body.

Fr. Michael Rennier is on the editorial board at Dappled Things *magazine. He has an MDiv from Yale Divinity School and is a Catholic priest in the Archdiocese of Saint Louis. A convert to the Catholic Faith and a former Anglican pastor, he's now a married priest and the father of six children. He is forty years old, and his hair is already turning gray.*

HEALTHY LIVING

Q. Why did God make me?

A. God made me to know Him, to love Him, and to serve Him in this life, and to be happy with Him in the next.

Many may recognize this familiar question and answer from the *Baltimore Catechism,* and the simplicity of the question-and-answer format makes it great to memorize, writing it in your mind and heart.

That said, how is it that something so simple can be, at times, so difficult to grasp?

As a convert to the Catholic Faith, I can joyfully tell you that while I did not always know God, I learned that He always knew me!

I had a feeling that what I did know was just not enough, and I wanted to know Him more. So I decided to ask a friend, who seemed to know God more than anyone else I knew at the time, how I could get to know God better.

Her gentle response was the recommendation that I pray. I felt an exasperated sigh come from deep within as I exhaled my plea: "How do I pray?" Without hesitation, she responded, "Pray like you work out!" Oh, she knew me so well! She immediately appealed to something I enjoyed, needed, and always made time for — brilliant!

During my next workout, I was literally at the height of the heart-pounding, heavy-breathing, intense moments, lifting my weights and focusing on my step when my thoughts completely shifted to my friend's words, and they were so clear and impossible to ignore: "Pray like you work out!"

Along with those words came the magnitude of what all of that meant to me: When I work out, I make time for it. I prioritize it. I give it my full attention. I follow instructions. I trust the instructor. I persevere through the tough stuff. And I know that the hard work is totally worth it.

All of this came forth as though infused into my mind in a mere moment! It was all so powerful, and I was all too aware that I was not alone as I stepped off my step, laid down my weights, and welcomed this overwhelming realization.

God met me right there in my workout! I knew that I would remember this forever.

Life is full of moments in which God reveals Himself to us, His beloved children, and it is so important to stop and reflect on this, so that we may discover He has been with us all along!

While my active life may have begun with jump ropes and hula hoops, they gradually turned into aerobics classes at the gym and workout videos at home. I was adopted into a large family in which collecting wood and berries, gardening and canning, and building and repairing were daily norms. My parents loved work and taught great work ethics at home, at school, and on the job. I married my high school sweetheart and converted to the Catholic Faith.

I must share that from that point on, and I tell you this with all my heart, once I understood the truth and beauty of Holy Mother Church, I even breathed differently! It was as though I had been holding my breath all my life and I was now given lungs of faith, and everything in my life took on new light and depth!

The decisions that my husband and I made were as close to being Christ-centered as we could make them, and we certainly embraced many struggles and joys in this way of living.

Our openness to life increased and took on a new meaning — an eternal meaning. What greater gift to give to God, to one another, and to our children than a new eternal life in a new sibling! God blessed us with sixteen beautiful children, nine of whom we got to raise for His glory, while the others He raised from my womb before they entered my arms — some of the greatest joys and deepest sorrows that mere earthly words cannot express.

Our family did nearly everything together: Holy Mass, housework, homeschool, shopping — there were no home deliveries back then! We prayed our Rosary, went on pilgrimages, and even worked out together!

I truly have always believed that personal health care was a responsibility, not a luxury, so I tried to recover well from each pregnancy with great care, hope, and expectancy for the next!

I enjoy all kinds of exercise: weightlifting, body-weight exercise, HIIT cardio with and without equipment, outdoor sprints, skating, and cycling. It is all so invigorating and beneficial to the mind, body, and soul.

Figuring out proper nutrition was a bit trickier for me. Gone are the days when I seemed to be able to eat whatever I wanted without consequences. I had no idea that I was nurturing indulgent habits because I didn't gain weight at that time. The truth is that you cannot exercise away bad nutrition.

I diligently researched healthy nutrition, but it was as if I had all these pieces of a puzzle without knowing what it was to become! So I simply started to clean up my choices and discovered that the cleaner I ate, the better I felt.

For years I followed a plan of four to six meals a day, including shakes. That worked for a while — until it didn't. As we age, our needs change, and so must our habits.

There is a freedom that comes with understanding that harmful "comfort" foods and binge eating are a form of self-abuse, and one must learn to treat oneself mercifully in a way that only God can teach — through love.

While I've always loved the spiritual benefits of fasting, I wasn't fully aware of the physical benefits until I began to fast more regularly.

Intermittent fasting affected my entire person — spiritually, physically, and mentally. The healing benefits were astounding, and I was amazed at how it drastically helped to decrease and alleviate inflammation, straighten my arthritic fingers, remove skin tags, which are often results of an overload of carbohydrates, and so much more!

My renewed mental clarity was refreshing, my spirituality was heightened and deepened, and my body literally felt free! Fewer, more nutrient-dense meals were satisfying and did not leave me bloated. Researching the balance of protein, carb, and fat takes a bit of time, trial, and effort, but it is well worth it. Each of us is unique, and we need to delight more in the wonder and miracle that is the human body!

The puzzle is becoming quite clear now, and it is wild to discover that the picture that those pieces were building was actually me — and this puzzle is one of a kind!

All the while, prayer is at the center of it all, as I desire God, not my emotions, to guide me. Temporary fixes are just that — temporary.

I was at Adoration praying and thanking God for the many ways He strengthens me, especially when I am so weak. It isn't always easy to get over the daily obstacles as I strive to be healthy with the different tastes of a large family. The Christian life is certainly not easy, is it?

Healthy living truly is an expression of gratitude for our very own lives. As I pondered this, I wrote out:

HealThy Living

Did you notice it?

This little way of writing these words led to a big way to see and tweak all of my habits!

God accepts all the broken pieces that we offer up to Him, and He leads us to healing, body and soul.

HealThy Living is a divine invitation! So let us love the Lord our God with all our hearts, all our souls, all our minds, and all our strength; and love our neighbor as ourselves" (see Luke 10:27).

How do we love ourselves?

How do you love yourself?

If you've ever struggled thinking that it is so much easier to love others than yourself, I have great news for you! This can be overcome!

How do you learn to love yourself? Remember that Jesus lives in you — the temple that is your own body. Meet Him there in your heart, in your mind, and in your body! Care for Him, feed Him, and love Him in you!

Susan Rohr describes herself as God's littlest daughter, Greg's wife, mother of sixteen, spiritual mentor, hairstylist, friend, and neighbor.

--------⋈--------⋈--------

Mr. Universe Meets the Universe's Maker

I was born in Newport, Rhode Island. My father left my family when I was three, and my five-year-old brother and I were raised by my mother and my grandmother. My mother's father also passed away around that time, so I grew up without positive male role models.

I started lifting weights at age seven because I was tired of getting beat up. It wasn't like bullying or anything. Boys were just pretty rough and tumble at that time, in the 1960s, and I was one of the younger kids. While I lifted, my diet was very poor, and at times I went for days without eating. My mother just didn't know how to cook nutritious foods. She and my grandmother developed insulin-dependent diabetes that required three shots every day. That scared me straight into eating right!

Still, I was able to do well in athletics, doing a high jump of six feet five inches in high school, for example. I did basketball and track at school and skateboarded professionally as a kid. I also boxed as a semipro for three years.

When I graduated from high school, I had no money and did not know about financial aid. I planned to join the marines but was rejected because of the four knee surgeries I had due to skateboarding injuries. Instead, I booked a one-way ticket to Santa Monica, California, to stay and work out at Joe Gold's famous World Gym.

A taxi dropped me off at the gym at 3:00 a.m., and I slept in its underground garage. I ran into champion bodybuilder Roger Callard (famous at the time for a guest appearance on the popular *Charlie's Angels* TV show), and he let me train with him. Within forty-eight hours, I found myself training with his training buddy, Arnold Schwarzenegger himself! I ate well and grew muscular and strong.

Unfortunately, as a powerful young guy who knew how to fight and liked to, I got involved in what you might call "dirty work" and what my friend Tom Peterson calls "unscrupulous things." I did bouncing and money collecting as I competed in statewide bodybuilding shows and then the Mr. America contest.

Six weeks before I won the Mr. Universe title in 1992 in London, my mother died of a heart attack, and that produced the biggest change in my life up to that time. I remember staring out at the ocean, reviewing my life and feeling as if I were paving my way to Hell. I felt useless. Here I was, this big, strong guy who thought he could do everything, and I could do nothing for my mother. It was a very low point. My brother suffered his first episode of bipolar disorder after my mom died.

As a result of my mom's death, being a man of faith, I decided to change my life to try to become a good man. How? I had no positive male role models. Where should I turn? I thought, "How about Jesus? The best man on earth will be my role model!" I bought a King James Version of the Bible and read it three times. Here I was, thirty years old, and it was the first book I ever read cover to cover!

I was back home in Rhode Island and going to Mass again. One morning, I had been reading the Letter of James, one of my favorite books of the Bible, and praying to God for an opportunity to do His work, to be a "doer of the word." When I went to Mass, the director of religious education made an announcement that the parish could not begin its religious education classes until two more teachers signed up. I volunteered to teach them both. The director was delighted. She asked if I had teaching experience, and I answered no. She asked if I had children, and I answered no again. But I ended up teaching fifth, ninth, and tenth graders for fourteen years!

One day, though, I was teaching about the immorality of sex outside marriage, and the kids were asking me questions. I felt like a hypocrite and knew I had to change my own life. I was done. No more! I am now married very happily to my wife, Carla.

Here is an example of how caring she is: About five years ago, my brother was on a bridge contemplating suicide, when he called me. He was distraught and said he had nowhere to go. Carla said he must come home and stay with us. While he stayed with us, I insisted that he go to Mass and Bible study. During one session, he told the group of about seventy-five people that he had wanted to kill himself his whole life, but praise be to Jesus, he no longer wanted to and had devoted himself to God. It ended up that he had lost his keys and walked five miles to the Bible study that night.

When I went to his house the next day, he didn't answer the door, and I heard water running. I found that there was food out. He had been planning out his day. I opened the bathroom door and found he had died in the tub from a heart attack. There is a strong history of death from heart disease in our family. What was remarkable was that I experienced a great calm and peace at that time, knowing the state my brother's soul was in and what God had worked in him.

And one last thing: I had COVID for about three weeks this year. Recently, I had a physical that went well. I had a low total cholesterol of 127 and a normal EKG. Still, when doing cardio work in the gym, my chest felt funny for the first time. When I described the pain, the doctor thought it sounded like indigestion. One day when I felt the same straightjacket-like feeling in my chest while at rest, I was brought to the hospital, where it was determined I was having a heart attack. My doctor later told me I had survived a 100 percent blockage in the left anterior descending artery, the blockage doctors call the "widow maker," because the vast majority of people die from it. In fact, my right coronary artery also had a 100 percent blockage, another was blocked 85 percent, and the fourth was blocked 75 percent. They were able to treat them with stents, and I was in the ICU for four or five days.

The most interesting thing was the total peace I felt when all this was going on. I calmly accepted that if Jesus was calling me, He was calling me. My only concern was for Carla. I remember a calmness, stillness, and sense of slow motion. Later, when it was clear I was re-covering, things gradually came back to normal. I was told not to lift weights for the next seven days, but I was back in the gym doing mild cardio work the next day. The doctor told me that the vast majority of people would have died with those blockages, but my training all my life had prepared me physically to survive. I was spiritually ready to go but physically here to stay!

Mick Souza is owner and operator of "Mick's Muscle Mania." He trains women for bodybuilding and physique competitions. The story of his faith journey can be seen on an episode of Catholics Come Home *on EWTN.*

···❧···———···❧···

Working Out My Place in the Body of Christ

I'm not sure when I realized that I was small. As the oldest of four boys, it wasn't really an issue when my first brother came along — or even the second one, when I was about three years old. I had a pretty happy early childhood, or so I'm told. But as we all got older, it became apparent that my brothers were growing a lot faster than I was, and when I started, as the oldest, to wear their hand-me-downs, I began to be more and more self-conscious about my size. During my high school years, when people would meet my family, they would remark to one of my younger brothers, "Ah, you must be the oldest." Nothing made me madder.

When we were old enough to play organized sports, it became clear not only that I was smaller but that I lacked the natural athletic talent that came so easily to my brothers, especially early on in youth baseball. I didn't even try out for football, although my brothers excelled at it. I did go to basketball tryouts a couple of years but was pretty quickly cut. I had always been a bit of a bookish kid, but after being met with failure after failure in the world of athletics, I descended pretty fully into the world of my mind, reading everything that I could get my hands on, writing poetry and songs, and finding friends in the worlds of Narnia and Middle Earth, but thankfully, most of all, in the pages of Sacred Scripture.

In all this, I know that my parents were concerned about my lack of athletic ability, especially in light of the success my brothers were experiencing, and they worried what effect it might be having on me. They encouraged me to get involved in more individual sports, where I could measure my success against my previous successes, and that got me into wrestling, which allowed me to compete against boys in my weight class.

Wrestling, however, was a bust for me, for two main reasons. First, I lacked the "killer instinct" necessary to be a good wrestler. In wrestling, it's every ounce of your strength against every ounce of someone else's, and perhaps there was just a bit too much of St. Francis of Assisi in me to take pleasure in slamming another kid's body to the mat. Second, even in weight classes, I was small compared with my peers; the lowest class in my group was for 80-pound wrestlers. At 74 pounds soaking wet, I'd be cramming peanut butter sandwiches in the weeks leading up to the meet, while 85-pound kids were sleeping in trash bags or spitting in buckets as they waited in line for the weigh-in so that they could squeak into the right class for the competition. I lettered by competing in exhibition matches, in which one kid from our team who didn't qualify would wrestle one kid from the other team who didn't qualify, meaning that my Saturdays consisted of waiting all day to spend about ten seconds of match time getting body-slammed by a 135-pound kid who didn't make weight. I hated wrestling.

All along, I had vowed to myself that I would go out for football in my junior year of high school, no matter what. To get ready for that, during the winter of my sophomore year, I took up the invitation from the football coach to join the powerlifting team, fully expecting that this would be another opportunity to get a sportsmanship award as the kid who tried really hard and kept a good attitude despite not being very good at anything. Boy, was I wrong about myself!

Powerlifting, at least of the competitive type I participated in, consisted of three lifts: the bench press, the dead lift, and the squat. Interestingly enough, almost all of those played to my smallness and compactness, and I began, through a pretty calculated pyramid training regimen, to experience significant gains in all three of those lifts. As the smallest guy in a weight room full of guards and linebackers, I didn't really have a sense of how I was doing until we started going to meets. Competing in the lowest weight class (under 114 pounds — I weighed 105 at the time), I started winning — as in winning everything.

I don't think I placed out of the top three in a single meet that year. And when it came to the Ohio state championships, my bench of 145, my squat of 250, and my deadlift of 265 (a school record for my class) were enough to win me the state championship in the 114-pound weight class. Looking back, those aren't exactly huge numbers. But they weren't too bad for a high school kid who was just over a hundred pounds in a winter coat!

I'll never forget the bizarre feeling of getting back on the bus the day of the state championship in 1994. I was surrounded by some pretty great football players who had picked up lifting to keep in shape during the off-season. There they were on their green vinyl seats, many of them holding participation ribbons. And there I was, squeezing down the aisle past them and lugging a trophy half as big as I was! They gave me a good-natured hard time about it. And for the first time in my life, I felt like a real athlete.

We moved that year, and I ended up playing my first season of football at a new school in Kentucky, where I broke my foot in a scrimmage the weekend before the first day of school. I came back my senior year and got in on a few running plays in the fourth quarter whenever we were losing by thirty or more. Football was not exactly my thing.

I didn't do much lifting in college or in my young adult years, but I feel very strongly that the lessons I learned through that year of focused time in the weight room have had a long-term effect on my thinking about the body, about perseverance, and about the diverse ways that God spreads His gifts among His people.

You Are That Temple!

Among other things, that experience got me thinking more and more about the genius of the body, not just in a biological sense, as the way the body is ordered, but also as the form of the soul. What does it mean, this odd mystery that causes the brain to command the muscles, that connects the intellect and will to action and pain and pleasure? As a Christian, I had some sense of that, but the more I explored that question through philosophy classes in college, and later through discovering the wisdom of St. Thomas Aquinas and Pope John Paul II's Theology of the Body, the more I marveled, and continue to marvel, at the mystery of God's gift of the human body. The angels are pure spirit, but we humans are amphibious, living in the worlds of matter and spirit and, because of the Incarnation, serving a Savior who Himself took on, of all things, a body. And the variety of things we can do with it is astounding.

I also believe that had I not had the perseverance to try yet another sport after failing in so many others, I would not have been quite as prepared to persevere in later physical, emotional, and spiritual challenges that I would come to face as I grew into adulthood. I credit my family and coaches for encouraging me to fight through those failures until I found something I could do well at. And I believe that perseverance through difficulty in the physical realm directly translated to my perseverance in the spiritual realm as a seeker of truth. As an Evangelical Christian in the late '90s and early 2000s, I felt deeply dissatisfied as I tested version after version of Christianity, all of which seemed to have bits and pieces of the truth, but none of which had the fullness of the truth. It was an echo of the frustration I had experienced trying different sports and feeling like none of them fit the reality of what my body was made for. I know many dear Evangelical friends who felt that same angst in those years and who have since given up on Christianity altogether. But I was given the grace to persevere, and that perseverance led me to the threshold of the Catholic Church in

2005, where all those bits and pieces and crumbs along the trail found their ultimate fulfillment.

And finally, that experience has given me a larger sense of the meaning not only of my own body but of the Body of Christ, the Church. My attempts to be a baseball player, a football player, and a wrestler were good as far as they went, but that's not what God built me for in those years. He built other people for those things. He also built artists and musicians and scientists and doctors and a hundred thousand other kinds of people. Any inferiority complex I may have had because I wasn't good at the thing I wanted to be good at was ultimately an inferiority complex of my own making because God didn't want me to be someone else; He wanted me to be fully myself. And once I was able to find a gift God had given me and to use it, I recognized more of the hidden gifts in my brothers and sisters in the Body of Christ. Later, I would have some success as a musician, and eventually in radio and writing and a few other areas, but even those were arenas I felt confident to explore in part because of my experience of trial and error in the realm of athletics and because I was able to realize the level of my gifts in relation to the level of giftedness in others who were also engaging in those pursuits.

These days, with work and parenthood and everything else, lifting isn't a part of my physical regimen anymore, although I think about getting back into it every now and then. I completed a half marathon a few years ago, and I still run from time to time just to offset office life. One of these days, I hope to be a lot more disciplined in setting out a formal exercise plan because I notice a difference not just in my physical but also in my mental health when I prioritize exercise. I have been focusing a lot more on diet than exercise in recent years, and some of the fascinating things I've learned about eating whole foods and cutting out alcohol and sugars has given me a much stronger appreciation for that aspect of how God designed the human body, and the gift of food in all its aspects, from nutrition to a philosophy of hospitality. But I will always look back on my awkward physical years, and the way they led me to powerlifting, as a deeply formative aspect of how God taught me more about myself — and more about how to understand who He created me to be.

Matt Swaim, age forty-two, is co-host of The Son Rise Morning Show *and producer of* The Journey Home, *as well as outreach manager for the Coming Home Network.*

An Olympian Effort at Fifty

I started Olympic weightlifting at age fifty, and it has changed my life for the better. It has strengthened me physically, mentally, and spiritually. It has helped me achieve a more balanced life, improved my nutrition and my sleep habits, and reduced my alcohol consumption; in fact, I have been completely alcohol free for a year. I am more in tune with God's mission for me than ever before.

I never lifted weights or played any varsity sports in high school or college except for intramural basketball, sandlot baseball, and softball or flag football. For more than twenty-five years, I was a hard-driving road warrior living a sedentary life. I now love the sport of weightlifting so much that I give back and volunteer as a referee at local events, and I am honored to have been on the USA Weightlifting Finance and Audit Committee since December 2018. This was not an easy journey; as a matter of fact, some of my toughest physically, mentally, and emotionally challenging days have been weightlifting related. It has all been worth it. I have attended two USA Masters Camps at the USA Olympic Training Center in Colorado Springs and have won bronze and gold medals at local and Texas state meets. I even did a Strongman competition in late 2019 and finished in third place for the master's group and qualified for Nationals. My strength journey also led me to explore the techniques of the "oldtime" strongman, who bent steel, tore telephone books in half, and slammed nails through wood with his bare hands. My twenty-year-old son and I have completed the Oldtime Strongman University weekend courses, studying under the famous Oldtime Strongman Dennis Rogers and Dave "the Iron Tamer" Whitley.

My journey started at age forty-nine, when my wife "strongly encouraged" me to get a hobby, as I was too focused on work and needed a change in my life. It had been a year since I tore my left rotator cuff, and after my surgery, I become less active: I needed to lose weight, having then reached 335 pounds at just under six feet tall. I researched popular gyms in my area and ended up doing CrossFit training at Tiger's Den Gym in the Dallas Design District. One day, I saw people in the corner of the gym sword fighting in what looked like medieval attire. "What's going on?" I asked my coach. "Oh, that's Russ teaching our medieval martial arts class." Being a history buff and a lover of the medieval and Renaissance periods, I immediately signed up. Russ was also a Masters Olympic lifter, and one weekend, when it was just he and I in the gym working out, I saw him training and doing Olympic lift drills, which I was now familiar with, having done CrossFit. Russ explained to me that he was training for a "Master's competition," which is essentially weightlifting for people older than thirty-five. I told him that I enjoyed the Olympic lifting in CrossFit, and that's when it happened: Russ told me, "I've seen you lift, and you have pretty good form for someone just starting out." He told me that he started lifting three years ago and would be competing in his first competition, and he encourage me to try it. I replied, "You mean I can do only the weightlifting portion of CrossFit?" I was all in. From there, I started focusing on Olympic lifts. I started with a coach, and for the first few sessions, it was all technique with the PVC pipe, then just the bar until I got the rhythm of the lifts down.

Unfortunately, in only a few months after training and when I had just started to put weight on the bar, I tore my right rotator cuff in a sword fight in a medieval martial arts chivalric tournament and had to have surgery. My weightlifting was put on hold, but I was determined to return. After all my rehab, I began slowly getting back into lifting. Ultimately, I lost more than seventy pounds on my weightlifting journey. While I may at times have gained some weight back I continue to focus on the healthy habits that weightlifting has encouraged.

My next wellness goal is to continue to drop weight while building strength and to compete in a National Olympic Weightlifting competition in the next year or so.

Nutrition is my biggest challenge; I eat healthy foods but also take in too many calories. At home, my diet is gluten and dairy free with a focus on organic produce, whole foods, and grass-fed beef and free-range chicken. I grind my coffee beans each morning using a pour-over method and add Laird's Super (Coconut) Creamer. I have my own "green shake concoction": one-third berries and two-thirds kale, spinach, cucumber, and celery, and I add fresh turmeric and ginger, cashew milk and water. I also throw in a scoop of Organifi's Green Juice. I make enough for my late breakfast and will have it with eggs and Irish oatmeal; I usually have some left over to have another shake late in the day. It's a way for me to make sure I am getting enough vegetables. I love bison, as it has greater protein and iron count and less fat than regular beef, and it tastes great! My carbs are now more potato, sweet potatoes, and rice and less pasta these days.

I follow time-restricted eating, and on Wednesdays and Fridays, I fast for about twenty hours, or until about 4:00 p.m.

I traveled 30 to 40 percent of the time before the COVID pandemic, so it was a battle to get a consistent training program. When I am at home, I plan each week to have two days at a gym under a coach, one heavy day on my own at home, and one overall day of movements. For each session, I spend ten to fifteen minutes warming up with some form of stretching with bands, followed by three to five minutes in a Concept 2 rower or SkiErg or another form of cardio to loosen things up and get my heart rate going. Then it's typically three different Olympic lifting drills followed by one or two strength-training lifts, such as squats or dead lifts. I then finish up with some form of metabolic conditioning such as farmer's carries, Arnold press, then row or SkiErg for two hundred to four hundred meters and then repeat three times. My "heavy days" are usually 1.5-hour workouts, and the other days are fifty to sixty minutes. Due to the nature of my work with global companies and virtual meetings at all hours of the day, there are some weeks in which I may get in only two lifting days. It's a constant battle between changing schedules and priorities. If I am training for a competition, I focus on being as consistent as possible for six to eight weeks.

This past year, I had to deal with physical therapy for some injuries and two surgeries along with some other issues, and I feel as if I am starting all over again. That's okay, as I know what I need to do, and I look forward to building up a strong routine again. I am much more focused now on stretching before and after I lift; I have a knockoff Theragun that I use before and after workouts, and the foam roller is my new friend. I rarely take Advil or pain reliever, but I have increased my turmeric and fish-oil supplements to help decrease inflammation.

After my right rotator cuff injury and surgery, I knew I had an uphill battle, at the age of fifty-one, not only to return to weightlifting but to begin Olympic weightlifting. I researched several athletic comebacks and focused on "mental toughness" and the mindset part of the sport, which I would always hear about but never appreciated until I had to do it. When I started to train again, not only did I drop some pounds and feel better but my blood work also improved.

My mental clarity and my ability simply to be more present in everything I did improved exponentially after focusing on all aspects of my training — lifting, nutrition, and recovery. All this work has helped me become more aware of the mind-body-soul connection and that my body is indeed a gift from God to be cherished, nurtured, and taken care of everyday. I am in the greatest mood after a good workout and am filled with optimism to conquer the world or any challenge in front of me. Yes, I do miss workout days, and I don't always succeed as being the best caretaker of my temple, but I feel stronger and more in tune with my body now than at any other time in my life.

A pilgrimage to Medjugorje this past year highlighted for me the spiritual and mental power of some form of fasting two days a week. I have been working on my own combination of an Eastern (India) Ayurvedic and Western monk lifestyle for the four rhythms of the day. This incorporates morning prayer and reflection time, which, for me, includes some spiritual reading and journaling. I hold off on eating my first meal until 10:30 or 11:00 a.m., depending on when I arise. Then I have a rest or low-activity period and then a strength and active period midafternoon followed by downtime and prayer and reflection in the evening. Although I struggle for daily and even sometimes weekly consistency, I find strength in my prayer life and in learning and reflecting on the lives of the saints, including St. Patrick, St. Brendan, St. Hildegard of Bingen, St. Thomas Aquinas, St. Peter, St. Alphonsus de Liguori, St. Philip Neri — I could go on.

Dan Torpey is a forensic accountant and the co-author of The Business Interruption Book: Coverage, Claims and Recovery (*National Underwriter, 2010*). *Dan is also a national board member at Young Catholic Professionals (YCP) and a public speaker on building strong corporate cultures, fighting fraud and corporate crime through strong ethics and corporate integrity programs that focus on values consistent with the fundamental life virtues. You can find Dan at www.dantorpey.com, where he writes about mentoring, coaching, and building teams that last.*

HE AIN'T HEAVY …

I've been married for thirty years and have two sons in their twenties. Being a husband and father has been the greatest joy in my life, but it has also been a bit stressful at times. Likewise, my career of many years in the IT field, though it has brought me great joy, has also been stressful at times. I've been in the IT industry for more than thirty-five years. For the first ten years, I was in technology sales; then I ran a midsize technology-solution company for almost twenty years. I currently work for a Fortune 100 IT integrator and distributor. I started to realize years ago that a big motivator for my passion for high-intensity workouts is stress relief. I believe my work stress is directly related to my self-imposed high pressure to provide for the top priority in my life: my family.

Today, I'm in the process of developing my next career as a fitness and wellness professional. In the last couple of years, I've become a NASM Certified Personal Trainer (CPT) and Certified Nutrition Coach (CNC).

As I reflect and track my health and fitness by decade, I'm continuing to learn how to adapt to Father Time's relentless aging process. At fifty-nine years old, I'm still about as physically active as I was in my thirties and forties. However, I'm much more conscious of my diet and cautious about the amount of wear and tear on my body.

Here is a timeline of my pursuit of fitness:

In my twenties and thirties, I could pretty much eat and drink anything I wanted and not gain too much weight. I was active in a wide variety of sports (including tennis, racquetball, and softball). I was dedicated to weight training three times per week. I felt this gave me a competitive advantage in sports. I started lifting in my early teens and have virtually never missed a week to this day.

In my forties, my sports participation was down to playing tennis six months per year, when the weather would cooperate. I picked up a new training method that I still use today: High-Intensity Interval Training (HIIT) — sixty minutes of brutal cardio, including sprints, kettlebells, free weights, body-weight strength, and so forth. This was ideal for my high-intensity personality and my need to relieve work stress. I wasn't playing team sports anymore, and these classes gave me an opportunity to push myself and compete with other serious fitness enthusiasts. I was still lifting once or twice per week.

In my fifties, my body started to feel the effects of an old dude working out with such high intensity. My stress at work was at its highest, and I began to gain weight. This combination resulted in a constant series of injuries — nothing major, just nagging things that I tried to push through, as when I was young. I realized I had to do two things differently.

First, I started taking seriously the food that I put into my mouth. In the last ten years, I've become a lover of healthy proteins, vegetables, and fruits. I try to eat as few processed foods as possible, keep the sugars on the low side and avoiding fried foods. I track my carbs and protein daily — always trying to keep my carbs complex and at a reasonable level and my proteins fairly high to support my weight-training regimen.

Second, I adjusted my workouts to reduce impact and add more strength training.

I still do HIIT training, but I'm a lot smarter. I keep it at about once per week, and I greatly reduce impact. When a body part is feeling overworked, I don't push it; I back off a bit and live to work out another day. Also, my renewed focus on weight training has me feeling stronger and fitter.

Today, my weight is about the same as it was in my thirties — mostly due to my greatly improved eating habits. The most important outcome, however, is not my waistline but my ability to be active and enjoy outdoor activities with family and friends.

In addition to my personal life, exercise has been an integral component of my professional career. The technology field is a tremendously competitive and stressful business. I usually work out during my lunch hour, and when I return to the office, I'm relaxed and have improved concentration. When I was in my teens, I experienced substantial bouts of depression and low self-esteem. Throughout my adult life, I have continued to suffer from mild levels of mood disorders. My workouts have kept me going and have kept my self-esteem above water in many ways.

My big takeaway from a lifelong passion for exercise is the peace of mind it has provided. Exercise has been a constant, positive influence in my life. When I was down, I could work out and then forget my troubles and relax. When I was a bit overenergized, exercise helped calm me down and burn off some of the excess energy in a positive way. Exercise has been a big help in managing stress. My ultimate coping mechanism has been to work hard and sweat out my anxiety. I feel fortunate that when I was young, in addition to my love of sports, I picked up the habit of weight training. This was my coping mechanism, as opposed to drugs or alcohol.

When I was in my teens, my brother, Kevin, was a big proponent of weightlifting, well before it was cool. He was an avid follower of Arnold Schwarzenegger in the seventies, pre-Terminator or even Governator. Kevin brought me to the YMCA multiple times per week and taught me how to lift free weights when very few knew how or thought it was worthwhile for sports or even fitness. Going to the gym and lifting has remained a positive staple in my life for more than years.

I begrudgingly need to give my brother some credit for his help guiding me toward this healthy addiction.

Jamie Vost is my sons' uncle, my mother's son, and my little brother.

⸺⸱✦⸱⸺⸺⸱✦⸱⸺

BITTEN BY THE IRON BUG FOR THE GREATER SERVICE OF GOD

For me, the opportunity to contribute to a book on physical fitness from a Catholic perspective is proof of God's magnificent sense of humor. Years ago, I was the awkward, nerdy kid who nearly flunked gym class in middle school. I'm also a convert to the Catholic Church.

While I was in high school, I began taking greater interest in my health, since my family has a history of medical problems. I discovered in a neighboring town the community fitness center — and that's a rather extravagant name for it. It was a collection of well-worn gym equipment in a dark, musty basement below a store. I paid the eighteen-dollar annual membership fee and picked up a barbell for the first time in my life. Some people would describe this experience as "getting bitten by the iron bug." I wish the bug had bitten a little bit harder because I didn't get really serious with my strength training until much later, but it was a beginning.

Several years ago, I read Dr. Kevin Vost's book *Fit for Eternal Life: A Christian Approach to Working Out, Eating Right, and Building the Virtues of Fitness in Your Soul.* This book helped me to recognize the potential of physical fitness in general, and strength training in particular, to enhance my spiritual life. That understanding renewed my desire to pursue physical strength. The phrase "virtues of fitness" in the book's subtitle especially resonated with me. Since then, I have begun to see strength training not only for its health benefits but also as a conduit for building virtue. The cardinal virtues of prudence, justice, fortitude, and temperance, as well as the theological virtues of faith, hope, and charity, can all be strengthened beneath the weight of a barbell. The idea of building virtue through weightlifting became the topic for a talk that I gave at our diocesan men's conference a few years ago.

Developing virtue requires small, incremental steps, just as muscular strength is built gradually. Many people keep prayer journals, which can track progress in the spiritual life. A weightlifting journal serves a similar purpose. Whether I'm lifting at the commercial fitness center near my office or in my own basement gym, I record each workout in a notebook with the date and location, followed by the specific type of machine or lift, the weight, and the number of reps for each set. I regularly look back at my journal to see the increments of progress — a heavier weight, a larger number of reps. One method of progression that I often use consists of two sets of five reps, followed by a third set of as many reps as possible (AMRAP). Depending on how many reps I can perform in the third set, I adjust the weight upward or downward during my next lifting session. This is when the journal is especially useful.

Above all, I need to remind myself constantly that my physical training should have the purpose, or "end," of enhancing my body for greater service to God. He is the source of all goodness, including physical strength. "For we are his workmanship, created in Christ Jesus for good works, which God prepared beforehand, that we should walk in them" (Eph. 2:10). Thus, I can pursue progress in bodily strength with the faith that God will use it for purposes that are not yet known to me.

With all of this in mind, I recommend beginning every workout with a prayer to thank God for the gift of strength and a promise to use it for His glory. I keep prayers and inspirational quotations in the front of my lifting journal for easy reference. A pre-workout prayer might sound something like this: "Gracious Father, I praise You for creating me in Your image and likeness. I recognize my physical strength as a gift from You to be used for Your glory. Protect me from injury as I train my body today. Stir up in me the fortitude to press through the difficulty. Through Christ our Lord. Amen."

Russell Yount has been married to his wife, Bonnie, for twenty-one years. He works as an accountant for the diocese of Madison and recently began formation for the permanent diaconate.

A MODERN MILO OF MIND, BODY, AND SOUL

My two brothers and I played sports all our lives, taking a particular interest in wrestling. All of us placed in the top three in the state of New

Jersey and went on to become nationally ranked wrestlers. Jeff and I were both All-Ivy League while being teammates at the University of Pennsylvania, and Greg was a two-time academic All-American at Rutgers University and ranked as high as sixth in the country. In 2012, the three of us founded a high-intensity fitness program called Z-Fanatical Fitness — the first three-dimensional model of fitness, providing a workout plan for exercise, nutrition, and mindset. The exercises were 10-minute high-intensity body-weight circuits; e.g., Killer Quad (legs), Z-ABdominator (abs), Explosive TricepZ (chest triceps and shoulders). The nutrition plan emphasized quality over quantity and provided five levels. The concept with nutrition is to start slow and let your commitment grow without limiting quantity or counting calories. The mindset plan included a curriculum of worksheets to address "mental muscles": goal setting, motivation, confidence, and so forth. We continued to lift weights and run, but we added these workouts into our plan for days when our time or resources were limited.

We eventually realized that exercise, nutrition, and mindset still do not add up to becoming the "total package." If we are not spiritually strong, the other strengths mean nothing in the long run.

In 2015, Greg discerned a call to the priesthood, and it led to a massive reversion of our immediate family. The three of us completed the thirty-three-day consecration to Our Lady and immediately learned much about apologetics.

Jeff and I are business partners and co-owners of Winning Mindset as well as leaders of the first-ever New Jersey chapter of the Militia Immaculata. Fr. Greg was ordained a priest for the Diocese of Metuchen in June 2021. All three of us continue to exercise (lifting or running, or both) almost every day.

For nutrition I choose quality over quantity. You don't want to get into a battle of willpower with food if you can help it. I think the better approach for most people, most of the time, is to switch to cleaner eating slowly for long-lasting change. Forget about dieting. The first three letters spell "die" — not a great start. People go on and off diets. Diets tend to be short-term. A nutrition plan is long-term. Begin by calling it your nutrition plan. It is also helpful to identify your poisons as early as you can and to decide on healthy substitutions.

You cannot reasonably expect to kick a bad habit immediately. If your poison is potato chips, maybe switch to whole-grain crackers or pretzels. If you drink a lot of soda, consider switching to seltzer. Substitutions like this go a long way over time. Don't check the scale every day. Instead, make healthy substitutions and then revisit how you're doing in three to six months, trusting that eating and drinking healthier will provide long-term results.

I like a combination of powerlifting and bodybuilding to work on body aesthetics of muscle while still being able to lift heavy weight in the three power lifts (bench, dead lift, and squat). For cardio, I usually run because it is easiest, but I also change it up from time to time with Airdyne bike sprints, the Z-Fanatical Fitness high-intensity workouts I created, jump rope, sprints, and so forth. With two young kids and a third on the way, it is not as easy as in the past to exercise the way I would like. Sometimes just getting it in is a win. Consistency is key. It's better to do something than nothing.

With my business being based on peak performance through mental health, I apply the lessons I teach others to my own life and marriage. I'm a big believer in teaching my family and friends around me the same mindset lessons so we will all be in an environment that is positive and nurturing, mentally and emotionally.

Spiritual life is most important, especially taking time for mental prayer and working on building virtues and eliminating vices. Striving for Christian excellence is much harder than any other area because it includes everything you do and how you do it. Padre Pio has always been a patron saint of my family. My great grandfather met him.

As a husband and father, I have a strong devotion to St. Joseph. My consecration to the three hearts of Jesus, Mary, and Joseph is very important to me.

The mind and the body are meant to support spiritual growth. It is important to remember proper order in your training. There is a clear hierarchy. I look at spirit, mind, and body as three levels of a pyramid with spirituality at the foundation. Mathematically, a pyramid is only as high as its base is wide. Without a wide base, the pyramid can never reach its potential in terms of altitude, no matter how strong the other two dimensions are.

I also love Pius XII's allocution on sports, which does a great job providing the framework from which to view sports and recreation.

Gene Zannetti, age thirty-seven, is a wrestling champion and coach, a husband and father, a licensed school psychologist, a Catholic author, a podcaster, a speaker, a lover of the traditional Mass, and the author of Develop the Predator Mindset: Win in Sports and Life.

POSITIVE ASCETICISM: PHYSICAL DISCIPLINE AS AN AVENUE TO SANCTITY

Growing up, I was obsessed with sports. Sadly, school, church, and any other priority was always put in second place after perfecting my jump shot or running faster than anyone else on the football field. When I was a sophomore in high school, however, I took a shot from a helmet to the side of my right knee while I was playing defensive end. I looked down, and my leg was bent in the wrong direction from the knee down. Out of sheer panic and adrenaline, I popped my leg back into place and limped to the sidelines. After the coach downplayed my injury, I went back on the field, and the exact same thing happened. I had dislocated my knee. My doctors stated that my tendons were fine, but my cartilage had been ripped to shreds, and the likelihood that my knee would pop out again was very high. They recommended that I start lifting weights to keep my knee strong. My father has always been a weightlifter, so we had plenty of weights and machines at home (in fact, my room was the weight room for my high school years). Almost immediately, I was "bit by the iron bug." I loved everything about the weight room and focusing on my diet. Within a year, I put on about thirty pounds of mostly muscle. I still played football and basketball, but bodybuilding and powerlifting became my new obsession — that is, until late in my junior year, when my appendix ruptured. Not only did it rupture, but I had the toxins from the incident in my system for almost four days before finally going to the emergency room. I had lost thirty-five pounds in two weeks, I had to have emergency surgery, and for about a month, I had to have two tubes to suck the poison out. The physicians told me that if it were not for my extra muscle mass and my level of health, I likely would have died from the incident. Lifting weights saved my life, both physically and mentally. At the time as these two injuries, I dealt with a lot of mental depression, but the weight room gave me a healthy outlet to focus and to feel as if I could change my life.

After those incidents, I continued to lift weights, but I also grew interested in varying fighting techniques. After marrying my wife, I started training in boxing, Jeet Kune Do, and Brazilian jiu-jitsu. Once again, the love of competing and pushing myself found a home in me. However, my first love of lifting weights has always been a priority. During this time, I started questioning where this physical game fit into my spiritual life. I never left the Faith, but I certainly was not a great Catholic at the time, and most of my reading focused on the Stoics and on Bruce Lee. However, I stumbled across John Paul II's Theology of the Body as well as Dr. Vost's *Fit for Eternal Life*, and I realized that my great love of building the body and focusing on my health could be an avenue of sanctity as long as I treated it as such. The great wealth of wisdom from Thomas Aquinas, numerous popes, and other athlete saints woke me up to the great tradition of the Church, and I better understood the body's beauty from a theological lens. Since then, my competitive drive has continued. I now compete in the Scottish Highland Games and have started training for Spartan Races.

As a husband and the father of six, I have found that I can glorify God through a mutual love of the weights with my wife and, since I train in my garage, being with my children while I lift. My wife and I have used Jim Wendler's 5/3/1 program a lot over the years; it even helped me reach a 500-pound squat (something I never thought I'd be able to do, given my knees), a 590-pound dead lift, a 295-pound shoulder press, and a 465-pound bench press. That, and a lot of calories! I have come to find that my children are growing up in a home where exercise and discussions about diet are a natural part of their lives. They know the necessity of getting enough water and protein and the dangers of too much processed food and sugars. The beauty of it is that we also highly emphasize life's spiritual and mental aspects. Daily prayer together is a must, and most days, we recite poetry or discuss books we're all reading. I hope to train my children always to consider mind, body, and soul in their daily lives. If they can understand disciplining themselves in these three areas of life, I'll know that I have set them up for success in their relationship with Christ and in their own identities.

My exercise regimen changes, depending on my goals. When I hit a few of my highest lifting numbers, I lifted only four days a week for about thirty minutes. No cardio and no extras. It was tedious, but I gained a lot of strength. When I get ready for a Highland Games competition, I focus on explosiveness, speed, and agility; lots of farmer's carries, power cleans, and kettlebells. I still lift heavy but with less of an emphasis on the numbers. Sometimes I focus on flexibility, especially when training in Brazilian jiu-jitsu. However, I am running at least two miles five days a week and adding many HIIT style lifts to get ready for a Spartan Race. Overall, I work out at least four days a week, always incorporating the four main lifts with variations, depending on my goals.

Honestly, the gym is where I can deal with most of life's stresses. Aside from prayer, Mass, and adoration, working out in the gym is how I can balance my mental health. I have long tended toward depression and negative self-talk, but in the gym, I remember that I am not made of glass and that much of life's difficulty comes from our attitudes toward our circumstances. Perhaps it is the Stoic in me, but the gym and physical discipline are major reminders that we are going to die one day, and we all need to make the most of the time we have.

One thing that needs to be revisited and promoted is the Christian tradition of asceticism. In the past, asceticism was often associated with neglecting the body, which is still a viable option. Regular fasting and abstaining from meat can be a good thing if done with the right mindset. However, a type of positive asceticism sees the body as an aspect of our relationship with God that we build for the mission of the Church and our vocations. Think about it. If you stay away from fast food and push your body to its physical limits, you experience a kind of suffering that can be united to the Cross and increase your capacity for Christ's love. We can also incorporate prayer and devotion into our workouts. We can devote a session to our Lady, that she may use any grace we might earn as she desires. Inviting our patron saints to use our time of healthy suffering to mold our hearts and minds to Christ's is an excellent way to incorporate exercise into your spiritual life.

Jared Zimmerer is the senior director of Bishop Robert Barron's Word on Fire Institute. He is a doctoral candidate in humanities at Faulkner University's Great Books Honors College and holds a master's degree in theology from Holy Apostles College and Seminary. He also holds an undergraduate degree in kinesiology and has trained and competed in bodybuilding, Highland Games, boxing, Brazilian jiu-jitsu, mixed martial arts, and more recently, in Spartan Races. He and his wife, Jessica, have six children and live in North Texas.

About the Author

Kevin Vost obtained his Doctor of Psychology in Clinical Psychology from Adler University in Chicago, with internship and dissertation research at the Southern Illinois University School of Medicine, Alzheimer's Center, Memory and Aging Clinic.

Dr. Vost has taught psychology and gerontology at Aquinas College in Nashville, the University of Illinois at Springfield, MacMurray College, and Lincoln Land Community College. He has served as a Research Review Committee Member for American Mensa and as an Advisory Board Member for the International Association of Resistance Trainers.

He is the author of more than twenty Catholic books, and his hobbies include lifting big weights and reading big books, such as those of St. Thomas Aquinas. He resides with his wife and their dog in Springfield, Illinois.

Sophia Institute

Sophia Institute is a nonprofit institution that seeks to nurture the spiritual, moral, and cultural life of souls and to spread the gospel of Christ in conformity with the authentic teachings of the Roman Catholic Church.

Sophia Institute Press fulfills this mission by offering translations, reprints, and new publications that afford readers a rich source of the enduring wisdom of mankind.

Sophia Institute also operates the popular online resource CatholicExchange.com. *Catholic Exchange* provides world news from a Catholic perspective as well as daily devotionals and articles that will help readers to grow in holiness and live a life consistent with the teachings of the Church.

In 2013, Sophia Institute launched Sophia Institute for Teachers to renew and rebuild Catholic culture through service to Catholic education. With the goal of nurturing the spiritual, moral, and cultural life of souls, and an abiding respect for the role and work of teachers, we strive to provide materials and programs that are at once enlightening to the mind and ennobling to the heart; faithful and complete, as well as useful and practical.

Sophia Institute gratefully recognizes the Solidarity Association for preserving and encouraging the growth of our apostolate over the course of many years. Without their generous and timely support, this book would not be in your hands.

www.SophiaInstitute.com
www.CatholicExchange.com
www.SophiaInstituteforTeachers.org

Sophia Institute Press is a registered trademark of Sophia Institute.
Sophia Institute is a tax-exempt institution as defined by the
Internal Revenue Code, Section 501(c)(3). Tax ID 22-2548708.